Live Simply in the City

Live Simply in the City

by
Jonathan Allan
and
Lynne Cantwell

Ardea Press
Seattle

Ardea Press
PO Box 23221 Seattle WA 98102

ISBN 0-9727112-2-8 (electronic book)
ISBN 0-9727112-3-6 (paperback)

Jonathan

To my family, who in one way or another
have affected this effort immensely.

Lynne

To Kat and Amy. And to all our children,
unto the seventh generation.

CONTENTS

More Challenging In The City

Sometimes Easier, Sometimes Harder

Wrapping Up

FOREWORD

Live Simply in the City is a real godsend—and should never have been written.

It's a godsend. It's a treasure trove of insights and practical tips. It's a feast of truly helpful and accessible information. It helps dispel the myth—and the oft-used excuse—that simplicity is only for those willing to live in huts in the woods a la Thoreau. Simplicity is really for everyone, because it's about the basic human task of asking, "What is the good life?" and then living your answer. In some ways, simplicity is *easier* in the city because there so many cultural and pragmatic resources are at hand, which are available inexpensively. Everything from worship to laundry is within walking distance—and you don't have to own it or create it yourself to have access to it. Life in the city can be rich, even on modest means.

Yet I ask, "Why should we live in a world where this kind of common sense, sanity, and integrity needs a guidebook anyway?" In sharing *Your Money or Your Life* internationally, I've discovered that the values and practices of simplicity are integral to "the good life" everywhere. The Chinese think it's very Chinese. The Spanish this it's "muy mediterraneo"—very Mediterranean. It's about who-you-are being more important than what-you-have. It's about being choosy—choosing what you are, do, and have in light of *your* highest sense of what makes life worth living. This has led me to the conclusion that the consumer culture, the whole system that promotes self-alienation and problem solving through products, is unnatural. We are not a greedy species. We are a generous and connected species that is being instructed by 3000 consumer messages a day that we must protect ourselves and improve ourselves in a world where love and even necessities are scarce.

They say, "fifty million Frenchmen can't be wrong." Well, about that many Americans are making concerted efforts to set a boundary beyond which the consumer culture is *not* welcome in their lives. They are buying less, working less, spending more time in relationships, service, and nature and generally creating lives they value. Can we be wrong?

So kudos to Jonathan Allan and Lynne Cantwell for bringing us such a valuable and helpful book on living simply anywhere. And kudos to all of you, dear reader, for applying yourself to living more simply in a world that says, with every billboard, you aren't enough, you don't have enough and you don't do enough. Simplicity is radical and courageous—and as more of us take it on, it will become less that and more what it naturally is: simply "the good life."

—Vicki Robin

PREFACE

This book began when Hillary White posted the following message to the online discussion forums of The Simple Living Network on October 7, 2001:

> I guess I sometimes have a hard time with some of the [Voluntary Simplicity] books and posts by some folks here in the forums, because they seem to suggest that you haven't bought into the VS thing if you live in the city. The goal (for everyone, presumably, from their point of view) is for all right thinking people to live a rural life on a large acreage or at the very least, in a very small town somewhere. This is not one of my goals! ... I love my city life! I don't think my life isn't any less simple because I live in an urban environment. I'd be lost in the country. ... Sorry if I'm ranting, but I was reading another VS book tonight. ... The authors' big advice was "sell your big house in the city and buy a little house in the country". All fine and well, but it was just another example of how sometimes even with VS folks, I feel like a weirdo and like I don't belong.

Hillary, you are not a weirdo. You **can** live a simpler life in the city. We, your authors, are doing just that in fact. A quick check of the local library confirmed Hillary's observation that the majority of the existing literature on Voluntary Simplicity (VS) equates VS with the "Back to the Land" movement or it does not mention the effects of where you live at all. And so the book began. Jonathan, with dreams of being a writer someday, put the idea out to Universe in the form of the mailing list of the Financial Integrity Associates (FIA) and garnered a co-author, Lynne, and a publisher, Michael.

Even with the proper folks on board, it has been a long, hard slog to gather the information and make it all relevant to the Simplifier living in the city.

We hope you enjoy the stories we have collected. We hope you find this book useful. And when you are done with it, we hope you pass it along to someone you know or your favorite library so someone else can understand: You *can* live simply in the city!

ACKNOWLEDGEMENTS

We would like to acknowledge:

Hillary White, for the rant that started us down the path of writing this book. All the giving folks we interviewed to make this book more than just the authors spouting off. All the fine folks who answered our on-line survey but did not get interviewed or quoted. They often provided us with corroborating opinions. We could not have done it without their help! The whole gang on The Simple Living Network discussion forums, for your fantastic ideas, especially Anne Lewis for not thinking Jonathan was a complete lunatic.

And all who believed and helped!

We also wish to thank the following for their kind permission to reprint previously published material: Duane Elgin, the New Road Map Foundation, R. J. Wilder, the Simple Living Network, the Center for a New American Dream, Hillary White, Lindi Hulse, Primrose Edmonds, and Katie MacInnis.

We must point out that some of the names in this text have been changed at the request of the individual to preserve some of their anonymity. Their stories have been left as-is.

Thank you all!

INTRODUCTION

If you live in an urban area – whether it's New York City or Los Angeles, Seattle or Orlando, or any other city in the world – you can live simply without having to move.

This book will give you the tools you need to begin a life of Voluntary Simplicity, no matter where you live. We begin by showing you how to identify your values. We expose the role of television and advertising in wreaking havoc with your spending habits, and give you techniques for bringing your spending in line with your values.

We show you how living in a city can make Voluntary Simplicity easier—from parking your car permanently to eating cheaply and well, from decluttering to getting along with others. We discuss the myth that living simply requires retiring to a rural area—retirement can actually be easier in a city! We also tackle the more challenging aspects of living simply in a city and provide tips for such things as minimizing your housing costs and raising children simply. And in these pages, you will meet many, many people who are practicing Voluntary Simplicity in cities successfully.

Whether you are a novice Simplifier or whether you have been waiting to move to the country before you *really* simplify–or even if you just love your city and don't ever want to leave it just to simplify your life—you will find *Live Simply in the City* a celebration of all that urban life has to offer.

We are doing it, others are doing it, and you can do it, too. You really can *Live Simply in the City*!

CHAPTER 1

WHAT IS A CITY?

Can I Live Simply In The City?

Absolutely! Without one shred of doubt! Your authors have been living a simpler and saner existence in the city for years. In fact, living simply may be easier in the city than in the country. For starters, you do not have to butcher your own lunch in the city: most likely you can get it at a nearby store! If you rent, you can call the super or landlord about maintenance problems. You seldom have to worry about your septic tank backing up in the city. Depending on where you live and where you choose to work, the patterns of your urban existence can be modified, simplifying your life to those people, activities, and things that hold true meaning and value for you.

There are many advantages to living in a city, some of which we will show you in this book. By living a simpler life in the city, you can make the most of those advantages. By living more simply in the city, you can avoid many of the disadvantages to city living as well. This book will introduce you to some basic concepts behind Voluntary Simplicity (VS), explore how VS is very compatible with living in the city, and then wrap up with a few ideas you can use as jumping off points for your simplified sojourn in the city.

Why Are You Here?

Voluntary Simplicity. What does that really mean?

If you read much of the literature on Voluntary Simplicity to be found in your library, you might come away with the impression that Voluntary Simplicity is about reducing your existence to the bare minimum, buying some land somewhere for cheap, and dropping out of society to grow and harvest your own food.

That is not Voluntary Simplicity; that is the "Back to the Land" movement. In the 1960s, pioneers like Scott and Helen Nearing, among many others, prescribed a simple lifestyle and a rural existence. However, the mass pioneer movement never really happened, even though many people chose to go "back to the land" individually. If you are motivated to live the rural existence, there is a wealth of literature available, but this book is not a resource for that topic.

Living a voluntarily simple lifestyle does not have much to do with where you live. Voluntary Simplicity is more of an attitude. It is about your perception of where you live, the sort of structure you choose to live in, and the ways you choose to express your values.

This book aims to wrap up in one package, intertwined with the stories of real people solving real problems, how you can simplify your life while living in a city setting. But what do we mean by "city"?

What is a City?

A city is an urban place. That may strike you as circular logic, but the definition of a city is not entirely straightforward. Suppose for the moment that you live in New York City, USA. If you live in an efficiency apartment in a high rise building in downtown Manhattan, clearly you live in the city. But what if you live in a single house with detached garage in the borough of Queens? Is that still "in the city"? Or is that living in the "suburbs"?

According to Webster's New Universal Unabridged Dictionary, a city is "a large or important town, or a municipality recognized by some authority". A "town", as defined by the same source, is a grouping of houses, sometimes walled in. We are guessing that most of the towns you are familiar with are not surrounded by a moat, but you get the idea. In the modern sense, the "wall" is the city limits, set by the city council. Anything outside the city limits might still be urban but it is not "the city".

Urban, however, means "the opposite of rural". And rural, by definition, is "in the country". So, what we see is that the dictionary is just as vague as anyone else on the topic. We suggest that defining "rural area" is simple. It is where you count the population in wildlife per square foot. Your nearest neighbor's house is too far away to see from your window. You can walk to town, but it will probably take you a long while. There is no mass transit; you have to own a car to get anywhere. It is unlikely that you will have to stand in line for any length of time to buy anything or get in to something. If you are really in a rural place, the traffic lights might not even work all night.[1]

Defining "urban area", however, makes one feel a little like that Supreme Court justice who said he could not define pornography, but he knew it when he saw it.[2] The boundaries today are murky, particularly when you try to draw a line between urban neighborhoods and suburbia.

Suburbs are somewhat easier to define. Post-WWII suburbs are typically made up of large-lot, single-family housing, with a single land use per area.[3] All the houses are detached from each other, and there are usually one or two designs per development. Streets are generally long and curving to fit the terrain, with cul-de-sacs spread around like flat lollipops to maximize land use. Developments are segregated by house price: $100,000 homes are not usually built in the same subdivision as $500,000 homes without a court fight. Often mass transit is not available and you have to drive your car to get to amenities like shopping, restaurants, and health care;[4] you cannot usually walk to those from your house.

Traditional city neighborhoods, however, typically offer row houses or, at the very most, tiny lots. Alleys commonly exist between the back yards. Streets are narrow and on-street parking is typical. At least in the past, the area was mixed use: storefronts and homes would be found in the same block since the corner grocery and druggist still existed. Apartments usually existed over the businesses. Houses of all sizes are usually found in the same block, or at least on the same street. Streets were, depending on the original grade of the land, laid out in rectangles with many cross streets to allow easier access[5]. Mass transit of some form is usually available.

But in today's urban/suburban areas, the urban and the suburban have met. Cities have expanded to swallow areas that used to be suburbs; suburbia now sprawls farther and farther away from the heart of the city. Mini-mansions regularly spring up in what used to be farmers' fields, and we have coined a new term, "the exurbs," to define the semi-rural fringe of the suburbs where the well-to-do builds their manses. Smaller cities that used to be considered bedroom communities have bulked up to attract tourists and new industry. In so doing, they have also attracted new residents, giving them a much more urban feel and more urban problems. Big cities have added shopping malls and improved green spaces. Suburbs have added condominiums and apartment complexes, increasing their population density. Therefore what you call the enclave where you live depends on you; that is, you probably live in the city if you think you do.

We had a lot of trouble coming up with a definition of "urban area" for this book. In the end, we agreed to let the U.S. Census Bureau decide. The authors of this book, and all of the people featured in it, live (or have lived) in cities listed on the 2002 census as having populations of 100,000 or more. Granted, living in New York City, with more than 8 million residents, is a different experience than living in Burbank, California, or Livonia, Michigan, with just over 100,000 residents apiece. But the strategies for living simply in New York City, or Burbank, or Livonia, or any city in between, are pretty much the same.

We also decided that living in "suburbia" is largely a state of mind. If you think you have to have a big house, on a large lot, with a lot of stuff, and that you need a car to get anywhere, have a nice life in suburbia. But if you recognize that you have alternatives, welcome to Voluntary Simplicity.

What is Voluntary Simplicity?

Voluntary Simplicity author Duane Elgin defines VS as living an outwardly simple life, with a rich inner existence. While Elgin originally called this concept Voluntary Poverty, the rationale remains the same: "To live more simply is to live more purposefully and with a minimum of needless distraction. ... Simplicity of life means meeting life face-to-face. ... It means taking life as it is – straight and unadulterated."[6]

Another way of defining VS is "living the examined life". Socrates and other ancient Greek philosophers dwelled at some length on how to live life. Both Plato and Aristotle discussed what the good life meant and how to live "on the Golden Mean". By living the examined life, one had the opportunity to consider attachments to people, places, things, and ideas, accepting or rejecting each as seemed good to the examiner. But perhaps the most accessible definition of Voluntary Simplicity today comes from an American, Joseph Beckenbach: "Voluntary Simplicity is about systematically removing things, activities, and people from your environment that unnecessarily complicate your life."

VS is not just about selling, donating, or trashing all your excess stuff. It is also about examining your relationships with others and your daily activities to ensure that you are receiving good value for the energy you invest in them, and that they are in accord with your personal values. If you are not receiving a reasonable return on the energy you invest in any of these things, activities, or people, VS gives you a framework for removing them from your life. In today's fast-paced, move-forward-or-die world, the concept of simplifying your life holds great appeal. But how? What kind of framework can help?

The Doors to Voluntary Simplicity

Vicki Robin, co-author of *Your Money or Your Life*, suggests that there are eight doors that people come through into the Voluntary Simplicity movement. That is, this framework is useful to think about when trying to label what brings you to the Voluntary Simplicity table. The doors are:
1. Environmental Concerns
2. Moral Concerns
3. Social Justice
4. Personal Finance
5. Time Famine
6. Debt
7. Spirituality
8. Retirement

In brief, the eight doors can be described as:

Environmental Concerns. Environmentalists everywhere can tell you all you ever wanted to know about how humans, as a species, are poisoning our own nest. Indeed, many of the most recent converts to Voluntary Simplicity have come through this door. You might enter the movement through this door if environmental degradation is your hot button.

Moral Concerns. Those who enter through the Moral Concerns door may also be exploring vegetarianism because they believe that the way animals are treated in feedlots and processing plants is immoral. Others may feel that it is immoral to force children in Third World countries to make soccer balls used by privileged kids elsewhere in the world. Still others may feel that it is morally wrong for CEOs to receive such huge salaries and bonuses while their workers receive far less — or are being laid off.

Social Justice: Is it fair to deny someone's human rights because that person looks different or acts differently? If removing hypocritical public behavior and attitudes from your life is one of your goals, then maybe you will enter through the Social Justice door.

Personal Finance: Are you bewildered by your money challenges or your investments? Are you concerned that you are invested in something that is not in line with your values? Maybe you will enter through the Personal Finance door.

Time Famine: If you have found yourself consciously wanting to eliminate activities, people, or excess things that drain away all your time; or worse, all your creative time; or worst, all your family time; then maybe you will enter through the Time Famine door.

Debt: Has bankruptcy or excessive debt bolted you to the work-and-spend treadmill? Are you drowning in debt with no clear understanding of why? Perhaps the Debt door will be a method of clearing up your financial problems.

Spirituality: If your spiritual path is leading you to question where we are going with all of our overt consumption, or whether your personal consumption is in your spirit's best interest, then maybe the Spirituality door is your entry point.

Retirement: If you would like to exit the rat race and unsaddle your raton time—or even early—then maybe you will enter through the Retirement door.

It does not matter which door you come in through; there is not a "most righteous" doorway that everyone "should" enter through. Each of us comes to the Voluntary Simplicity movement with our own ideas, perceptions, judgments, and baggage (both emotional and physical). In fact, each of the authors of this book came in through different doors. And do we have baggage! But once you get through the door, you find a garden, even if it is not quite Eden. Elgin wrote an essay describing his vision of the Garden of Simplicity (*see* the sidebar on page 8).

The Path of Voluntary Simplicity

Vicki Robin sees VS as a house with many doors. Duane Elgin sees it as a garden. If two of the big names in the Voluntary Simplicity movement cannot exactly agree on what VS means, then why would anyone else even try to sort this all out? The answer of course, is that Consumer Society is so anxious to possess everyone's time and money, so lacking in returned value, and often so soulless as to not care the personal cost, that many people just cannot remain sane and do what everyone around them is doing. They have to *escape!* And often, they are not sure what they are escaping.

Voluntary Simplicity is not a destination. You cannot go to the store and buy Simplicity (although there are several brands that use that name, from snow blowers to sewing patterns). You cannot install it as an option on your latest gizmo. Your company cannot mandate it, even though there are some management texts on the simpler organization. Exceedingly few of us can read a single book, have an epiphany, and simplify our lives for all time to come; life is just too messy for that. We all come with too much baggage.

Duane Elgin's essay, "Garden of Simplicity" describes ten categories of simplicity. They are:
• Choiceful Simplicity
• Commercial Simplicity
• Compassionate Simplicity
• Ecological Simplicity
• Elegant Simplicity
• Frugal Simplicity
• Natural Simplicity
• Political Simplicity
• Soulful Simplicity
• Uncluttered Simplicity

To read Elgin's full essay describing these expressions of voluntary simplicity, please visit www.ardeapress.com

Voluntary Simplicity is a path, beginning with a doorway, into a garden where Hope lies. And like the fallow field, Hope is waiting for each of to turn it over and let it grow. The problem is that most of us do not have the required tools.Realistically, Hope is all around us, if only we would take off our blinders and see it. The process of peering around the edges of our societally-conditioned blinders is the process of becoming conscious. Conscious that we have choice in our daily life. Conscious that we do not have to do the same thing everyone else does. Conscious that we have a mission, a calling, something unique for us to share. Conscious that we *are*.

But the baggage, the schtuff, the people around us, the boat anchors, sometimes even the boat, all conspire to weigh us down. We perceive pressure to conform, to follow the straight and narrow, to be one of the in-crowd. And yet the Simplifier, someone looking to simplify their life, is asking why these are all important. In fact, the sorting of wants and needs, the determinations of value or not valued, the practice of confronting our own behavior as we tread our paths, occur daily whether we are conscious of the decisions or not. VS is largely about becoming conscious of our own decisions and modifying them to fit our mission or calling.

Talk to ten people practicing Voluntary Simplicity, and you will find at least 200 reasons why this is a good thing to do. Add to that all the complicating baggage we each carry around with us and you begin to see why nailing down exactly *what* Voluntary Simplicity really means can be tricky. But the fact remains: living in the city does not preclude you from living a simpler, and maybe a saner, life. It truly is not necessary to own forty acres—or even five—to have your independence.[7]

How To Read This Book

Before you jump off into the rest of the book, please remember that with eight doors, ten garden plots, and all the baggage each of us brings to Voluntary Simplicity, there is no single right answer to any question. Each of us might perform the same behavior, but each of us is likely to be doing that behavior for a completely different set of reasons. Do not make the mistake of assuming there is only one good reason for doing something; there are as many good reasons as there are people, and then some. Each of us is in a different situation, with different concerns and levels of tolerance for "different" or "risky" behavior. The people you will meet in this book are all strivers who have examined their mundane consumer existence, found it wanting, and are seeking a more fulfilling, examined life. We hope this book will show you someone or something that will spur you on the journey of simplifying your life too. VS really is easier than it looks at first glance, and gets easier as you more fully reintegrate your lifestyle around your true values.

We have divided the remainder of the book into five sections. Section I, which you're now reading, is "Voluntary Simplicity Basics". Here, we explain the core ideas behind the book *Your Money or Your Life*, which is considered by some to be the Simplifiers' financial bible, and try to help you apply the ideas to your personal situation. The authors of this book are members of FI Associates, which means we have followed the principles outlined in this book for at least six months and can personally attest that they work. We also explain why, if you want to simplify, you really should turn off the boob tube, or get rid of it entirely.

Sections II, III and IV are the meat of the book. Following the path of Voluntary Simplicity requires numerous detours from the superhighway of Consumer Culture. Your lifestyle may change in many ways. A lot of these changes are easier to make if you live in an urban area; some are harder to make in an urban area; a few are just difficult, no matter where you live. Section II features the parts of VS that are easier to do if you live in a city. This is the largest section of the book. Section III talks about the things that are harder to do if you live in a city. What we found in writing this section is that even though some parts of VS are harder in a city, they are rarely impossible. Usually all you need is a little creative thinking and some extra effort. Section IV outlines the short list of things that are challenging to do as part of a VS lifestyle, no matter where you live. Section V is where we wrap up the book. Here, we feature tips for living the simple life from all of the Simplifiers who responded to our online survey and discuss the survey itself.

Just as there is no single right way to begin to simplify your life, there is also no one right way to read this book. We suggest that you read Section I first, to put you in the right frame of mind. Then skip around in the other sections and read whatever strikes your fancy. Each chapter features resources at the end, to help you along your path. Try some of our Practical To Do's; read one of the books in the Library section; we have included a full bibliography with notes at the back of the book to help you. If you have access to the Internet, check out one of the web sites we suggest. You can plug one of our suggested search terms into your favorite search engine and see what turns up. There is a wealth of information available, far more than we could digest for you here. So dig in and find something meaningful for you. Then get started simplifying; we have done it and we know you can do it, too! You can be an example for your peers, friends, and acquaintances just by living your own life.

See you on the path!

Practical To Dos

In each chapter we will present a list of things you can do to work on these ideas in your own life. Like all lists of suggestions, some of them will be completely off the wall with respect to your situation and interests. Hopefully you will see a few that do make sense for you to try. Try them, and see how they fit with your world. This chapter's list is pretty short:

- Read the rest of this book.
- Be prepared to spend some time defending your "new and strange" ideas. Coming up with a "cover story" that is socially

acceptable is often done. Like: "I'm saving for a trip around the world," or some other hideously expensive thing you "plan to pay cash for."

- Check out books of interest from your library that might have some bearing on your Voluntary Simplicity journey. Check the Library Guide below for more.
- If you have access to the Internet, items in the Internet Resources section below may be useful to you. If you do not have access to the net at home or at work, try your local library or coffee shop.

Library Guide

In this section, we will list book titles that you can find in the Bibliography section in the back which might be of interest. There is a short description of each and enough information that you can find the title in your library, through inter-library loan, or in your favorite bookstore.

- *Your Money or Your Life* by Joe Dominguez and Vicki Robin
- *Voluntary Simplicity: Toward a Way of Life That Is Outwardly Simple, Inwardly Rich* by Duane Elgin
- *The Circle of Simplicity: Return to the Good Life* by Cecile Andrews
- *The Good Life: Helen and Scott Nearing's Sixty Years of Self-Sufficient Living* by Helen and Scott Nearing
- *Walden and Other Writings* by Henry David Thoreau
- *The Cultural Creatives: How 50 Million People Are Changing the World* by Paul Ray and Sherry Ruth Anderson
- *Four Arguments for the Elimination of Television* by Jerry Mander
- *The Plug-In Drug: Television, Children, and the Family* by Marie Winn
- *Choosing Simplicity: Real People Finding Peace and Fulfillment in a Complex World* by Linda Breen Pierce
- *Suburban Nation* by Andres Duany

Internet Resources

In this section, we will list some web sites or other Internet related resources that you might be able to find and try. Due to the volatility of the Internet structure and the lag time between when we did the research and you are trying these addresses, some of these addresses might not work, so you may have to do some searching.

www.simpleliving.net
www.yourmoneyoryourlife.org
www.newdream.org
www.culturalcreatives.com
www.adbusters.org

Search Terms

These are terms you ought to be able to plug into a search engine and get a reasonable number of hits on. Remember to put quotes around phrases (like "voluntary simplicity") or you may get a lot of unrelated results. Enjoy surfing!

simplicity
frugality
simple living
voluntary simplicity
Joe Dominguez
Vicki Robin
Duane Elgin

CHAPTER 2

CHOICES AND VALUES

If you are completely new to Voluntary Simplicity, you may be asking yourself right about now, "What's in it for me?" After all, VS looks like a lot of work, with not a lot in the way of material payoff. Why should you downsize your desires? Why should you limit yourself? Why put yourself through the agony?

The answer is that Voluntary Simplicity demands no agony, no downsizing of your desires, and no strict limitations. In fact, it demands nothing but that you be true to yourself. What VS does is to give you a framework for weighing *all* the options available to you, and then choosing the ones that are best aligned with your values.

Think of the freedom that implies! The whole world is open to you. All you have to do is choose to live in the way that will make you the most contented. For true contentment comes not in the acquisition of this or that material thing, but in living in harmony with your values.

A Little Soul-Searching

Before you can begin to make choices according to your values, you have to know what your values are.

It is possible that it has been quite some time since you thought about what it is that you value most in life. Maybe you talked about values when you were a kid, in Scouts, or in Sunday school. Your values may, in fact, come directly from whatever religious upbringing you have had—or they may be diametrically opposed to that religious upbringing.

Or you may have found yourself lately thinking back to the idealistic young person you once were, and wondering whether you have turned into the sort of person that your younger self expected to become. If you have not, that might not be a bad thing; life throws all of us a curve ball once in awhile, and it forces us to grow in unexpected ways. Our values also grow and evolve over the years, so it is a good idea to revisit the topic periodically.

Try this: On a piece of paper, write down ten things that you want out of life. They could be material things, such as a house or a car. They could be non-material things, such as good health or a loving family. This exercise has no wrong answers, so do not feel that you have to avoid writing down "New SUV" or "Make more money than my stupid boss does" just because you found this idea in a book about living simply! This is *your* list, and the only person who you have to answer to is *you*.

Once you have your list, look it over and rank the things you have listed, from most important to least important.

Next, make another list. This one is a list of ten things you want that money cannot buy. Again, rank them from most important to least important. You may find that some items are common to both lists. For instance, love, family, and good health are important to almost everybody, and none of them can be purchased in a store.

Now, make a third list from these two: The top ten things that are most important to you. If you see some things on your first two lists that are similar to one another, it is okay to combine them into a generic listing for your top-ten list. For instance, you may have listed both "travel to Tibet" and "visit the pyramids in Mexico" on one of your initial lists; you could combine those into "travel to exotic places" (or simply "travel") on your top-ten list. Rank them from one to ten (or David-Letterman-style, from ten to one, if you would rather).

Look over your top-ten list. We suspect that the material wants that you started off with have largely dropped off the list. You may still list a few, particularly if your life right now is not particularly physically comfortable. But by and large, we are betting that your list is made up mostly of things that you cannot buy in any store. Congratulations! You have discovered your values.

If you work better in a group, or if you would just like to get your whole family on board with the idea of living according to your values, Marie Sherlock's book *Living Simply with Children* offers one way to get everybody onto the same page. She suggests a series of family meetings that include brainstorming about the things that everyone in the family believes is most important. You can then boil down your brainstormed list into a Family Values and Vision Statement, which can be posted on the fridge.[1]

Similar exercises with more depth and quite a bit of rationale behind them can be found in *The Passion Plan* by Richard Chang and *Creating Your Future* by Dave Ellis. Jonathan has used both books and found them very well organized.

Now that I Have Them, What Do I Do with Them?

Armed with this list, your life can become quite an adventure. Every buying decision, every choice of a way to spend your spare time, *everything in your life*, becomes an opportunity to practice your values.[2]

Say that number one on your list was, "Spend more time with my family." That is not an uncommon value, by the way; in *The Overworked American*, author Juliet B. Schor quotes a 1978 US Department of Labor survey in which 84 percent of workers said that, given the choice between a raise in the future and more time off, they would rather have some time off than the whole raise — and 47 percent would have traded all of a 10 percent raise for more time off.[3] Now, say that your boss calls you into his office on Friday afternoon and asks you whether you would like to put in a little overtime this weekend. Sure, you could use the money.

Couldn't everybody? But if your number-one value is spending time with your family, you may well decide that the extra cash you would earn would not offset the loss you would suffer from being away from your spouse and kids. (For strategies for carving out more time for the things you really want to do, see our chapter on "Finding Time.")

What if the number-one item on your list was, "Retire early"? Faced with the scenario above, you might make the opposite decision and agree to the overtime, and plan to put your earnings into your retirement fund. (See our chapter entitled "Retirement" for reasons why you may want to stay in an urban area after you retire.) But if you want to retire early, or if you intend to save money toward some other big goal, you may also find yourself weighing every purchase you make in order to get the best deal for your money. You may even begin putting off buying more stuff in order to sock away as much money as possible. You might find that saving money becomes a game to you. You might surprise yourself by finding joy in adding up the money you are saving by skipping your morning latté every day. (Budding cheapskates may find joy in our chapters, "All That Ugly Stuff" and "Consumer Culture.")

What if one of the items on your list was, "Be kinder to the environment"? Then you might trade in your gas guzzler for a hybrid car, or park the car and take the bus to work. You might replace the incandescent bulbs in your lamps at home with compact fluorescent bulbs, or even install solar panels on your roof. (Check out our "Energy" chapter for more information on these and other ideas.) You might look for ways to recycle everything from furniture to clothing to plastic baggies. You might even have fun seeing how many times you can reuse a plastic baggie. (See "Your Home as Art" for ideas for decorating on the cheap.)

And if your list includes an item like "Have more fun", you may begin to reevaluate the ways that you spend your free time. You may decide that you would rather stay home and read a book than go out and party with your friends – or you may decide that you have been spending too much time sitting at home, and instead you need to get out and mix with people. (Our "Entertainment" chapter has lots of ideas for having fun on the cheap, while either getting out of the house or staying in.)

You will find that items on your list play off of one another. If your values include both "Travel" and "Be kinder to the environment," you could search the Internet for ecotourism trips, or you could use your vacations to volunteer to improve trails in a national park, or you could simply decide to bike and camp when you travel instead of driving and staying in a hotel. You may even find that you prefer waking up in a tent in the great outdoors to waking up in an impersonal hotel room. If you want to "Retire early" because you think that will help you "Have more fun," you may realize that you are putting off doing what you really want to do with your life until after you retire. In that case, you may choose to begin living your retirement lifestyle now, by starting that hobby or taking that class or planning that round-the-world trip (maybe even by biking and camping your way around the world!).

The more you think about your list, in fact, the more you may realize that a greater truth lies behind some of the values you have listed. "Retire early" and "Have more fun" together could mask an overall dissatisfaction with your current career. You may need to do some further soul-searching to discover what has been called your "right livelihood" – the line of work that best showcases your abilities and allows you to look forward to getting up and going to work every morning. Once you find your right livelihood, you may never want to retire. (Look in "More Money" for more about figuring out the livelihood that is right for you.)

You may also realize that what you need to do in order to both "Spend more time with my family" and "Have more fun" is to give up some activities that you have felt forced into doing, or projects that you took on for the prestige of the position but that you do not enjoy. Chairing the school PTA's fundraiser for the new playground is important work, but if calling people for money makes you crabby, maybe another PTA member should make those calls. (Our chapter, "Finding Time," includes some strategies for getting rid of such soul-sapping commitments.)

In the process of making all these decisions, you are certainly choosing to exclude things from your life. But the things you are excluding are things that never made you happy in the first place. We are not advocating hedonism – unless it is on your list! But seriously, it makes sense to build your life around the people and activities that you value the most.

Some of the choices you will face will be difficult. Friends and family members may not be supportive, and in fact may actively oppose your attempts to simplify. (We suggest ways to cope with these naysayers in "Complicated Relationships." If your naysayers are of the youthful variety, then "Simplifying with Kids" offers some strategies for you.) The ever-present Consumer Culture lurks around every corner, pleasantly offering you Yet One More Product to satisfy some need you didn't know you had until you saw the commercial for it. (See our take in "Downsize Your TV" and "Advertising" for help with this one.) Again, look to your values. Be true to yourself.

Setting an Example

We have one more exercise for you to try. Take another piece of paper (our more frugal readers may use the back of the one they used before![4]) and make a list of ten things that you would change in the world, if you had the power to do so. Lynne used this exercise with a group of high-school-age Girl Scouts, and the results were entertaining; the suggestions ranged from "world peace" to "better cafeteria lunches" to "end the rule against bandannas in school." Your responses may be different (although if you have school-aged kids, maybe they won't be).

Next, using your values as a framework, think of three things you can do to contribute to bringing about one or more of these goals. No one person can end war, but one person can sign a petition against war, or learn mediation skills, or vow to not indulge in road rage. No one person can end discrimination, but one person can treat everyone else as an equal. No one person can end hunger, but one person can participate in a canned food drive, or volunteer at the local food bank. No one person can save the environment, but one person can buy products with less packaging, or use fewer chemicals on the lawn, or organize a cleanup of a nearby stream.

Not only does this sort of behavior allow you another outlet for living according to your values, but it also adds to the greater good of society. By your actions, small as they may seem, you are serving as an example. Your behavior might encourage others to behave as you do. As the behavior snowballs – as more and more people begin to behave the same way – suddenly it no longer seems as difficult to change the world.[5]

And to think it all started with a list of the ten things you wanted out of life.

Practical To Dos:

- Make a list of ten things you want out of life. Then make another list of ten things you want that money cannot buy. Then make a third list of the top ten things on the first two lists. This third list is a list of what you value most.
- Use your list of values to begin weighing the decisions you make.
- Think about whether some of the values on your list are really masks for your *real* values. For instance, "Retire early" and "Have more fun" might mean that you need to do some work to find your right livelihood.
- Read through this book for hints on living according to your values in an urban area.
- Make a list of ten things you would like to do to change the world. Using your values as a framework, think of three specific activities you can do to work toward one or more of these goals. Do these three things.
- See how your contentment increases, the more you live according to your values.

Library Guide

- *The Overworked American: The Unexpected Decline of Leisure* by Juliet B. Schor
- *Living Simply with Children* by Marie Sherlock
- *A Resource Book for Senior Girl Scouts* by Rosemarie Cryan et al. (the exercise listed under "Setting an Example" is borrowed from the requirements for the Senior Girl Scout Challenge)
- *The Passion Plan* by Richard Y. Chang
- *Creating Your Future* by Dave Ellis

Internet Resources

www.simpleliving.net
www.newdream.org
www.positivefutures.org

Search Terms

values
value definition
values clarification
right livelihood

CHAPTER 3

ADVERTISING

Advertising is one of the prime creators of the work-and-spend treadmill. As Jerry Mander writes in *Four Arguments for the Elimination of Television*, "[Advertising] has been assigned the specific duty of keeping people buying, buying, buying, and therefore working, working, working to get money to do so."[1] And people do spend, spend, spend. Juliet B. Schor reports in *The Overspent American* that middle- and upper-middle-class Americans save $208 less per year for every hour they spend watching TV each week.[2]

Advertising is so effective that consumer spending has become the biggest growth engine fueling the US economy. In the US, consumer spending accounts for two-thirds of the nation's gross domestic product.[3] And experts on the economy are acutely aware of this. Now that the dot-com bubble has burst, says Richard Hastings, the chief economist for Cyber Business Credit, "[t]he really big risk is that consumers will reawaken to the timeless truth that the best way to save money is to stop spending."[4] Advertising is a big part of what keeps us spending, even when we can no longer afford it.

Resistance is Futile

It is easy to demonize advertising. Advertising did not create capitalism; of course it was the other way around. Advertising creates markets for the products that capitalists manufacture, so that the capitalists can make money. Intrinsically, there is nothing wrong with making money. But advertising today has become more powerful than anybody ever expected it would.

Everywhere we turn – from billboards to TV and the Internet to gasoline pump handles to the floor of the local supermarket aisle – we are bombarded with images designed to convince us to buy something. This is especially true in urban areas, the home of many advertisers' most desirable demographic groups. Demographics is the art of dividing a population into specific niches, such as, say, 18-to-45-year-old Asian-American females that own a car and have two children under age 12 living in their household. Manufacturers find demographic information invaluable when targeting their ad dollars to venues that their products' prospective consumers frequent. Jim Twitchell, the author of *Adcult USA*, claimed in 2000 that the average American was exposed to 5,000 ads per day, "and that's nothing compared to what you'll see in the next 10 years."[5] Each of these 5,000 ads is designed to create a need in the viewer – usually a need that we did not know we had until we saw the ad. Advertisers create this need by making us feel uncomfortable in some way. Then they offer us a product supposedly designed to alleviate our discomfort.

In an effort to rise above the noise level of this ever-more-crowded marketplace, advertisers reach for more and more shocking images. We are surrounded, screamed at incessantly, engulfed in a torrent of sounds and images specifically designed to make us uncomfortable, all day long, day in and day out. Is it any wonder that so many of us are dissatisfied with our lives?

And yet, we shrug off advertising's effects. Jean Kilbourne, the author of *Deadly Persuasion: Why Women and Girls Must Fight the Addictive Power of Advertising*, has made a career of lecturing throughout the US on the effects of advertising on our culture: "Almost everyone holds the misguided belief that advertisements don't affect *them*, don't shape their attitudes, don't help define their dreams. What I hear more than anything else, as I lecture throughout the country, is 'I don't pay attention to ads....I just tune them out....they have no effect on me.' Of course, I hear this most often from young men wearing Budweiser caps."[6]

Kilbourne's research shows that ads do indeed affect us. We may think advertising is unimportant because it makes us laugh; we think we pay no attention to it. But advertisers know this, and capitalize on it. In *Boxed In: The Culture of TV*, Mark Crispin Miller quotes a couple of advertising firm honchos: "'People don't watch television like they're taking notes for an exam,' says Lou Centlivre, Executive Creative Director at Foote Cone Belding. 'They're half-conscious most of the time when they're watching television.' 'People don't really attend to TV commercials. It's more of a subconscious or subliminal effect,' observes Fred Baker, a Senior Vice-President at McCann-Ericksen."[7]

Advertisers use this subliminal effect to their advantage. No, ads for Ritz crackers do not feature the word "sex" imprinted on the crackers, as the old urban legend claimed.[8] What advertisers do instead is more insidious. They play their ads off of cultural dogma, things that most people (or at least, most people of a certain economic class or ethnic group) believe are true without thinking about them, thereby reinforcing those beliefs and further damaging the fabric of our culture. The more often an ad is shown in which all the discount store shoppers have Southern accents, or in which African-Americans greet each other with a jive-accented "whassup?", the more firmly entrenched become the cultural attitudes that only rednecks shop at discount stores and all African-Americans speak ghetto.

Ads Corrupt Our Relationships

In her book, Kilbourne cites numerous examples of ads in which both women and menare objectified, with women suffering the lion's share of it. Women are repeatedly "dismembered" by the camera. In an ad for women's shaving cream, the blades of a pair of scissors have morphed into a pair of women's legs. In an ad for jeans, the brand name is tattooed on a naked woman's buttock.[9] Joe Camel's face features an amazing array of sexual body parts.[10] Kilbourne argues that this focus on women's body parts encourages men to see women, and women to see themselves, as nothing but a collection of body parts, which of course have to be perfect in appearance.

Ads depict relationships between people as imperfect at best. An ad for the Honda Civic shows an open wallet; a picture of two kids and a dog is in the left-hand side, and a picture of the car is in the right-hand side. The caption: "If anybody should ask, go ahead and show them your pride and joy."[11] Suggesting that a car can be as important to someone as his kids is bad enough; allowing the car to supplant the spouse is worse; but worst of all may be the subliminal message. Since ancient times, Judeo-Christian culture has considered the left side to be the side of evil and the right side to be the side of good. For example, the word "sinister" comes from the Latin word for left, and in the Bible, Jesus ascends to heaven and sits at the right hand of God. This ad places the family on the side of evil and the car on the side of good.

Car ads are not the only places where we are encouraged to consider relationships with products as more constant – more "right" – than relationships with people. An ad for a women's shaving gel shows "two ways a woman can get hurt": a guy, and shaving with soap and water. In other words, this brand of gel will never let you down the way a man could.[12]

Some ads send out a subconscious appeal to unusual or unhealthy social behavior. A series of magazine ads for Newport cigarettes (their slogan: "Alive with pleasure!") show laughing couples in situations that demean one or the other. In one ad, the woman wears a yoke for oxen about her neck and the man appears to be pulling her by it. In another, the woman crouches in seemingly mock terror behind the man, apparently holding on for dear life, as he prepares to ski away from her. In a third, the woman uses a pair of scissors to create cutoffs for the man out of a pair of pants, while the man is still in them.[13] Sure, these are funny. Laughter is partly an involuntary reaction to something which surprises us, and certainly when seen in isolation, these ads are surprising. But taken in aggregate, they show a disturbing mindset that promotes unacceptable behavior in male-female relationships. Anyone who found himself or herself on the receiving end of such behavior from a loved one surely wouldn't find it funny.

Kilbourne argues that ads like these have a cumulative effect in our subconscious. As we see these warped relationships over and over – the yoking of our girlfriends, the relationship we have with our car as paramount to the relationship we have with our kids – our subconscious begins to register them as normal. Our self-image becomes warped. We begin to feel subconsciously, as the advertisers have hoped, that "our most significant relationships are with the products that we buy."[14] Advertisers deliberately arouse our discomfort, then offer us products to soothe that discomfort. But of course, a relationship with a thing can never give us the same warmth as a relationship with a human. Thus, advertising becomes a vicious cycle: products never fulfill our needs the way we expect, and advertisers stand always ready to provide us with another product that they claim will make us whole.

Ads Foster Our Addictions

Nowhere is this cycle more dangerous than where the product being advertised is an addictive substance. Alcohol, cigarettes, and junk foods are all marketed as products that can transport us to a perfect world of peace and happiness. Alcohol ads display the "magic bottle": the one that is full and unopened, sitting next to a full glass, suggesting that the bottle will never be empty. A cigarette ad shows two slim cigarettes bending toward one another as a half moon hangs in the sky above them. Ads for ice cream show women all but having an orgasm from a single bite. The truth, of course, is that alcohol and cigarettes can kill you, and obesity is one of the nation's biggest health problems.

Killbourne states that the addict is an advertiser's best customer. Advertisers of addictive products know they must create a climate in the culture such that the compulsive, greedy behavior of an addict is viewed as normal by everyone around him: "This is absolutely essential because the makers of addictive products must prevent addicts from being confronted and perhaps forced into recovery. *Every time an addict recovers, someone loses money, whether it's the pusher on the corner or the pushers in the boardroom. This is the bottom line.*"[15]

The alcohol industry's support of the "designated driver" program is one example of this. Designating one person to stay sober does not cut into alcohol sales much, but more importantly, it does nothing to fight the idea that it is normal, and even desirable, to go out and get wasted on a Saturday night.[16] Industries that make addictive products use this approach because it focuses on small changes in personal behavior, which the industries know will not make a difference in their bottom lines:

> If you drink so much you wake up with a hangover ... take an Alka-Seltzer, don't worry about your drinking. If you're afraid you might kill someone while you're drinking and driving ... get a designated driver. If you're getting fat, the answer is to use a diet product, not to cut out the junk food and get off the couch. If your dieting is destroying your bones ... take some calcium. If your teeth are rotting because you are bulimic ... use a whitening gel. Don't ever look at what this all might mean or try to put it in a larger context. That would disrupt the climate of denial that is so vitally important to the sellers of addictive products. (*Deadly Persuasion*, p.295)

Kilbourne observes another way that advertisers normalize addictive behavior is by encouraging all of us to dream of becoming children again, "usually spoiled, narcissistic children used to instant gratification, endless recess, no restraints."[17] Escaping responsibility is a theme of many ads, and the "adult" world of work and relationships is depicted as boring: "According to an alcohol ad, the 'perfect week' is 'Saturday, Saturday, Saturday, Sunday, Saturday, Sunday, Holiday."[18]

Above all, Kilbourne says, ads for addictive products encourage the addict to have a relationship with nothing but the addictive substance:

> Advertising most contributes to the addictive mindset by trivializing human relationships and encouraging us to feel that we are in relationships with our products, especially with those products that are addictive. This not only disappoints us. It also diverts attention from what would really satisfy us and make us happy – meaningful work, authentic relationships, and a sense of connection with history, community, nature, and the cosmos. We end up looking for love in all the wrong places – which could be the very definition of addiction. (*Deadly Persuasion*, p.233)

Ads Make Us Cynics

In *Bowling Alone*, Robert D. Putnam charts the decline in civic involvement in the United States over the past several decades, and blames about a quarter of the drop on TV. (See "Building Community" for a full discussion of our loss of social capital, and some ideas for what to do about it.) At least a portion of that 25 percent drop could arguably be blamed on advertising. Kilbourne says advertisers have redefined freedom as "our right to buy things" and democracy as "our ability to choose from a variety of consumer goods." That, she says, has helped create a climate of apathy in the United States: "When people are working hard to earn money to buy a lot of stuff and then spending their free time shopping, it's hard to get involved in community issues or civic affairs – especially if they believe that nothing they do will make any difference anyway."[19]

Miller calls this cynicism "televisual irony", and says it is the latest incarnation of an advertising ploy developed during the Great Depression, when people began to become distrustful of big business. The idea then, he says, was for ads to poke fun at themselves, thereby co-opting consumers' desire to jeer at them and aligning the ad with the consumer. However, Miller says, today TV is nothing but ironic:

> "I call it talk-back TV," says actor John James, a regular on *Dynasty.* "You turn on the set, sit back and, between scoops of Haagen-Dazs, you say, 'Do you believe he said that?'" Thus, within the televisual environment, you prove your superiority to TV's garbage not by criticizing or refusing it, but by feeding on it, taken in by its oblique assurances that you're too smart to swallow any of it.[20]

Miller says this causes a problem for Baby Boomers, who worked to upset the status quo in the 1960s and now find themselves in charge of maintaining it:

> The generation that once laughed off TV, in short, is trying still to laugh it off while disappearing into it. In Bruce Willis, and/or in David Letterman…or in any of a hundred other aging wise guys, the old children of the Sixties half-recognize an emanation of their own self-irony – the corrosive cynicism of those who have had to trash the ideals of youth so as to keep on shopping.[21]

Ads Sold Us on Suburbia

Among the things the Boomers have been shopping for are homes in the suburbs, and it is largely thanks to advertising that life in suburbia has become our ideal. Mander says the government decided in the 1940s that encouraging the construction of massive suburban housing tracts was good for the nation, because it gave the GIs returning from World War II both a job and a place to live. Mander says the task of creating a need for these homes fell to advertisers: "If suburbs are capitalism's ideally separated buying units, and suburbs can be built profitably, then we must create humans who like and want suburbs: suburb-people. Since before the existence of suburbs there were no suburb-people, advertising has the task of creating them, in mind and body."[22]

Mander says this opened the door to the creation of a whole new ideal world – the 1950s ideal of Mom, Dad, and the two kids:

"The nuclear family was idealized to a greater extent than ever before, because the family was the consumption unit... Separate family units maximized production potential. Private homes. Private cars. Two cars. Private washing machines. Private television sets."[23]

If the people who encourage our addictions to alcohol, tobacco, and junk food; our habit of spending instead of saving; and our cynical world view; are the same guys who sold us on living in the suburbs, perhaps it is time to reject the supposed ideal of suburban life and come back to the good life in the city.

How We Can Fight Back

Kilbourne has several recommendations for reining in the advertising industry and the companies that sell addictive products. Among her suggestions:

- Take a "systems approach" to fighting against addictive behaviors by focusing not on the addicts, but on the organizations that promote the behaviors. Instead of encouraging people to "designate a driver", the government should raise taxes on alcohol, mandate better warning labels on packaging, and discourage events that promote cheap alcohol. Instead of condemning dieters for lacking willpower, the government should mandate labels on diet products indicating that 95 percent of all diets fail.
- Teach media literacy in schools, because "[h]uge and powerful industries – alcohol, tobacco, junk food, diet, guns – depend upon a media-illiterate population."
- Teach media literacy at home by limiting your children's TV watching and watching with them.
- Limit your own TV watching. Turn off the tube and go do something.
- Practice Voluntary Simplicity.
- Reclaim the concept of freedom from the advertisers and redefine it: "We are free when we are not addicted, when we can

be our real selves, when we are as healthy as possible in body and soul ..."[24]

Imagine...

If we did rein in the advertising industry, what would the world be like? The Center for a New American Dream's *More Fun, Less Stuff Starter Kit* has one view:

> The consumerist definition of the American dream will have some strong competition. More people will turn off commercial television, reject shopping as a pastime, and reclaim non-material pleasures. These people will attract others because their lives will exude fun, energy, and purpose. There will be a renaissance of dance, small plot farming, carpentry, music, visual arts, gardening, reading, hiking, bird-watching, and people will embrace moments of just "being" instead of always "doing". We will play more interactive games and get rid of our "Gameboys", and children will have enough time to ponder clouds, clover leaves, and the sound of the wind.[25]

Such a vision may not be Heaven, but we think it sounds like a much more appealing place to live than where we are right now.

Practical To Dos

- Avoid advertising as much as possible. That means limiting your consumption of TV, radio, magazines, and the Internet.
- Take a look around and notice how many ads surround you every day. Conduct an experiment: On your way to work or school, spend five minutes counting the number of ads and product mentions you are exposed to. Do the same thing while watching your favorite TV show.
- Campaign for media literacy in your city.
- Encourage the use of "systems approaches" in fighting against addictive behaviors.

- Watch TV with your kids and educate them about advertising.
- Practice Voluntary Simplicity.

Library Guide

- *Deadly Persuasion* by Jean Kilbourne
- *Four Arguments for the Elimination of Television* by Jerry Mander
- *The Overspent American* by Juliet B. Schor

Internet Resources

www.newdream.org (The Center for a New American Dream's
    More Fun, Less Stuff Starter Kit)
www.adbusters.org
www.jeankilbourne.com

Search Terms

advertising
media literacy
low-involvement advertising

CHAPTER 4

DOWNSIZE YOUR TV

If you asked a group of Simplifiers for the single best thing that novice Simplifiers could do to improve their lives immediately, the most popular answer would probably be, "Kill your television." (The second most popular response would likely be, "Get rid of your car"; see the "Transportation" chapter for more details on why and how.)

Television is a ubiquitous presence in US homes. As late as 1980, more Americans had TV sets than had indoor plumbing.[1] TV, together with the advent of air conditioning, has been popularly blamed for the fact that we don't know our neighbors any more; whereas in pre-TV days, folks would sit on their porches on hot summer evenings and watch the neighborhood go by, now they race from their air-conditioned cars to their air-conditioned houses and sit in front of the tube all night. One survey has shown that TV watching is the third most popular activity that adult Americans engage in; the number-one activity is working,[2] and sleeping is in second place.[3]

This would be bad enough, if TV were nothing more than a benign time-waster. But television viewing has so many negative effects associated with it on our health, our emotions, and our wallets, that your authors heartily agree with the majority of Simplifiers that downsizing your TV is a great way to start simplifying your life.

TV is a Vehicle for the Ads

In the chapter on advertising, we talk about how ads are designed to convince viewers that their lives are somehow incomplete, and how, after generating that feeling of discontent out of whole cloth, the advertiser then proposes a product as the cure.

On TV, however, this effect is amplified, because not just the ads, but the programming itself, is designed to make us feel vaguely uncomfortable – in other words, perfectly primed to buy whatever product the ads present to us. In *Boxed In: The Culture of TV*, Mark Crispin Miller said the typical TV viewer is forced to assume the ironic attitude of the people he sees on the box, because if he does not appear to be in on the joke, he will become the butt of the joke, like all those sitcom parents:

> Guided by its images even while he thinks that he sees through them, the TV-viewer learns only to consume. That inert, ironic watchfulness which TV reinforces in its audience is itself conducive to consumption. As we watch, struggling inwardly to avoid resembling anyone who might stand out as pre- or non- or antitelevisual, we are already trying to live up, or down, to the same standard of acceptability that TV's ads and shows define collectively: the standard that requires the desperate use of all those goods and services that TV proffers, including breath mints, mouthwash, dandruff shampoos, hair conditioners, blow-dryers, hair removers, eye drops, deodorant soaps and sticks and sprays, hair dyes, skin creams, lip balms, diet colas, diet plans, lo-cal frozen dinners, bathroom bowl cleaners, floor wax, car wax, furniture polish, fabric softeners, room deodorizers, and more, and more. Out of this flood of commodities, it is promised, we will each arise as sleek, quick, compact, and efficient as a brand-new Toyota; and in our effort at such self-renewal, moreover, we are enjoined not just to sweeten every orifice and burnish every surface, but to evacuate our psyches. While selling its explicit products, TV also advertises incidentally an ideal of emotional self-management,

which dictates that we purge ourselves of all "bad feelings" through continual confession and by affecting the same stilted geniality evinced by most of TV's characters (the butts excluded).[4]

When you think about all the effort that TV requires of us — purchase this, look a certain way, act like you understand the joke, wrap up all your problems in half an hour — it is almost enough to drive you to become "pre- or non- or antitelevisual" immediately.

Please allow us to prod you further in that direction.

What TV Does to Us

The pervasiveness of advertising on TV is one of Jerry Mander's four arguments for the elimination of television, in his book of the same name.[5] But Mander, a former TV advertising executive, takes the medium to task for other problems, as well.

Mediation of the experience. No matter how giant your screen or how high-definition your set, watching something on TV will never be like being there in person. We all have five senses, and when we are experiencing something live and in person, all five of our senses are engaged. However, television can engage only two senses: sight and hearing. Even those senses are engaged by TV in a limited way; no video camera can reproduce exactly the field of vision of the human eye, nor can the best sound equipment match the full range of the human ear. And the sounds we hear on TV may not even be what they purport to be. What seemed to be the sound of Coca-Cola being poured over ice in one commercial was actually created by a synthesizer.[6]

As for the other senses, taste, touch, and smell are engaged only by the bowl of hyper-sweetened cereal we are eating while the images dance before us on the screen. You can *see* the hole in the Pentagon where the plane went through on TV, and you can *hear* the reactions of those who lived through the horror of the crash. But the reality of the event will likely not hit home for you until your morning commute is disrupted and you can *smell* and *taste* the smoke from the still-burning building as you get off your commuter bus half a mile away (as Lynne did near the Pentagon on September 12, 2001).

TV also plays with your sense of time, as anyone who has spent half an hour watching the last two minutes of a ball game, including three or four "official's time outs" for commercial breaks, can attest.

Effects of TV on the viewer. If you watch television — *really* watch it, sitting in a darkened room, as opposed to using it as background noise while you do something else — you are operating at close to total sensory deprivation. Experiments with people who volunteer to undergo such sensory deprivation show that the subjects' perceptions change profoundly: they latch onto any stimulus, no matter how bizarre, and build a fantasy around it. So in yet another way, TV watchers are in a perfect sensory condition to accept any suggestions to purchase products that the advertisers throw at them.

Other studies show that television viewing induces the brain to create alpha waves, which typically increase when a person is meditating or in a hypnotic trance. When you meditate, however, *you* control the focus of your attention. The TV viewer focuses on whatever is on the screen, which makes the TV viewing experience more similar to hypnosis, in which the hypnotist controls the stimuli that the subject receives.[7]

This TV-induced trance state creates other problems. Some researchers have noted that people who watch a lot of TV often sleep less at night.[8]

Because TV is a sensory tease, the viewer evaluates the information on the screen, begins to react to it, and then suppresses the reaction because it is only an image. This constant gear-up and shut-down of the body's arousal mechanism creates energy, which the body stores[9]. The pent-up energy is released, often in a negative way, when the tube is turned off. If you have ever turned off the TV on a child when his or her TV time is over, you have seen this in action.[10]   Adults also exhibit this release of energy after the TV goes off. How often have you felt your heart pounding during a scary movie, and still felt frightened or wired even after the show was over? We are not trying to say that all entertainment is bad. Certainly there is nothing wrong with seeing an occasional horror movie, or turning on the tube once in awhile. It is regular TV watching that puts the body into this hyperenergetic state on a more-or-less constant basis, and that can take a toll on your physical and mental health.

The Issue of Bias

Mander's final point is that television is inherently biased. In putting together an entertainment program, the director tells the camera operator which pictures to shoot. The camera operator shoots only the pictures that are the most dramatic, or that show the most movement, or feature the most artistic camera angles. The video editor takes the raw footage and culls from it what she considers to be the best shots to illustrate the story that will fit within the time limitations of the piece. The producer, who bankrolls the show, oversees the finished product and decides whether it will air as is, or whether it needs to be re-edited or re-shot.

At each level of the process, someone has exercised some judgment about what will finally air. Much of the event was never committed to video; much of the video that was shot ends up on the proverbial cutting room floor. Everyone involved is a professional trying to do a good job, working within the limitations of the medium. The constraints of the medium itself force this winnowing process.

Once the final product is "in the can," it is shown to advertisers and network executives. Advertisers are picky about where they spend their money. Demographics comes into play here: if an advertiser is selling a new type of skateboard, it is not going to want to advertise on a show that appeals mostly to 45-to-54 year old women. Producers make shows that they think will attract a lot of viewers in a particular demographic, so that the advertisers will buy lots of time on the show and make the producers rich. This effort to appeal to the broadest market means that the shows that get on the air are generally geared to the lowest common denominator. If your taste ranges well above the lowest common denominator, you will be hard pressed to find much of anything on TV that does not insult your intelligence. You might think that the diversity of cable programming would allow for more niche programming. Unfortunately, however, the plethora of cable channels has fragmented the market, so that the producers and the advertisers who are looking to make the most money find themselves appealing to an even lower common denominator in order to attract the biggest possible audience.

Advertisers want to put their ads where the most people are going to see them; therefore, they will pay a premium for ad space on a show that a lot of people watch. Ratings services (for television programming, the primary service is A.C. Nielsen) determine statistically which shows are watched most often by people in the various demographic categories. Popular shows attract the most advertising dollars, particularly if the show delivers an audience in a demographic coveted by advertisers. Sometimes, popular shows attract too many viewers of an undesirable demographic, usually retirees to whom it is supposedly pointless to advertise because their brand loyalties are too entrenched and their disposable income is too small, and so the show is canceled. "Dr. Quinn, Medicine Woman" was highly rated, but it was canceled because its viewers skewed old.

TV News and Objective Journalism

News programming does not rely on advertising for its continued existence the way entertainment programming does. This is because television station owners are licensed by the federal government. To keep their license, station owners must air a certain number of hours of news and public affairs programming every week, so news programs are unlikely to be canceled.

However, local news is a cash cow for local stations. News is often the only programming that a TV station produces itself, which means that all of the advertising time available on local news programs can be sold to local companies. As advertisers spend the most money on the best-rated shows, ratings are still important. Lynne was a broadcast journalist for many years, and she believes that the real problem is that TV news has morphed into something that no longer delivers very much real news because the desire for higher ratings has become more important than the delivery of important news stories.

A yawning chasm once existed in TV between entertainment programming and news programming, with newscasts and documentaries on the news side, and comedies, dramas, and variety shows on the entertainment side. News people took their role as independent watchdogs of the government seriously. They simply did not do entertainment. You would never have seen long-time CBS news anchor Walter Cronkite trading jokes with David Letterman. Cronkite was a newsman. He was paid to be objective. He was paid to give viewers the information they would need to be effective citizens of their nation and of the world.

Sometime in the 1980s, the line between news and entertainment began to blur. Entertainment programming started to bear a strong resemblance to news programming. The television industry started producing shows like "Entertainment Tonight," which looks like news but which delivers information that has nothing to do with informing the electorate; talk shows, which would like you to *think* they are news but aren't; infomercials and "investigative" specials about paranormal activity hosted by some has-been celebrity; and so on. Then management in local TV station newsrooms started scheduling features, or "news you can use" segments, during local news broadcasts, in an effort to win better ratings. Better ratings, of course, allow the sales department to sell advertising time for more money, which generates more revenue for the stockholders and bigger bonuses for the sales people. Features have their place in a news broadcast; without them, the news would not be much more than accidents, fires, and governmental meetings. But elaborate feature segments eat up a lot of air time — sometimes so much that some of the more important news of the day doesn't make it.

At the same time that this shift in news content was occurring, overall news viewership was dropping. Some news viewers went to cable, lured by 24-hour access to the headlines via CNN and its subsequent competitors, but other viewers stopped watching TV news altogether. In *Bowling Alone*, sociologist Robert D. Putnam makes a convincing case that this dropoff in news viewing was largely generational in nature. Putnam argues that older Americans are the most interested in watching TV news (and as a corollary, they are also most likely to be involved in civic activities). This interest drops off among the Baby Boomers, and even farther among the Boomers' children.[11]

In response to the drop in viewership, TV news management at the networks began to "modernize" their network news shows in an effort to get viewers back. In other words, they began adding "news you can use." Cronkite himself decries this attempt to put feature pieces on the network news: "Nobody's asked me, which is strange, but I think the networks ought to be doing the headlines – compressed as they must be – and no features. Drop that 'Your Pocketbook and Mine,' 'Your Beauty and Mine,' 'Your Garbage Can and Mine.'"[12]

In addition, the broadcast networks – and local stations, too – tried to make their product look more like the 24-hour cable news operations by going live for the sake of going live. Cable news outfits go live a lot because they have so much air time to fill. The danger is that because they have all that time to fill, the reporter will babble anything that sounds like a new fact. This means they report things which later turn out to be false. The old journalism practice of having two sources confirming a questionable report before publishing it has sometimes fallen by the wayside in the rush to fill air time and get the scoop.

Despite glitzing up the news with features and bogus live shots, viewership continues to drop. In March 2002, rumors surfaced that ABC was in negotiations to bring Letterman's show to the network from CBS – and, in the process, put Ted Koppel's venerable "Nightline" out to pasture. One TV critic, Howard Rosenberg of the *Los Angeles Times*, sees this as a symptom of the eventual downfall of broadcast news: "There's enormous atrophy in terms of quality. The genre is becoming less and less relevant to Americans. It's like the entire Titanic is going down."[13]

Some critics argue that the only way to solve these problems is to dump the current editorial process and let everybody have access to all the news. While this idea is appealing, it is unworkable. If you tried to keep up with all the news that is generated every day without the filter of TV or a newspaper, your life would be far less than simple. Somebody has to be the editor. The alternative would be similar to the unedited experience you get when surfing the Internet. When you are web surfing, you must constantly evaluate the accuracy of the information on sites you visit. Relying on people to do this would be fine if we had a media-literate populace, but we do not. If you doubt that statement, think about the longevity of some urban legends; for example, no matter how many times Proctor & Gamble has denied over the years that its corporate logo is a satanic symbol, the story persists.

Regardless of the future of the medium, viewers today should understand what TV news is and is not. TV news is not, and never has been, a comprehensive source of information. TV news is driven by pictures; sound bites are just long enough for a slogan; a package (with the reporter and source or sources on tape) runs a maximum of two minutes. If the story cannot be told in pictures, it is not going to get on the air. And yet, one survey showed that in the aftermath of the attacks on the World Trade Center and the Pentagon on September 11, 2001, nine of ten Americans got their news exclusively from TV.[14] At the same time, public confidence in the trustworthiness of journalists is eroding. In at least one recent poll, journalists are now ranked uncomfortably near used car salesmen in terms of trust.[15]

We saw a faint glimmer of hope, in the aftermath of September 11, that TV news might yet redeem itself. Coverage during and immediately following the plane crashes and the collapse of the World Trade Center towers was generally restrained, accurate, tasteful, and appreciated by most Americans. A Pew Research Center poll taken just after the terrorist attacks showed public confidence in the media had skyrocketed – 73 percent of respondents called the news media "highly professional". However, within a few months, TV news was back to business as usual, and a Pew Research Center poll in July 2002 showed just 49 percent of respondents — fewer than before September 11 — saying they thought the news media were "highly professional".[16]

Kids and TV

Earlier, we talked about how kids (and adults, too) must release their pent-up energy as soon as the TV is turned off. This is not the only effect of children's TV watching. We go into much more detail in the "Simplifying With Kids" chapter about why TV is bad for kids, but we would like to add a point or two here.

One interesting fact is that in 1984, the Federal Communications Commission issued a rule that allowed toy manufacturers to create whole shows around their toys. Just a year later, nine out of the top ten best-selling toys in the US had their own TV shows.[17] The media mergers of recent years have not slowed this greedy practice. In October 2001, The Walt Disney Co. (which already owned the ABC TV and radio networks, the Disney Channel, and the Disney theme parks, among other properties) bought Fox Family Worldwide, Inc., from Haim Saban and Fox Broadcasting Co. for $5.2 billion.[18] Saban is the brains behind the Mighty Morphin Power Rangers, toys which, not coincidentally, have spawned a string of kids' series for Fox Kids, Fox Network's children's programming division. In January 2002, Fox Broadcasting reportedly narrowed its list of suitors for programming its Saturday morning lineup to two companies: DIC Entertainment, which developed "Sonic the Hedgehog" (based on a video game), and 4Kids Entertainment, producers of "Pokémon" (a Japanese import based on a trading card game). Of the reported deal, *Broadcasting & Cable* said: "Insiders say the $25 million price tag will be a loss-leader for whichever studio is selected. Advertising revenue alone will not cover the cost, but both DIC and 4Kids want to use the Saturday-morning time to sell toys to young viewers."[19]

Additionally, constantly using TV as a babysitter can mean that children become dependent on the tube to structure their time. This turns their effort away from the development of the personal self. In effect, watching TV can be "dullness training"[20]:

> A child who is left for hours in front of a television set with nothing else to do, a child who has never been encouraged to independently create information – who does not know how to draw, how to make music, how to pretend, or even how to read – such a child cannot be expected to turn the set off. The child is condemned to develop a viewing habit, the choices determined by the poverty of the [viewing] environment. What is true of the child may also be true of those adults who, screened by societal deprivations from surrounding complexity, may be as helpless as the child when they are left with nothing to do.[21]

You know this is going on in your household if your kids know exactly when certain shows are on and whine about missing them because you have involved them in some other activity at that time. This is just as problematic for adults as it is for children. Without a way to structure their own time, TV effectively becomes an addiction for many children and adults.[22] It is easy to see how it would be almost impossible for people addicted to TV, which constantly peddles products to them, to formulate their own values.[23]

How Can I Get Off TV?

For most of us, TV is a habit. You get up in the morning and turn it on to hear the weather or traffic report, or to keep the kids amused while you get ready for your day. You turn it on in the evening to hear the news, or to keep the kids amused while you catch your breath and make dinner. And then, well, okay, you watch some of the programming. But only a little bit. Just one show on Mondays. Well, and the Thursday night sitcom lineup. And any time your favorite team is playing, you *have* to watch that. And there's that new drama on Fridays, that's so similar to that other show on Tuesdays that you like a lot... But aside from that, how will you keep up with what's going on in the world if you don't watch TV?

And there is the social aspect of TV to consider. Well, it might be more accurate to call it the "water cooler" aspect: What will you talk about with your coworkers, if you can't chat about last night's episode of whatever? You will feel so left out.

Our question to you is this: Is it worth it to you to allow yourself to be placed in a semi-vegetative state and marketed to, in order to catch a couple of headlines and to be able to join in the office chatter?

The only way you can tell whether it is possible for you to live without television is to do it. Go on a TV-fast for a week. Adbusters sponsors National TV Turnoff Week in April every year; you could plan your TV-fast for that week, or try it another time. Hide the remote, or unplug the box, to remind yourself not to turn it on reflexively. We know some folks who keep the TV set in the closet, and only roll it out when there is something on that they want to watch. (We know others who have gotten rid of their televisions entirely, but you don't need to go that far at the start.)

If you want traffic and weather reports in the mornings, turn on the radio or TV only as long as it takes to gather the information you need. If you have a weather radio, the National Weather

Service seldom plays advertisements. Or you could live dangerously and leave the house in the morning without knowing what
the weather and traffic will be like. Carry an umbrella with you
every day, in case you get caught in a cloudburst. Take public
transit, so that if you get caught in a traffic jam, you can blame it
on the bus driver. Jonathan has been doing this for years now, and
does not miss either the traffic or the talking weather-head.

If you want to be informed, read a newspaper, either in print
or online. You will get a lot more information from the paper
than you ever will from a TV newscast. Again, you have ads to
contend with, but print ads are easier to ignore. You could also do
the more daring thing and take a break from the news. It may
seem impossible, but our culture is so saturated with media that
you can learn about the *really* important news without even trying.
Lynne pretty much quit watching TV after she got out of the
business, but she has still managed to find out everything she needs
to know about current events from reading her local newspaper
online every day.

If you are worried that your social life at the office will suffer,
you are in for a shock. Since the advent of cable and its 500
channels, the audience has become so fragmented that hardly anybody is watching even the most popular shows any more. When
someone asks you, "Did you see...?" just smile and say, "No."
Chances are pretty good that they will just keep talking without
noticing what you said. It is quite possible to stay completely up
on the twists and turns of your old favorites just by listening to
your office mates.

Eventually, someone might catch on that you never seem to
see anything on TV any more and ask you why not. Here, you
have a choice. You can tell the person what you were doing instead of watching that particular show, evading the subject of
whether you watch television at all. Or you can tell him or her
that you do not watch TV any more, which is sure to trigger some
interesting responses. You will often find that the person will
then tell you that they hardly watch TV any more, either, except

for the one show on Mondays, and then all the sitcoms on Thursdays, and so forth. Be gentle with them.[24]

If I Don't Watch TV, What Will I Do?

When you quit watching television, you will likely find yourself with a lot of free time on your hands. We have numerous suggestions in "Entertainment" for things you can do in your newfound spare time, but as a quick reference, we offer here Ten Things You Can Do Today Instead of Watching Television:

- Have a conversation with someone. Talk to your kids. Chat with your Significant Other. Call a friend on the phone. Try to do this when the person is not watching TV, so that you will not have to compete with the TV for their attention.
- Play cards with a friend.
- Take a walk or engage in some other exercise you enjoy—especially if you can do it outside.
- Take a nap or turn in early to catch up on all your missed sleep.
- Go the library and check out a book. Bring it home and read it.
- Tackle that towering stack of unread magazines.
- Clean out a closet or the garage or….
- Take up a hobby you have let languish.
- Perform some community service.
- Bake bread or make cookies with someone special.

Free your mind and your time. Downsize your TV (or at least watch it less)!

Practical To Dos

- Turn off the TV for a week.
- Live dangerously: Walk out of the house without knowing if it will rain.

- Read the newspaper to get the news, or take a break from the news entirely.
- With your newfound free time, try one of our Ten Things You Can Do Today Instead of Watching Television, or some of the suggestions from the *Entertainment* chapter.

Library Guide

Four Arguments for the Elimination of Television by Jerry Mander
Boxed In: The Culture of TV by Mark Crispin Miller
Television and American Culture by Carl Lowe
Television and the Quality of Life by Mihaly Csikszentmihalyi and
   Robert William Kubey
The Plug-in Drug by Marie Winn
Unplugging the Plug-in Drug by Marie Winn

Internet Resources

www.adbusters.org
www.newdream.org
www.museum.tv
www.turnoffyourtv.com

Search Terms

TV Turnoff Week
Marie Winn
Gerry Mander

CHAPTER 5

A BATHTUB MODEL OF CASH FLOW

Debt can be a killer to your financial life. But too little income can also do you in just as fast, if not faster. However, many folks paper over a lack of income, or too big an outgo, by using loans of one variety or another. In this chapter, we will examine cash flow in the microeconomic sense: we will walk through your cash flow and relate it to a bathtub.

The Bathtub Model of Cash Flow

Let us assume that money is a liquid, like water; after all, we say cash is "liquid" and we call it cash "flow". We can then visualize this liquid money falling from a faucet into a bathtub. You and your family are in the tub. The money from the faucet is your income, be it from job(s) or investments. The size of the tub expands or contracts, depending on the amount of income you have, and it can get infinitely big; you cannot overflow this tub.

This tub has just one drain, for starters. The money flowing out the drain is spending or expenses; all your "business of life" and extraordinary expenses go down this drain. So when you pay the electric or the ambulance bill, down the drain the money goes. (It sure feels like that sometimes!) Whatever cash stays in the bathtub is savings. The money's movement is your "cash flow". If the tub empties, if the cash flow runs out the drain faster than it comes out of the faucet, then the drain will suck you all down. Not a happy thought; we will talk about this a bit more at the end of the chapter.

So with the terminology down, consider a few cases. These numbers are just an example; you can plug in your own numbers as you read.

Assume you make $30,000 per year, and you spend $27,000 per year. That is, your earnings faucet is delivering more liquid money than your spending drain is taking away. We would observe the tub to slowly fill over time, right? Remember that this tub cannot overflow; it will expand if needed. This is the best case: you are spending less than you earn, so you accumulate some savings (water in the tub).

Now consider the case where you earn $30,000 and spend $33,000 per year, which so many people seem to do. Assume for the moment that you have some savings in your tub. Over time,

as you spend 10% more than you earn, your savings would be depleted. That is, your tub will slowly empty. If this goes on, of course, your tub will become completely empty. That is not good because then YOU will be sucked down the drain.

Now comes an interesting dilemma: since you want to keep right on spending but must keep the drain filled, you have to come up with more cash flow. How do you do that? It will depend on your situation, of course, so we will consider several possibilities. You might be able to think of more.

You could sell something you own. These would be things you have already bought: household goods, tools, etc. These might also be your interest in something (a car, a house, etc.) but do not completely own. You might cash in a certificate of deposit, sell stocks or bonds, or empty your savings or your retirement accounts. Basically, you have found a bucket of cash flow and poured it into the tub. But since you probably will not decrease your spending, the cash flow will eventually drain away, leaving your tub empty again. Not good.

You could get a gift or an inheritance. You could beg a bucketful of cash, in the form of a grant, from your friends, family, or some governmental body, and pour that into your tub. Because this is a gift, you do not have to pay the money back. But since you probably will not decrease your spending, again, the gift cash flow will eventually drain away and leave your tub empty again. Still not good.

You could get a loan. It might be a signature loan, a payday loan, or a home equity loan. You might refinance your house, pawn some valuable, or make a visit to a shady loan shark. But whatever form your loan takes, in order to get it, you have to sign a piece of paper that says you promise to pay the loan back, usually with interest. So what have you done to your tub? As you did with the gift money and with the money you got from selling something, you threw a bucket of cash flow into the tub. But when you got the new loan you also drilled a new drain in the bottom of the tub. This drain is your loan payment, another outflow that you must keep filled or you will be sucked down. Under the drain is a bucket that will hold the loan amount plus all the interest you choose to pay. You cannot close a loan drain until the loan bucket is full! And the longer you take to pay off the loan (that is, fill up the loan bucket), the more interest you will pay.[1]

Notice that credit cards are a special kind of loan. With a credit card, you can get a variable amount of money thrown into your tub whenever you want it, so it is more like a faucet than a bucket. That is very convenient. But as you did with the conventional loan, you have agreed to pay the credit card company back, so you have drilled a hole into your tub and installed yet another drain. And under this drain is that darn loan bucket waiting to be refilled with what you poured in, plus all the interest you care to pay (probably at a rate that rivals the loan shark's!).

Now, as long as you pay off your credit card every month, there is no problem because you keep the drain happy and the loan bucket filled. But what happens when you do not pay off the whole amount each month? The drain for your credit card has a variable-size opening. It will take a minimum amount, the minimum payment due, or more if you want. But there is still that bucket under the drain waiting to be filled, and over time, the bucket gets bigger and bigger as you keep right on charging. Over time, the drain hole  gets larger and larger as the minimum payment goes up. The loan bucket keeps getting bigger and the drain hole keeps expanding until the day you reach your credit limit and max out the card. At that point, the drain hole will not get any smaller until you start filling up the loan bucket.

Now, most sane people would stop spending so much at this point, and start working on refilling the bucket under the credit card drain. Unfortunately, many people are a little nuts when it comes to credit cards. They keep on making just the minimum payment on this credit card. Then they go get another credit card. With a new drain and bucket installed, they keep right on charging. And charging. And charging. Until they discover that they cannot get another credit card. Bummer.

You know what happens here, when you are about to be sucked down the drain. You buckle down, cut your spending so your main drain is less than your income, and then start filling up all your loan buckets, paying interest all the way. Or you declare bankruptcy and get a new tub with only one drain. But even then you will probably still have to buckle down and live within your means because it will be more difficult (although not impossible) to get another loan, credit card or otherwise. (There are plenty of lenders out there who are happy to take on bad credit risks, because it means that they can charge a really high interest rate on their loan bucket.) Mega-bummer. Enjoy buckling! Too bad this is not like swashbuckling.

There is another way to keep from getting sucked down the drain, and that is to crank the earnings faucet open wider. In other words, you must earn more income. That sounds easy, but it seldom is.

And there is a third way to keep from getting sucked down the drain: do not overspend in the first place. That is what folks on the Voluntary Simplicity path try to do. It does not really matter where you live; you can overspend your income anywhere. Our survey respondents agree. Simplifier Everette Orr is a certified public accountant, who said, "I've seen people get in debt in rural areas up to their eyeballs and I've seen people in urban areas get in debt up to their eyeballs. I think it has to do with — there's something else going on with the debt issue. I've seen people live prudently in an urban area, and I've seen people live prudently in rural areas."

Canadian Simplifier alex glenlee[2] chose to live in the city after living in the country for several years and saw the same thing:

There's a tremendous amount of debt that one gets into. Most of the farmers here incorporate, as they do in the States, but the matter of the fact is you have to carry a tremendous amount of debt. There's a lot of dollars that go out for operational costs and equipment, and the profit margins some years can be very small, non-existent, or a loss, depending on all sorts of factors. ... Farmers are no different, they're involved in the same go round... "This is Dad's land, and it was Grandpa's land, and it was Great-Grandpa's land, and I love the land," and they really do! ... It's not a lot different from the sort of thing that the city guys face or the guy in a corporate job that's on automatic pilot, and the boss says: "You know, to keep your job this year (because you're in middle or upper management), we want you to produce/squeeze 5% out of this." ... And then the next year, you gotta squeeze 6%, and then 8%, and... How long do you have to squeeze blood out of a brick? ... How long and how hard do you have to do this just to make sure you have that house on the hill and the three cars in the garage? You know, gee, the farm people aren't much different. ... [I] see a lot of them looking at doing the same thing. This is all part of the consumer experience, isn't it? [I] think that we think that we value our worth in terms of our ability to be able to consume. It's scary!

Scary, indeed. It does not matter where you live; you can over-spend your income.

Practical To Dos

- Track how much you spend.
- Track how much you earn.
- Decide if you really want to spend that much.
- Follow the nine steps found in *Your Money or Your Life*

Library Guide

- *How to Get Out of Debt and Live Prosperously* by Jerrold Mundis
- *Your Money or Your Life* by Joe Dominguez and Vicki Robin
- *Affluenza: The All-Consuming Epidemic* by John De Graaf et al.

Internet Resources

www.debtorsanonymous.org
www.debtadvice.org
www.cccsintl.org
www.yourmoneyoryourlife.org

Search Terms

debtors anonymous
bathtub model of debt
affluenza

CHAPTER 6

MORE MONEY

Society grinds into us that we are identically equal to our job or the amount of money we make. If you doubt that statement, think about how we customarily greet people: "Hi! I'm Bill. I work for XYZ Widgets," or "I'm Sally, a computer programmer". What Sally does to make money is program a computer. Sally might have a whole other life as a mother, a pilot, a church elder, and so on. Why *is* Sally *a programmer?* Because in our society, status is conferred on those who make a lot of money. If Sally really wanted to mess with someone's mind, she could say: "I'm Sally, and I'm a human."

The next things to consider when you are looking for more income are your core values. This is important because your core values need to be upheld in any work situation you might find yourself in. For example, if you strongly believe that using tobacco is not something anyone should be doing, you might be miserable running the cash register at the tobacconist's shop. You must decide what sort of work situations you would feel the best about.

Drawing your ethical limits too broadly may put you out of the job market entirely. If so, you will have to be even more creative about earning money. Once you have a good handle on your values, then you can determine what attributes the ideal work situation might have. There are no rules, other than the ones you bring with you, so you can be creative and make the rules you need in many cases. *What Color is Your Parachute?* is a popular book that can help you explore all your options.

Here are some things you can consider to earn more money. Obviously, there are lots more ways than this; you are limited only by your imagination.

- Move up one step on the ladder at your current job.
- Change your employer.
- Work from home.
- Start your own business.
- Spend some time and money upgrading your skills.
- Freelance on the side, in an area that uses your underused skills.
- If you are paid by the hour, work overtime.
- Figure out how you can exercise more skills on the job.
- Offer a class in a skill you have.
- Write freelance articles for newspapers or magazines.
- Perform (act, dance, public speaking, etc) for money.
- Sell or rent books and other content-based or intellectual property (patents, etc.) you have created.

Passive income is any income that arrives in your account without you having to do much, if anything, to have it arrive there. Some forms of passive income are:

- Rental of property, usually a building;
- Leasing of owned land for mineral extraction, farming, or windmill power generation[6];
- Investment income: for example, dividends on stocks or interest from bonds;
- Anything else you can do or sell that causes a royalty stream.

Job or Career

The best ways to maximize your income is to do what you are best at, in a manner that best supports your values. We can refer to this as your calling, or your life's work. So how do you find your life's work, if you don't already know what it is? Unfortunately, there are no easy answers to that question. Some people seem to be born knowing it. Others suffer a traumatic event that causes them to redirect their life energy. Some relate that an off-hand remark or some odd situation that caught them unaware was the spark of an epiphany. A small group will talk about that still, small voice in the night or in their heads. However, the vast majority of us (and your authors fit in this category) kind of stumble around and either never find their calling or happen on it almost by accident. Finding a calling can take a long time. Likewise, as time passes, you may find that your old calling is being replaced by a new calling (often from a direction you never expected).

So you have a sense that there is more to you than you currently are. How do you find out what that more is?[1] First, what are your strengths? Don't say that you don't have any strengths; everybody has something that they do better, or more easily, than other folks. Maybe you make great widgets, or great sauerbraten. Maybe you're good at listening, or being sympathetic, or making decisions quickly, or sticking to the job until it is done. Make a list of those things. If you cannot think of anything, ask someone you trust for a list of what they think you are good at; work together on this if at all possible. Do the same thing for your weaknesses. For both lists, a sympathetic partner can help you. Then, compare your strengths against your weaknesses. What additional strengths and weaknesses now come to mind? Add them to the appropriate list.

Third, make a list of all the things you ever want to do in your life.[2] This is a brainstorming session, so do not let "reality" stop you from writing down what you want. This is a reality-free exercise; if you want to walk on Mars without a pressure suit, write it down!

With your three lists, what do you see? You may see some pleasant and unpleasant truths on those lists. Think about what your little voice (if you have one) is telling you. What was your last "Aha!" moment? What recurring dream have you had that seems to call to you and beg you to make it so? Having all this stuff on paper is liberating for many people—what does it say to you? What is important is that you begin to see how your strengths and weaknesses[3] might become useful tools for helping you achieve your dreams.

Another exercise for discovering your calling is this: Take the list of personal strengths from the exercise above. Second, make a second list, of things you love to do. Third, make a list of things you can think of that people would be willing to pay for. Now for the fun part: Take one thing from each list, and combine them into a job or business. For example, if you are good at making sauerbraten, you like to garden, and you think that people would buy herbs, you could grow and sell sauerbraten seasoning packets. Admittedly, the market for sauerbraten seasonings is probably pretty small, but you could morph this idea into seasonings for other foods, as well.

If, after completing any or all of these exercises, you are still stumped about your calling, or if you are getting a sense of it but the details are still a little fuzzy, you could try a Web search. *What Color is Your Parachute?* author Richard Bolles has listed links on his website, jobhuntersbible.com, to interactive online tests (some of them free) which suggest good careers for people with various personality traits.

What habits do you have that keep you from your dreams? Look at your three lists again. Do you see any patterns? What values do you see there? Think about the ways you reward yourself. Is there a better way to reward yourself that fits in with your values? Is there a way to reward yourself that will drive you along the path toward your dreams? Is there a reward you want more than the ones you have been giving yourself already? These can be tough questions for several reasons. The biggest reason is resistance.

Resistance

Resistance is the manifestation of the forces within you that seek to minimize your success. Often resistance begins as a small failure at something trivial. This failure festers in your subconscious. The next time something a wee bit risky comes along, the subconscious starts spewing out failure scenarios. "You failed last

time, didn't you, why should this time be any different?" your subconscious seems to say.

So listen to your subconscious and start making a plan for
every reasonable case it churns out. (Not every scenario will be
reasonable.) You can plan for a piece of machinery breaking down:
your car, your personal computer, or any other gadget your new
venture may depend on. You can plan for people to let you down,
especially if they have done so in the past. You can plan for events
that will hinder your progress.

So with a little bit of thought, and maybe a pencil and paper at
your bedside to record things late in the night, you may well be
able to come up with all the reasonable scenarios that could cause
you to fail. Start thinking through plans to lower the risk of those
bad scenarios happening or eliminating them altogether. Writing
your plans down is a useful device for helping you think them
through.

Three Laws of Resourcefulness

Resourcefulness is an attitude. Everyone knows someone who,
if they get stuck with a truck full of lemons, puts up a lemonade
stand within an hour and opens lemonade stands all over the city
inside of a week. No matter what life seems to hurl at some
people, they always find a way out of every jam. They may not
emerge with their dignity or their wallets completely intact, but
you just know, somehow, that they are not the least bit fussed.
Those people are resourceful; they have an inner strength that
seems to let them see through the muck and mire of life to grab
for the jewels (whether they get them is another matter, but it
seems they usually do). Dr. Marsha Sinetar suggests that these
folks have learned the three laws of resourcefulness:

First, the person must have faith in his or her ability to solve
problems. Whether we call this self-trust or high self-regard matters less than that we understand how the person learns to depend
on his own brain's ability to solve problems. The second law or

requisite of resourcefulness would seem to be to practice independent thinking and decision-making – practice that puts the individual at risk if he does not solve his own problems. The third "law" or requisite is determination: the individual must decide deep in himself that somehow he is going to discover the answer to puzzles he faces.[4]

Living in the City Resourcefully

Living in the city can make it easier to have multiple revenue streams. The truly interesting thing about having multiple revenue streams is that not only are you building your net worth faster (if you are saving some of your earnings and not living at the edge of your income), but you are more likely to withstand a downturn in the economy. If one job succumbs to cost cutting, then you still have the other to pay the bills. Many folks start their own business when the pink slip shows up in their pay envelope, using a side job as the basis for their new adventure.

Living in the city can make having a job or a career much easier. When you live in the city, this can be simpler to manage because there are more jobs available in a much smaller area. Being resourceful in your choices and outlook is a habit you can learn, and makes working more enjoyable. Whichever route or routes you decide to take is really up to you. Living in the city just increases your options.

Real Hourly Wage

One of the measures of how well we are doing is our hourly wage. Many times people have changed jobs in order to increase their hourly wage. But what shows on the top line of your pay stub is not your real hourly wage; there are a lot of other factors that determine your Real Hourly Wage (a concept from *Your Money or Your Life*, by Joe Dominguez and Vicki Robin).

What is Your Real Hourly Wage?

Your Real Hourly Wage (RHW) starts at the top line of your pay stub with your gross income. If you are an hourly worker, you have an hourly wage assigned to the job or jobs you are working. If you are a consultant, you probably bill for some number of hours on the client's site or job at an hourly rate.

Regardless of how you get to this initial figure, this is *not* what you truly make per hour.

Compare a typical working day to a typical "post-lottery" day, so the true costs of working become visible. Record all the time and money you spend doing things that are associated with your job(s). Here is a partial list.

Time Spent on:
- Working, including any unpaid overtime
- Preparing for work before or after the day's work (work done at home, preparing your body for work, buying and maintaining work clothes, etc.); commute time to and from work
- Unwinding time from work, before you can deal with fighting kids or speak civilly to spouse (some call this 'daily decompression')
- Organizing or attending special work-related functions outside of working hours
- Keeping up with your special field
- In therapy or at the doctor's from work-related illnesses (physical, mental, etc.)
- Preparing for your next job (at this employer or client, or at the next level: classes, certifications, etc.)
- Going to and from daycare
- Taking vacations to get away from work
- Doing unpaid union or professional society work
- Socializing "at the club" or elsewhere as a way to network for business
- Dealing with your child's behavior problems because you were not there parenting

- Filling out and filing income tax schedules related to work
- What are other ways that work takes time from your life?

  Money spent on:
- Uniforms or office clothes you would not buy, own, maintain, or dispose of otherwise
- Meals on the run to/from work and meals at work (if you regularly brownbag what you would eat at home anyway, then do not count the cost of your meal)
- Coffee or other substances to wind up for work, alcohol or other substances to unwind from work
- Commuting costs (car and gasoline, bus or subway fare, etc.)
- Office contributions (weddings, funerals, retirements, baby showers, etc.)
- Unreimbursed work supplies (paper, forms, tools, cell phone, pager, etc.)
- Money spent on items needed to keep up with your field: books, magazines, classes, etc.
- Money spent preparing for your next job (advertising, classes, certifications, etc.)
- Money spent on illness related to work
- Day care costs
- Money spent on vacations to get away from work
- Union or professional society dues
- Bar and restaurant tabs from networking sessions
- Income taxes (any of federal, state, or city), FICA, FUTA, OASDI, etc.
- What other money do you spend in order to keep your job?

  Add up all the time you spend that is associated with your job (time you would not spend if you did not have a job): this figure is your "total work hours". Next, add up all the money you spend associated with your job (money you would not spend if you did not have to work): this is your "total work costs".

  Take your annual salary (gross income) and subtract your total annual work costs (you may have to adjust your work costs to be annual instead of per week or per month). The result of the subtraction is the amount of money you really earn per year.

Now, take the total work hours per year that you calculated above, and divide this number into the annual amount you really earned. This is your Real Hourly Wage for the year. Expressed as a formula, this is what you are calculating:

$$RHW = (\text{Gross income} - \text{total job costs}) / \text{total work hours}$$

If your RHW is positive, what is your reaction to that number? Are you surprised? More than one person has been shocked at how little they make per hour even though they have a high-status, high-paying job. Is there some way you could rearrange your work life to increase your RHW (cut the amount of time you spend on work, or lower your work expenses, or both)?

Having calculated your Real Hourly Wage, you can use it in quite a few situations:

- When you are contemplating spending some money, figure how many hours it takes to earn the money you will use to pay for this thing. Use this to evaluate whether the purchase is worth the effort.

- When you are contemplating adding a new job or changing jobs, you can take a guess at the new job's RHW, and use that to help you figure out if you want the job at all, or to negotiate a larger hourly rate, or an office nearer to or in your home, or slightly different job duties, or something else that adjusts your RHW upward.

- If you have investments, tracking how much time you spend thinking about and handling your portfolio to derive a certain amount of income can help you figure out what type of investor you are: buy and hold, couch potato, day trader, gambler, etc. It will also put a spotlight on the fact that investing is not a "free" activity and investment-derived income requires some amount of time spent to acquire it (if nothing more than filing in a couple of extra lines on your tax forms).

- If someone comes along with an activity you do not really want
  to do, you can determine how much it might be worth your
  time just to send the person away with money (that is, make a
  donation or hire the job done instead of participating in the
  activity).

Values-Based Spending

You may have begun to wonder why we trade our life energy
for money indiscriminately. The answer is that we are not in touch
with our true values. In fact, people who can articulate their values in a clear way, especially on paper, are the very rare exception
in our society. If you doubt that, sit down and write out your
values. Notice that we are not saying that people don't have values; we are saying that most people's values are so well hidden
internally that they have to work at finding and exposing them.

We suggested a method for helping you to identify your values in "Choices and Values." A method that will help you identify
your values in terms of your spending decisions is to track your
spending closely for a period of time. Make the effort to write
down every penny[5] you spend for a limited period, say a week or a
month.[6] Then sit down and look at all your spending for that
period; put each transaction in front of you. What kinds of patterns do you see? It is easy to do the budget-book analysis and
lump everything into Food, Clothing, Shelter, and Miscellaneous—
don't do that! Take a deeper look at your spending. What categories of spending make the most sense to you while you are looking at your figures? What personal values might lie behind each
of those categories?

When we go to work, we trade our life energy: our time, effort, creativity, and "juice" for money. When we buy something,
we are spending our life energy for something. Without casting
blame on ourselves, we must ask three questions every time we
are about to spend some of our life energy in the form of money[13]:

1. Will I receive fulfillment, satisfaction, and value in proportion to life energy spent?

2. How would this expenditure change if I didn't have to work for a living?

3. Is this spending in alignment with my values and life purpose?

By working with your categories and observing what you are spending your money on, you can start to see how you express your values to the world. These expressed values may be different than the values you identified in doing the exercises in "Choices and Values"—and at this stage, that really is fine. Once you start to see your values as expressed in your spending, you can start to change your buying habits to bring them in line with your real, internal values. You will know you have arrived when you look over the last month's spending and can say to yourself: "I spent every penny according to my real values".

Practical To Dos

- Track how much you spend.
- Track how much you earn.
- Decide if you really want to spend that much.
- Follow the nine steps found in *Your Money or Your Life*.
- Figure out your total debt. Start paying it down.
- Track how much you earn.
- Decide if this is what you really want to earn.
- Make a plan for earning more.
- Get several books from the library on careers or jobs you might like.
- Investigate courses offered through your local college, vocational school, or other school district.
- Investigate offering a course through your local college, vocational school, or other school district.

- Make time to write your book.
- Put in some overtime at your current job.
- Take a second job part time.
- Take a third job part time.
- Learn about investments at your local library, and then open an investment account.
- Think about alternative ways of making money that fit with your values. Then go try one.
- Research job or career alternatives at the library.
- Decide to be resource-full.
- Cut up your credit cards and use cash for all transactions.
- If that is too drastic for you, at least pull the cards out of your wallet and hide them someplace difficult to get to.
- If that is still not enough to keep you from using them, put them in a baggie full of water and freeze them.
- If that does not work, stash them in your safe deposit box.
- If that does not work, cut them up now and cancel the account when fully paid.

Library Guide

- *Your Money or Your Life* by Joe Dominguez and Vicki Robin
- *The Overspent American* by Juliet B. Schor
- *Do Americans Shop Too Much?* by Juliet B. Schor
- *Money and the Meaning of Life* by Jacob Needleman
- *What Color is Your Parachute?* by Richard Nelson Bolles
- *Is There a Book Inside You?* by Dan Poynter
- *Bird by Bird: Some Instructions on Writing and Life* by Anne Lamott
- *Wishcraft* by Barbara Sher
- *The Artist's Way* by Julia Cameron
- *The Bond Book* by Annette Thau
- *Making the Most of Your Money* by Jane Bryant Quinn
- *See You at the Top* by Zig Ziglar

- *How to Get Out of Debt and Live Prosperously* by Jerrold Mundis
- *Affluenza: The All-Consuming Epidemic* by John De Graaf et al
- *Do What You Love, the Money Will Follow* by Marsha Sinetar
- *The Passion Plan* by Richard Y. Chang
- *The Wealthy Barber* by David Chilton
- *Creating Your Future* by Dave Ellis
- *Now, Discover Your Strengths* by Marcus Buckingham and Donald Clifton
- *Do What You Are* by Paul Tieger and Barbara Barron-Tieger

Internet Resources

www.debtorsanonymous.org
www.debtadvice.org
www.cccsintl.org
www.newdream.org
www.simpleliving.net
www.personal-budget-planning-saving-money.com
www.nfcc.org
www.myvesta.org
www.monster.com (and other major job-placement sites)
www.parapublishing.com
www.treasurydirect.gov (Treasury Direct site where you can buy US Treasuries directly)
www.vanguard.com (and other major brokerages)
www.wsj.com (and other major financial news outlets)
www.sba.gov (The Small Business Administration)
www.jobhuntersbible.com
www.dice.com
www.yourmoneyoryourlife.org

Search Terms

Debtors Anonymous
affluenza
values-based spending
debt counseling
Federal Reserve
self-publishing
Anne Lamott
Dan Poynter
(the name of whatever special skill you might have)
investing
right livelihood
job vs. career

CHAPTER 7

ALL THAT UGLY STUFF

In 1997, Lynne bought a three-bedroom house with a basement, about a mile from the two-bedroom townhouse she had rented for several years. When they moved, their possessions filled a large moving van; in fact, they had to go back for the refrigerator. Packing and unpacking that much stuff was exhausting, although some of the packing was easy, as several of the boxes were full of things that had never been unpacked after their last move in 1993.

In the fall of 1998, in the midst of several personal crises (including her fourth layoff in nine years), Lynne put the house on the market, packed up the kids, the cats, and the car, put as much stuff in storage as would fit, sent five boxes of household goods to herself in the mail via General Delivery mail, and left the East Coast for Colorado. Gone were the three extra sets of linens per bed. Gone, in fact, were the beds, as well as most of the rest of the furniture.

Yes, it was traumatic to get rid of all of their familiar stuff. But a funny thing happened: between thrift store purchases and donations from new friends, within about a month, Lynne and her girls were once again living in a fully-furnished house. And when they moved back to the East Coast, five months after their arrival in Colorado, they needed a U-Haul!

But even more interesting was the sense of freedom Lynne felt from not owning all that other stuff, and the realization that most of the stuff she had had, she had used rarely, if ever. In fact, after she unpacked all of the stuff that she had put in storage, two-thirds of the kitchen stuff ended up going to charity. Lynne is not alone in this discovery. One of the fellows in Jonathan's VS study group moved from Texas to Minnesota, placing a bunch of household and personal materials in storage before he left. A few years later, he had the space for the stuff and went back to Texas to get it, only to find that he had already repurchased most of the things he wanted and did not want the rest anyway. Ouch!

Lynne learned a number of lessons from this experience:

1. You do not need anywhere nearly as much stuff as you think you need.

2. If you lose something and you truly need it, it will come back to you somehow. Maybe the new sofa will not look exactly the same as the old one, but it will still be a sofa.

3. Stuff is just stuff. It is not money; it is not friends or family; it is not food; it is not health or a roof over your head. In short, stuff is not critical to your well-being, however good it may make you feel.

4. Living without a lot of stuff can be a major blessing.

Simplifying Your Stuff

You do not have to go through a life-altering crisis in order to be inspired to pare back your inventory of stuff. It could be that you are planning to tackle Step One of *Your Money or Your Life*, but you keep putting it off because you know how long it is going to take to count every pair of shoes you own. It could be that you are beginning to become more environmentally aware, and you are starting to realize (and, if the truth were known, feel embarrassed about) how much of the world's Gross Domestic Product has taken the short route from Malaysia or China, through a discount retailer, to the storage shelves in your basement. Or it could just be that you have been searching for the past three months for the left-hand-threaded frammis you bought three years ago and stuck in a junk drawer, and now you could use the dang thing, if only you could remember which junk drawer you stuck it in.

Or as Lynne did, you may find yourself in a situation where you suddenly have a lot less stuff, and you realize that you can breathe a lot easier without it. The easy way to try living with less stuff is to get rid of it temporarily. Make the time to empty out a room and clean the carpet. While the carpet dries for a few days, get the feel of the room without all that stuff in there. Jonathan recently did this with his living room and is now contemplating what furniture to get rid of, since the living room feels so much more "alive" without all that ugly stuff taking up so much space. Lindi Hulse has taken this to what some people may think is an extreme, but it suits her perfectly: "I've always lived a very simple, low impact, debt-free, non-consumer life style. I realized ... that I could do more good for myself and my world by doing with less stuff. I love the simple, time and hassle free, uncluttered lifestyle I lead and would never want a different one. So it's easy for me to follow. What makes it hard is the lack of understanding I get from others about the choices I've made. Having to deal with the mindset that the only worthy thing one can do in life is work for money and to make and spend as much as possible regardless of the moral and physical costs to their own life, their family's, their society or their planet."

Whatever your reason, know that you are not alone. We are all trying to tame the Stuff Monster! One of the nice things about city living is that it is harder to let the Stuff Monster get out of hand. Living spaces are generally smaller, so there is less room for clutter. It is more difficult (although not impossible) to have multiple junk drawers in an apartment than in a three-bedroom house.

What Should I Get Rid of...and How?

Trying to tame the Stuff Monster all at once is a recipe for failure. Start small. The clutter did not grow overnight; you are not going to get rid of all of it in one day. (Unless you just burn the whole place to the ground, but that is felony arson.) Instead, do one drawer, or one closet, at a time. When each is complete, move on to the next drawer or closet.

Label five trash bags or boxes: one for items you intend to keep, one for items you intend to sell or give away, one for items that are not nice enough to sell or give away, one for items you are not sure whether you wish to keep, and one for items that belong somewhere else in the house. Each time you take an item out of the drawer or closet, put it into one of your five containers. When the closet or drawer is completely empty, put back the items you wish to keep, put the giveaway box in the trunk of the car, take the bag of stuff that is not nice enough to give away to the trashcan or dumpster, seal the box of stuff that you are not sure about and label it with today's date, and take the fifth box around the house and put the items in it away.

Do Not Re-Sort Your Giveaway Box or Your "Unsure" Box! Do not even let another member of your family go through these boxes: that is the quickest route to having the stuff disappear back into the drawer or closet that you just cleaned out! The exception to the rule is if a family member is an adult child with their own space. Then you can add another bag or box for each child, and give or ship it to them at the next reasonable opportunity. As long as the stuff you are getting rid of is clearly yours, do not let anyone else mess with the containers. But if the stuff belongs to some other family member, you have some negotiating to do.

The next time you are out running errands, drop the box in your trunk at the charity drop-off point. In about a year, check your boxes of "unsure" items; if you have not opened a box within that time, do not even bother opening it; just give it away. The "one year" rule is a good rule of thumb for clothing, too: If you have not worn something in a year, get rid of it.

Numerous systems for uncluttering exist; one of the most popular is the Flylady's system (see the Resources at the end of the chapter). While the Flylady aims at hard-core clutterholics (her first rule before cleaning is to get dressed, all the way to your shoes; her second rule is to clean out and scrub the kitchen sink), even the less case-hardened may find some hints on her web site for paring down stuff.

One of the advantages to having less cluttered surroundings is that cleaning is easier; the fewer geegaws and gimcracks you have to pick up and dust, or put away, or vacuum around, the quicker your chores will go. Many years ago, Don Aslett developed a system of "speed cleaning" that stresses decluttering as the secret to completing cleaning chores in a hurry. He published the details in a book called *Make Your House Do the Housework*. He has also written a number of books about the process of decluttering. You might want to check them out if you are searching for inspiration.

Now That I Do Not Want It Any More, Where Do I Put It?

One of the joys of living in a city is the abundance of charities and agencies that are thrilled to have your junk. In fact, they are so happy to get it that they will often come and pick it up from you. Most will give you the paperwork required for getting a charitable contribution deduction on your taxes as well. Some charities even run regular routes through certain neighborhoods; if you get a phone call from one of these groups, offering to pick up your castoff junk, consider it a sign. Say, "Yes, thank you," and go clean out a closet. Or a whole room.

Preschools, elementary schools and daycare centers are usually happy to take old magazines and catalogs for art projects. Animal shelters and animal hospitals often need sheets, towels and blankets. Shelters for the homeless and abused men, women, and children can also use these items, as well as clothing, toys, and individual-sized toiletries. Many churches also have collection points for items that you may be able to use (ask your church-going neighbor if you are not religiously active yourself). If there is not a public drop-off for these kinds of materials, call each place you are considering and ask if they can use your old stuff. Even if they do not want your stuff, they might be able to tell you someone who does want it.

A caveat, though, if you go the giveaway route: please make sure that the things you are giving away still have some use left in them. Charities have to pay people to go through the donations and cull the truly reusable from the trash. That cuts into the amount of revenue they can spend on helping the needy. Giving all your odd socks to charity only means that they pay to throw out your trash. If you will not wear your own odd socks, throw them out yourself, or start an odd sock exchange. In general, if you would not buy it from the thrift store yourself, then it is questionable whether it has any value to a charity.

If you would rather try to recoup part of your investment in all this stuff, you might consider having a yard sale. If you do not have enough stuff, or enough space, for a sale on your own, you could get together with neighbors and hold a joint yard sale, or investigate whether there are any local flea markets where you could rent a table.

If you are certain that you could get more than yard sale value for some of your stuff, you could list it for sale on the Internet. Web sites like eBay.com and half.com encourage both buyers and sellers. These are also good places to check for a ballpark figure for what your antique whatsit or collectible whosit is worth (although if your antique whatsit is really nice, you will probably want to hire an appraiser).

If this all sounds like too much trouble to you, another option is to stick your stuff by the curb with a sign on it that says, "Free!" This is called a "free garage sale" if you advertise it in your local paper. It might be fun to see how long it takes before everything is gone. Some cities even have a "free week" where anything put on the curb is free for the picking and after the week is up, the leftovers are picked up as part of the regular garbage collection. If your city does not provide this kind of organized "treasure hunting days", work with a sympathetic city administrator or council member to see if you can start one. Not only is it a good way for everyone to recycle items easily, but it also gives everyone an incentive to keep trash piles from accumulating in the backyard, which makes your city a nicer place to live.

If you live in an apartment, see if your management office will designate a spot for giveaways. Many frugal Simplifiers "shop" at their local dumpsters regularly. An enlightened office manager might consider formalizing the practice. There is precedent for this; Traci Freebairn lives in an eight-unit building in Tacoma, WA: "There is a community 'discard pile' where items that are no longer of use to one couple can be placed for anyone to take."

If you are willing to hang onto the item while you search for a new home for it, put the word out that you have one available. Many classified ads for free stuff can be found in newsletters for credit unions or similar organizations. This means you have to store the thing for a while, but it can be useful. Jonathan bought a drill press to use while fixing up his basement. Eventually the basement was done, and the drill press collected dust for several years. He finally decided to get rid of it and, after asking around for about six months, finally found a community theater that wanted it. The best part is that Jonathan already volunteers at this theater. Not only did he get a tax deduction for the value of the drill press, but he can still use the tool with a bit of planning (which he has already done once)!

As a last resort, throw it out! Just be sure to dispose of it properly. Many items that are commonly found in the house are actually hazardous waste: old chemicals, some dead batteries, paints, fluorescent bulbs, useless electronics, etc. Your city or county may have special rules for getting rid of your toxic trash or a particular site that handles toxic materials. When in doubt, get on the phone with your trash hauler or city/county garbage collections department and find out what the applicable law is. They will be far happier to talk with you now than to clean up a mess you caused later by incorrect disposal.

Note, however, that many items are just plain dangerous. Many old chemicals are either proscribed poisons or explosive. Your hazardous waste folks can tell you which is which. (You can read R. J. Wilder's simultaneously humorous and frightening experiences in dealing with mysterious hazardous materials at www.ardeapress.com.) As you are cleaning out your stuff, please pay attention and see that it is all disposed of properly. Everyone will be better off.

Practical To Dos

- Remind yourself that stuff is just stuff.
- Declutter one drawer or closet at a time.
- Don't second-guess yourself — if you put something in the giveaway/sell box or the "unsure" box, don't take it out again.
- Give away or sell the good stuff.
- Put stuff by the curb in a box labeled "Free!"
- If it is really no good, throw it out!
- If it is hazardous, dispose of it properly.
- If you are keeping stuff to give your children later, give it to them now so they can enjoy it now.

Library Guide

- *Clutter's Last Stand* by Don Aslett
- *Not for Packrats Only* by Don Aslett
- *Make Your House Do the Housework* by Don Aslett and Laura Aslett Simons

Internet Resources

www.flylady.com
www.cleanreport.com
www.ebay.com
www.half.com
www.clutterersanonymous.net

Search Terms

declutter
speed cleaning
"hazardous waste" + your county or city name

CHAPTER 8

LOCAL ALTERNATIVES TO MONEY

Money is a funny thing. It's perhaps the most pervasive symbol ever created by humans. It is symbolic of the time and life energy people spend earning it. To some it represents power, or freedom, or safety, or love. Although it can't be eaten or worn or lived in, the power of its symbolism is so strong that its mere presence helps us to get food, clothing, and shelter.

However, because of this powerful symbolism, many people confuse the symbol for the real thing it represents. A person may want more freedom or safety and so they hoard money rather than thinking about the best way to obtain true freedom or greater safety.

Money as we know it is like a game—it follows certain rules that govern how people interact with each other while participating. Things like interest rates, inflation, debt, and the stock market and how they interact and influence each other are all governed by the rules of the money game. What many people don't realize, however, is that there are other games.

Lots of different money systems exist in the world. Virtually every national currency on the planet follows the same rules. The technical term for this kind of money is "scarce fiat"—meaning that the money is created to be in short supply (scarce) and created by the government, central bank, or federal agency by decree (fiat, or Latin for "let it be" or "make it so").

The opposite of 'scarce' is 'sufficient'. This is money that works like information rather than a resource. It's like an inch (as a measurement of value) rather than a bucket (a 'container' or 'store' of value). You can run out of buckets, but you can't run out of inches. An IOU is an example of a sufficient currency. It has value, but there is no limit to the number of IOUs a person can write.

The opposite of 'fiat' is 'backed'. A backed currency is one where a unit of money represents a unit of some real thing. For example, the original United States Dollar was a backed currency; it represented a specific amount of gold. Now we have the Federal Reserve Note (which, just to confuse things, people still call a U.S. Dollar) that is not backed by anything but the promise of the government that it's worth something; or as it's often described, the "full faith and credit of the United States Government." A share of stock is, in a sense, a backed currency because it is traded between people, has value, and represents something real—a tiny piece of a corporation. Frequent flier miles are backed by services, although it's not really currency because people don't generally use them for transactions other than travel-related services.

And before getting into the meat of things, two other distinctions. First, 'money' is used to mean the thing used to register the exchange value, whether that's bank credit or tick marks on a ledger. This is distinct from the method of payment, which could be paper notes, swipe cards, checks, coins, certificates, coupons, punch cards, computerized 'smart cards,' or other forms which the exchange or carrying of 'money' might take. The second distinction is that the word 'cash' will be used to refer to the scarce fiat money, whether or not it's in the form of federal reserve notes and coins (the usual use of the term 'cash') or bank credit, or the other forms it takes.

If 'cash' is the term we'll use for what's used in the federal money game, we'll need a term for money in other games. Common terms include 'local money,' 'community currency,' and 'complementary currency,' among others. Since most of these systems directly support the building of the local economy or community connections, and because they're generally small in scale, we'll use the term 'local money' for these alternatives as a group.

With those terms defined, we can look at the other money games out there and how the different rules of the game address different weaknesses of the federal money game. Understanding these differences will allow you to play by whichever rules are most in alignment with your values.

In the federal money game, interest rates are used to make sure there is always demand for money. If the government wants people to save and invest, they make interest rates high. If the government wants people to borrow and spend, they make interest rates low. But in both cases, the money is like a resource—there's only so much of it in circulation at any one time. When interest rates are low, people borrow more which puts more money into circulation; when rates are high, people save more which takes it out of circulation.

Some other money systems, however, are created as sufficient currencies. These are like having money that is always at zero percent interest for both saving and borrowing. If you need money you can get some more without penalty; if you have extra money, you might as well spend it on something because it does you no good to hoard it. One such system is called LETS, which will be covered in more detail later in this chapter.

Others address the issue of value. The marketplace values some things more than others—for example, the average person who has a good deal of knowledge about law can earn much more in the marketplace than the average person who has a good deal of knowledge about raising children. The value reflected in the marketplace does not always reflect the 'use value' of the product or service provided—that is, some things that are extremely useful are hardly valued at all in the market, while other things that are less useful are highly valued in the market. A local money system directly addressing this issue is the TimeDollar system.

Still other local money systems address how and where money is spent. Because federal money can be spent anywhere in the country, large businesses can earn money in your community, and collect it at its home office, slowly siphoning the financial resources out of your local community. This makes it more difficult for smaller, local businesses to survive and thrive. The majority of new jobs—two-thirds to three-quarters of net new jobs, according to the U.S. Small Business Administration's Office of Advocacy—are created by small businesses (defined as fewer than 500 employees).

Every dollar spent locally circulates in the community many times before leaving, while a dollar spent at a large business will leave the community within a few days. This is called the "local multiplier" or "economic multiplier." The multiplier of any given location may vary, but most average estimates range from three to seven; that is, the average dollar changes hands three to seven times before leaving the community. Federal money spent at a local business can have a multiplier up to five times that of federal money spent at a national chain store, according to an article from reclaimdemocracy.org.

As Michael Shuman writes in his book *Going Local*, "The expenditure of a dollar generates more than a dollar's worth of activity. A worker who receives a paycheck of say $500 might spend half on food and half on rent. The market that sold the food might use its $250 in revenue to buy more produce from local farmers and the landlord might spend his or her $250 on electricity from the local utility. Every expenditure cascades into a larger number of transactions that enrich the community. Once a multiplier leaves the community, the benefits of subsequent transactions are lost. A community in which money flows out quickly and never returns slowly bleeds to death." On the other hand, a community with a high multiplier enjoys greater wealth and financial liquidity.

Think back to the bathtub model of personal finances. The local multiplier is like the ratio of flow into the tub relative to the flow out the drain. The higher that difference (the higher the multiplier), the faster the bathtub fills. Most local money systems have an infinite multiplier because the money simply isn't accepted as payment outside of the community it serves. The more a community currency is used, the more the drain is plugged in the economic bathtub.

In addition to this multiplier benefit, some local money systems encourage specific actions, such as encouraging the purchase of sustainably produced goods and services, or spending at local businesses. An example of this type of currency is Ithaca HOURS.

EXAMPLES

Three local money systems will be briefly explained in this section: the LETSystem, Time Dollars, and Ithaca HOURS. These explanations are meant merely to whet your appetite rather than to provide the technical details on how each system works or how to set one up in your neighborhood. However, at the end of the chapter are web addresses to sites that have more detailed explanations of these systems.

LETS: Local Exchange Trading System

This system was created in 1983 by Michael Linton in British Columbia, Canada. At the time, the economy was poor and people were unable to do business because of a lack of money. He and others got together and decided that it was silly that the medium for exchange was actually *preventing* exchange because of its scarcity. So they decided to act *as if* they had money. Everyone who participated got an account in a registry. Transactions happen much as they do when someone writes a check in the federal money—the buyer's account goes down and the seller's account goes up.

For example, if Alice and Ben signed up on the registry at the same time, they'd both start with a balance of zero. Let's say Alice then bought something from Ben for the equivalent of $10. Alice's account would go down to –10 and Ben's would go up to +10. The negative represents that Alice has created 10 units of LETS money and is obligated to redeem 10 units in the future. The positive balance means that Ben has provided 10 units worth of value to the community and is entitled to receive 10 units of value from the community in return.

This kind of system is called "mutual credit" because everyone in the system has credit with everyone else in the system. Unlike an IOU, credits in a LETSystem can be spent or redeemed from anyone in the community. For example, Alice can redeem her 10 units from any other account holder—she doesn't need to pay back Ben specifically; and Ben can spend his units with anyone.

The payments have been done using all kinds of methods. The most common are perhaps checks and phone calls. In some systems, an account holder can call the registry and authorize a payment. In others, printed documents like checks are used to keep track of payments—the LETS checks are deposited when the seller sends the check into the registry to transfer credits on the books. Other systems use online Web-based accounts to keep track of everyone's balance, or smart-card systems where account holders use a card containing a tiny computer chip that keeps track of their current balance and trading history.

In most LETSystems, payment is typically done in a combination of federal and local money. For example, at an auto repair shop, a customer might pay federal money for parts and 75% of the labor in LETS. This gives individuals and businesses flexibility in their use of the local system. The mathematics for these mixed exchanges are made easy because a unit of LETS is equal in value to a unit of the federal money of the country in which the system operates. Thus, in America, a LETS unit is equal to a dollar; in England it's equal to a pound; in Japan it's equal to a yen.

Time Dollars

The Time Dollars system was created by Edgar Cahn, author of *No More Throwaway People*. It is also a mutual credit system, but instead of one unit being equal to a unit of national currency, it makes the value of a unit equal to an hour. This shifts the focus of the currency away from goods and monetary transactions and towards social or service transactions. An hour of service to someone else earns a Time Dollar.

In the Time Dollar economy, undervalued social behavior is valued. Childcare, writing letters to inmates, giving people rides, serving on student or citizen councils, and doing errands for the sick or elderly are all examples of things for which Time Dollars can be earned. These are traditionally things that are considered to be the work of unpaid volunteers, or generally near the bottom of the pay scale. Yet these activities arguably provide more value to society than, say, a producer of advertising, cigarettes, or weapons.

A final benefit of Time Dollars is that several IRS findings have determined that Time Dollars are tax free because the typical services exchanged are domestic—that is, it helps people do for each other what is typically done in and around the home— and that the Time Dollar doesn't have a monetary value since payment is equal regardless of what is exchanged.

Ithaca HOURS

The Ithaca HOUR system was created by Paul Glover in Ithaca, New York. His system, like Time Dollars, is based on the value of an hour; however, to allow people to exchange goods as well as time, they have said that one HOUR is worth approximately $10, which is roughly the average wage in Ithaca. Another difference between HOURS and the other two is that Ithaca HOURS is not a mutual credit system. It is not self-regulating in the sense that individuals can create money when they need it like in a mutual credit system. Rather, it requires a central agency to issue printed notes into circulation.

Printed notes is another difference between the two mutual credit systems and Ithaca HOURS. While LETS and Time Dollars are sufficient currencies, Ithaca HOURS is still a scarce currency. However, it's a scarce currency with a geographical limit, which means that it still has the essentially infinite local multiplier effect. The bills are printed and issued into circulation by a central agency (like a central bank does for a nation). The printed money, however, acts like an advertisement for the system itself ("Hey, what kind of funny money are you paying with, anyway?") as well as making it easier for people to understand—which makes it easier to get people to use. Everyone understands paper money; explaining credits in a database or ledger requires a little more thought and more trust in those keeping the records.

The notes are put into circulation in two ways. The primary way is when advertisers take out an ad in the *HOUR Town* newsletter. They pay for an ad in federal money, and get the ad, plus some HOURS. The advertiser then can spend those HOURS into circulation for other goods and services. For example, a small business might advertise a sale, and give the HOURS received because of placing the ad to the salesperson that makes the most sales that month as a bonus. That person could then go to a store that accepts HOURS at lunch for a sandwich. The merchant could either continue to circulate the notes, or use them to purchase an ad in *HOUR Town*. This redeems the note until the next time an advertiser buys an ad to start the process over again.

The primary benefits of the HOURS system is that it's easy for people to understand, doesn't require opening an account on a registry to get started, and has the inherent local multiplier to increase the wealth of the local businesses.

Conclusion

Local money is a possible solution to lots of problems caused by quirks of the rules of the federal money game. Whether your interests are in addressing economic disparity, increasing social actions, building the wealth of your community, or any of a number of other issues, a community currency may help.

If your city has a local money system, it may be just the way to align your spending with your values. Or, if you're looking for a large project to be of service to your community, starting your own may be an option. Either way, a city with its large numbers of people invariably has a host of different communities and organizations that may find a local currency to support their values as well. Although local money may not simplify your life directly, it offers you and others in your community more choices for building connections and financial health. And making conscious choices in alignment with your values is what voluntary simplicity is all about.

Library Guide

- *Money: Understanding and Creating Alternatives to Legal Tender* by Thomas Greco
- *Going Local* by Michael Shuman
- *No More Throwaway People* by Edgar Cahn
- *The Future of Money: Creating Wealth, Work, and a Wiser World* by Bernard Lietaer

Internet Resources:

www.transaction.net/money/
www.gmlets.u-net.com/design/home.html
www.ithacahours.org
www.timedollars.org
www.reclaimdemocracy.org/pdf/articles/
   benefits_going_local.pdf

Search Terms

LETSystem
time dollars
local currency system
community currency system

CHAPTER 9

COMPASSION AND TOLERANCE

The city is a cosmopolitan melting pot, full of people from all combinations of all races, religions, nationalities. It is a great place to be to learn about community, tolerance, and compassion. And it is a great place to be if you are interested in practicing a discipline that is a little bit outside the mainstream. As Kevin Cornwell puts it, "There's a vitality to the city that you don't find in other places. To me, it's more likely that you'll have community when you have people closer together, and it forces the issue, which is not only just fine with me, but I think it's preferable."

Learning Compassion

Simplifier Joseph Beckenbach says, "As I see it, the core value of Voluntary Simplicity is 'compassion', not only for ourselves but for those around us and those around the world. Most of the eight Doors into Simplicity seem to open from (and into) compassion."

Compassion and tolerance are best learned by living them. A person learns tolerance for others most easily by associating with people who are of different races and creeds. The act of association eliminates the fear of the unknown, the Other. We learn that we are all people, with similar hopes and fears, dreams and goals, and that our existence is interconnected with the existence of every other being in the world. Compassion for others, and for all creatures, follows swiftly.

Beckenbach found this in his hometown of Carbondale, IL, which is not a big town, but it is a university town that draws students from as many as 75 countries: "It was very cosmopolitan. It was very open. You could learn a lot about different cultures, different societies, learn about how people are really, at root, all the same. We all have the same underlying urge to grow peaceably and to realize our individual potentials and help others do so as well."

He now lives in San Jose, CA, in a neighborhood that is predominantly Chinese, where his wife, who is Chinese, feels at home:

> I know that, for my wife, she wants a very definite set of things in our lifestyle. That involves the climate, that involves the type of people that are around us, the type of community around us. So in that respect, this is a more appropriate place for us to be than [my parents' home city]. She is from China and she wants to be around a very large Chinese community. She wants to live in a place that is cooler than where she grew up, but doesn't have snow. So that pretty much leaves us with Mediterranean climates. The neighborhood that I'm in, half the houses are owned by folks from China, mainly Taiwan, but some from the mainland. There's Jews, there's Indians, there's folks from all over the United States. It's an incredible mix of people.

Across the country, another Simplifier, Tracy, also appreciates the racial tolerance she has found living in Boston: "My family is composed of multiple races. We picked our neighborhood based on its diversity." Lynne also picked her neighborhood for its diversity. She believes that it is extremely important for her children to grow up with children of many races. At "International Night" this year at one of her daughters' schools, fellow students showed off their heritage by performing dances and modeling clothing from their native lands. Countries from every continent but Antarctica were represented.

Of course, not everybody in the city is tolerant of others. Simplifier Kevin Cornwell volunteers as a community mediator in Vancouver, WA:

Most of the problems people have that they wind up calling the city for help on are things that, in my mind's eye,
30 or 40 years ago, they would have just leaned over the
fence and said, "Hey, would you stop your dog barking?"
Whereas now everything is escalated and everybody's –
nobody wants to talk with one another to solve problems…
[P]eople tend to forget that all you have to do is, first of
all, introduce yourself when things are not tense, when
you first move in or something, and then just be a good
neighbor. It pays off in spades.

Kevin says he tries to be kind when neighbors are in a jam,
even if their jam affects him directly. For example, if someone's
tree fell on his fence, rather than rant at the neighbor about the
damage to the fence, he might bake cookies and take them to the
neighbor: "You probably felt pretty awful when your tree fell
over, so I thought I'd bring you a treat or something. We still need
to talk about what WE do about this tree…"

Situations like these, and the conflicts that inevitably arise when
large numbers of people come together, can be addressed in many
different ways. Marshall Rosenberg describes one of the methods for connecting compassionately with others and resolving
conflicts in his book, *Nonviolent Communication*. By recognizing
that all humans have the same basic emotions and universal human needs, and by paying attention to which feelings and needs
are in play at the present moment, it becomes much easier to deal
with each other compassionately. This skill can be especially useful in urban areas, where people live and work so close to one
another. More information on Nonviolent Communication is available in the resources at the end of the chapter.

Tolerance for Voluntary Simplicity

That tolerance is higher in cities is good news for those of us
who practice Voluntary Simplicity as city dwellers. We may still
get comments and criticism from our friends and loved ones, but

people who live in cities are likely to be more accepting. Simplifier Fred Ecks says:

> [E]specially American cities, we've attracted so many immigrants largely to our cities, that people, I think, become more open-minded: Not everyone is "like me." There's an embarrassment factor to being frugal. You know, how I don't want people to think I'm cheap.... But if you're living in the city and there are people howlin' at the moon down in the ghettoes and there are people living in million dollar homes at the other end of the city, at least I feel more comfortable being whoever I feel like.

All this diversity living so close together can make the city a noisy place. Jonathan combats the noise by wearing noise-canceling headphones during his commute. (See "Transportation" for more on these little marvels.) Many people swear by earplugs for blocking out the sounds of the city while they are sleeping. Or you can look at the noise the way Simplifier Francine Jaskiewicz does: "The first thing I hear in the morning, and the last thing at night, are the people on the street below. Nothing makes me happier than this reminder that we are not alone in this world."

Following Other Paths

Compassion cuts both ways. If you are interested in exploring a lifestyle that is not in the American mainstream, city dwellers are likely to be more tolerant and supportive of you than if you had settled in a rural area. It is also easier to find people in a city who are doing what you are interested in trying.

For instance, some, though certainly not all, Simplifiers are vegetarian or vegan, their compassion for life on this planet having extended to the animals we consume. Soy products are becoming more mainstream now, but it is still easier in a city to find vegetarian foods at the grocery store, and vegetarian entrees that go beyond grilled cheese at a restaurant, than it would be in a more "meat-and-potatoes" rural area.

Many people practice some form of meditation as a way of coping with stress. It is much easier in a city to find a class or group to get involved with. Simplifier alex glenlee is active in a Buddhist sangha, or meditation group, which meets in St. Catharines, Ontario, where he lives. Buddhist temples offer meditation instruction for free. There are numerous other forms of meditation practice, from Transcendental Meditation to Christian prayer to Native American drumming circles and vision quests. Some churches also host meditation groups. Check the phone book, or do an Internet search with the type of meditation you are looking for and your city name.

Tai chi is a soft-style martial art that has been called "meditation in motion". Check the phone book for studios that offer tai chi. Your city parks and recreation department may even offer classes.

Yoga has become fashionable as a way to stay fit, but classes begin and end with centering and meditation. There are several different styles of yoga, some more athletic than others. An Internet search can generate a list of local studios. Your city parks and recreation department, the YMCA, or even your workplace may offer a class. You can also rent or buy videotapes, or borrow them from the library. Because form is so important in yoga, you should plan to take at least one class.

As a plus, disciplines such as meditation, tai chi and yoga allow you to find the calm center of your mind. When you are calm and centered, and not so quick to fly into road or some other sort of rage, it is much easier for you to be more tolerant and compassionate toward others.

Even something as simple as taking a walk can be restorative, as Simplifier alex glenlee recommends: "When you walk, you can smell the flowers. You see life. It's almost like a living meditation. The pace of your feet—it's a natural thing."

Unitarian Universalist, Quaker, Wicca, and many other out-of the mainstream religions, are easier to practice in the city. With a larger pool of people to draw from, the odds are that somebody in your city is doing what you are interested in doing. Check the phone book or do an Internet search. Even if your religious preference is in the mainstream, you have many more choices for places of worship, making it easier for you to find a congregation where you feel at home. In a rural area, you may find just one church of your denomination within a fifty-mile radius of your house; in a city, you may find five or ten.

Twelve-step groups for various addictions are easier to find in a city. You might even have a choice of locations and meeting times.

Feng shui has become popular as a way to harmonize your surroundings with your goals and desires. Numerous books about feng shui have been published; check your library. A library in a city is more likely to have books on a topic like this. Feng shui has become very popular in recent years, and some people are skeptical. But if you believe in it, and you decide that you need a statue of a particular color in a particular part of your room in order to attract more money or luck or peacefulness, you are going to have more luck finding that statue in a diverse city.

The happier and more comfortable that you are in your own life, the easier it is for you to view others with compassion and tolerance — and that makes life more pleasant for everybody. And learning about other traditions and beliefs will increase your comfort when you meet people who practice them.

Practical To Dos

- Practice tolerance and compassion.
- Introduce yourself to your neighbors.
- Consider sending your children to a school where their classmates come from many cultures.
- Investigate non-mainstream religions or disciplines in which you have an interest by doing an Internet search or by checking the phone book.

Library Guide

- Videotapes on tai chi and yoga
- *The Complete Illustrated Guide to Feng Shui: How to Apply the Secrets of Chinese Wisdom for Health, Wealth and Happiness* by Lillian Too
- *Nonviolent Communication* by Dr. Marshall Rosenberg

Internet Resources

www.yogasite.com (one of many sites about yoga)
www.do-not-zzz.com (on Zen buddhism)
www.geomancy.net
www.qi-whiz.com
www.cnvc.org (Center for Nonviolent Communication)

Search Terms

(discipline you are interested in) and (name of your city)
meditation
tai chi
yoga
feng shui

CHAPTER 10

ENTERTAINMENT

One of the best things about living simply in the city is all the free, or nearly free, things to do. From eating on the cheap to cultural offerings to just sitting and watching the world go by, cities have many more options for fun than rural areas do, and you don't have to go as far to find them.

Fine Dining

You can drop a fortune in the city on good food, but you don't have to.

• *Ethnic restaurants.* Large cities are gathering places for immigrants from every continent and have an abundance of restaurants that provide a sampling of world flavors. The food is often fabulous and the prices are very good. Simplifier Jane Zeender of Arlington, VA, goes out once a month with a group of friends to a different ethnic restaurant. They leave the kids at home and have a girls' night out for very little money.

• *Ethnic food stores.* Some cities have large enough immigrant populations to support grocery stores that cater to them. These stores can be great, and cheap, places to shop not only for staples, but for those exotic and wonderful foods that leap off the pages of cookbooks.

• *Pushcarts.* You may laugh, but in our McDonaldized world, pushcarts are one place where you can still get the flavor of your local region. One of Lynne's favorite meals in Denver was a breakfast burrito from one of the pushcart vendors near the Market

Street bus station. Nobody sells breakfast burritos from a push-cart in DC (attention, entrepreneurs!), but they do sell hot dogs and hot pretzels.

Literary Events

You don't have to know how to deconstruct modern fiction to take advantage of these. Anyone, bookish or not, can enjoy these outings.

- *Readings and book signings.* City bookstores often host free lectures and book signings by well-known authors. The store may require you to buy a book there before the author will sign it for you, but if you were going to buy the book anyway, you come out ahead. This is an especially terrific idea for parents with elementary or middle school children. Lynne's girls have met three of their favorite authors at such events: Brian Jacques, Phyllis Reynolds Naylor, and Tamora Pierce.
- *Local author appearances.* If your city has a writers' center, it probably offers public poetry readings and the like.
- *Visit the library.* You can read the latest bestseller, listen to music, or rent a video, as long as you have it back before the due date. Some libraries will even lend back issues of magazines or give them to you free. You may not even have to go to the library to check out a book: Simplifier Katherine Kiger uses the "Books by Mail" service offered by her local library in Orlando, FL. She goes online and orders the books she wants sent to her in the mail. Libraries are great places to read newspapers and magazines, too, saving you the cost of subscribing and the hassle of recycling them when you are done. In addition, most libraries now have computers with Internet access for public use, although there may be a time limit.
- Your local library may have rooms available after business hours that the public can rent for a small fee. Where available, these are used for meetings by various local groups. Often the meetings must be open to the public, so you can check the schedule

and visit some interesting community groups. The meetings must be quiet, of course, and the rooms must be straightened when the meeting is over.   Check your library for availability and scheduling.

Performance, Art, and Culture

You could pay big bucks to see a big act in a coliseum, or you could try something on this list.
- *Visit a museum*; museums are a great deal, especially on advertised special days. For a low admission price (and maybe even our favorite price – free), you have a climate-controlled place to hang out, look at famous art and world culture, and maybe even learn something about the history of your local area. Many museums are putting together exhibits that have something of interest for everyone. There are museums for everything from art to aviation to hands-on science to history and culture. In Washington, DC, all the Smithsonian museums (including the National Zoo) are free.
- *Local arts fairs.* On any warm weekend, your city, or a nearby city, or a neighborhood within your city, is probably throwing a street fair or an arts-in-the-park event. You can find free music, cheap food, and Frisbee-catching dogs there. Bring your pooch and a blanket or lawn chair.
- Some cities even have spots where local artists can show their works for free or cheap. One of the skyways in Jonathan's city, Rochester, MN, has a 40-foot-long locking case in which local artists exhibit their works regularly. The skyway interiors are decorated for many holidays by local school kids, scout troops, and other recognized organizations. For the winter holidays in December, the city itself decorates the outsides of the skyways with light displays and the insides of the windows are usually painted with holiday themes by local groups. The local library usually has an exhibit, especially around the holidays, that will appeal to most library users. Some libraries may have a place

where anyone can put up an exhibit. Many have public bulletin boards. See your librarian for details.

- *Free concerts.* Your city probably has a band or orchestra that plays free concerts in an outdoor venue. This could be as simple as your city's band, or as elaborate as the National Symphony Orchestra on the steps of the U.S. Capitol. Some cities with convention centers will have an outdoor "concert in the park" on an annual or series basis. These are usually free or very inexpensive.

- *Amateur theatricals.* Want to see "Guys and Dolls"? "Annie Get Your Gun"? Check with your local high school or community college for show times. Tickets will be cheap.

- *Community theater.* If you usher, you often can get in free. Simplifier Fred Ecks regularly ushers at a local art theatre: "I saw Lily Tomlin doing 'The Search for Signs of Intelligent Life in the Universe'. Great show, it's written by Jane Wagner. It's a 2 1/2 hour monologue, but you're riveted the whole time. ... I got to see that for free. I discovered that I could usher for the show. ...Ended up sitting in a seat that costs $50, for free."

- *Professional theater* can also be free or cheap. The Municipal Opera in St. Louis has free "seats" on a hill behind the outdoor stage. You can bring your blanket and enjoy the show without ever having to see the performance! Bring your binoculars and a tripod if you want to see. If you want to sit a little closer, there are cheap bleacher seats as well. And if you are a last minute sort of person, "jump seats" can often be had inexpensively after someone cancels. Or go the day before the show opens and watch the dress rehearsal for free, and learn a little bit about the process of putting together a show at the same time. Check with the theater troupe first to make sure it is okay with them for you to attend the dress rehearsal. If you know someone in the troupe, they may even have tickets for the dress rehearsal you can have for free.

- *Matinee movies.* Bring a big purse and smuggle in candy (you did not read this tip here, though!). Or look in the newspaper for

second-run theaters, where admission prices can be as low as a
dollar.

- *Readings and lectures.* Your local library, community center, club,
  or professional group may sponsor poetry readings or slams, or
  lectures on topics of local interest. Bonus points if you live
  near a college or university: keep an eye out for free lectures by
  well-known people. Simplifier alex glenlee regularly attends lectures by environmentalists at his local college. Since he is a
  member of the environmental group that helps sponsor the
  lectures, he gets in at a reduced rate off the already low cost.
  Jonathan attends regular lectures put on by a local employer,
  regional quality council, and other professional society chapters.

- *People-watch.* You can do this anywhere, of course, but places
  frequented by tourists, or the local exotic flora and fauna, are
  especially good. Every major city seems to have at least one
  relatively safe park where the "odd folk" collect. People-watch
  with a friend and bet on where the next person to get on the
  bus will sit, or play people-watching Bingo. Stay away from the
  mall if you find the temptation to spend money is too great.
  Or, you can just leave your credit cards and checkbook at home
  before heading for the mall: you can't spend it if you do'nt have
  it with you. But the best place to people watch may be the
  venue with the highest stakes: City Hall. Who says politics is
  not a spectator sport?

- Many businesses hold an open house or sponsor a "lecture"
  that is really a sales pitch. As long as you are "sales proof", you
  can go to the lecture and learn about something, typically some
  form of investment. In a similar fashion, many studios (music,
  dance, martial arts, etc.) and gyms will offer a few free or deeply
  discounted initial lessons in hopes of luring you in for the whole
  course.

Shopping

Most Simplifiers will not identify shopping as something they do for entertainment, but it does seem to be the central ritual for many people bound in Consumer Culture.

- *Yard sales, thrift stores, and flea markets.* Even if you are not there to shop, these are fun places to spend a weekend morning. And in the city, you can find more yard sales closer together.
- *Urban treasure hunting* (known in certain circles as dumpster diving). People throw away the darndest things when they move. You could furnish a whole apartment, right down to the stereo system, with the pickings from a dumpster behind a college dorm at semester break. Also scout apartment complex dumpsters for furniture at the end of the month. You could keep these finds yourself, or fix them up (if they even need fixing), and sell them at a yard sale. Please be careful, however, to stay off private property; you don't want to have to put the money you make from reselling your finds toward bailing yourself out of jail on a trespassing charge.

The Social Scene

Getting together with family and friends is becoming a lost art. Turn off the TV, disconnect yourself from the Internet, and try one of these for some face time with your friends.

- *Volunteer.* Pick your favorite cause or charity; chances are very good that they would be glad to find someone who is willing to do more than just write a check. Volunteering is cheap and a good way to get perks, as well as being an avenue for broadening your social circle and giving back to your community.
- *Join a simplicity circle or a study group.* Check the Simple Living Network to see if there is a circle in your area. If not, consider starting one.

- *Invite people over for an evening.* This does not have to be elaborate, nor do you need an excuse. Lynne's backyard is not big enough for a crowd, so last summer she invited friends and neighbors to meet in the courtyard in front of her townhouse for an ice cream social. It was so successful that she plans to make it an annual event. If ice cream is not your thing, you could organize a picnic or a barbecue, or even a potluck. It need not even be that involved. Simplifier alex glenlee thinks getting together ought to be simpler than that, and even involve your children:

  > You know, sometimes it would be healthy to talk to or look into the eyes of another human being. i try to encourage people to talk: "Guys, let's get together. Heck, c'mon over to my place we'll have a cup of coffee. This place, our house, the door is always open, it's like 1950 here." People don't believe it. i encourage the kids to bring their friends over [and] we sit in on the conversations. You always get, "Really?!? You do that with your parents?" Sure you can, too. Why not?

- *Remember the progressive dinner?* The group goes from one person's house to the next, eating a different course at each house.
- *Play cards or a board game.* Dust off your Baby Boomer edition of Trivial Pursuit; for once, you will know more than your kids. Or invite friends over for a games night.
- *Do a science experiment.* One of Lynne's daughters' favorite activities is to put some cornstarch in a bowl, and add just enough water to make a paste. The resulting glop both oozes and breaks. Try it sometime. The best part is that it leaves no mess and any spills can be cleaned up with a wet cloth. It is also edible, and therefore safe, for all but the smallest children. Look in your newspaper's Sunday funnies for more science experiments in the "Beakman & Jax" comic strip.
- *Homemade Art.* With a little paint, clay, or even food, your family or a group of friends can have a lot of fun being artistic. If people start getting anxious about whether or not their art is good or not, have a "bad art" break where everything has to be awful or tacky. That'll get the fun back into it right away!

Sports

You could shell out big bucks for the coveted tickets to see the local pro sports franchise, or you could support your local athletes as a spectator, or be an athlete yourself.

- *High school and college sports.* See the pro stars of tomorrow – today. When you think about the fact that the pros are playing for money while the amateurs are playing for the love of the game, why would you watch the pros?
- If you just have to watch the pros, you may be able to get what some stadiums call Uecker Seats: seats where the view is partially obstructed. Miller Park, in Milwaukee, WI, sells these seats for $1 during regular season baseball. Available only at the stadium, the seats sell out every game even if the whole stadium is not sold out[1]. Buyers try to find an empty seat elsewhere in the stadium.
- *Work out at your local recreation center.* City recreation centers usually feature Olympic-size pools, weight rooms, saunas, tennis courts, and handball and racquetball courts. Many offer classes in aerobics, tae kwon do, swimming, and yoga, all for lower cost than a big-business health club.
- *Join a league.* Check with your local bowling alley for a bowling league membership, or call your city recreation center about leagues for softball, soccer, basketball, volleyball, hockey, curling, or other sports.
- *Ride your bike.* Some cities have upgraded their bike trails so that you no longer take your life in your hands by riding in traffic. Remember to wear your helmet!
- In the winter, if your city gets enough snow, you can go cross-country skiing, or maybe your city runs an ice-skating rink.
- *Take a walk.* One of the nicest things about living in a city is that things are close enough together that you can hit the sidewalk and actually walk *to* something. Or you could volunteer to be a dog walker for your local animal shelter.

Simplifier Jef Murray is a nature artist in Atlanta, GA, who has many options in his neighborhood when he needs a nature fix:

About two blocks from here, on the north side, and one block on the west side, is Peavine Creek, which runs kind of in an arc around our neighborhood.... It connects with Peachtree Creek, which in turn connects to the Chattahoochie River, which in turn goes down and connects with the Flint River, and becomes the Appalachicola River, and dumps into the Gulf of Mexico. ... I mean, we literally are in the Appalachicola watershed, and so if I drop a feather in the water here, in theory, it'll eventually be swept out into the Gulf. And that's a really cool feeling. Even though we're a good 300 miles from the gulf, it's kind of neat to know that nature is still here....

If you find birdwatchers in your community, [they can lead you to] all kinds of wild, little niches, nooks and crannies where Nature still has her foot in the door. And we have a wetland, it's about a mile from here, which we had never discovered until some friends of ours pointed it out to us. It's this wonderful bog that's behind a Saturn dealership. And it's protected. They've put a boardwalk out so you can walk out and you can see the dragonflies in the summer. It's beautiful.

And I think that's true of almost any city. If you really nose around and you find people who pay attention to these things, you'll find nature is even in the cracks in the sidewalk. There are whole little worlds around us.

Nature

- Need a little peace and quiet? Visit a local park. Simplifier Everette Orr, who lives near Washington, DC, likes the diversity of his local parks. He says:

    > There are trails, for example, within fifteen minutes of my home where there are very few people on them and they're back doors into Great Falls [National Park]. And they're free, they're beautiful, they're good exercise. So I see the same beauty that I see in a rural area – it's preserved through the national park system in this area. …. [W]e've actually managed to bring both worlds together here. We've got some of the most extraordinary scenic areas of nature at the same time that we have the positive aspects of city life.

- Local parks and nature preserves often need volunteers for their annual bird, butterfly, or other wildlife counts. Your local Audubon Society can put you in touch with the right people. Some parks even sponsor a "cleanup day" where you or your group can help the park staff clean up trash, pull weeds, and otherwise maintain the park, similar to the Adopt-a-Highway cleanup campaigns.

- City parks can be quite enjoyable as well. Well known ones like Golden Gate Park in San Francisco and Central Park in New York City are great for a stroll and people watching. But even smaller parks can be quite fun. You just have to bring your own entertainment. Please clean up any mess you create before you leave!

Travel

Living simply does not mean never going out of town again. Many Simplifiers live simply in order to have the money to travel. Or you can find ways to travel cheaper so you can travel more often.

- *Surf the Internet for cheap airfares.* Sites abound; Orbitz and Travelocity.com are two of the more popular at this writing. Another resource is Cheaptickets.com.
- *Travel by train.* The price of a sleeper berth on Amtrak includes meals in the dining car, and you get to see America.
- *Bus service* is a time-honored way to get across country inexpensively. Before you depart, be sure to check the locations of the stations you'll be using, so that you are familiar with the nearest accommodations, police station, and other services you might need upon arrival.
- *Consider driving.* If you calculate door-to-door time rather than just flight time, you may find that you do not save as much time by flying as you might think.
- If you have the time and the inclination, look into other modes of travel. Some ethnic neighborhoods are home to very inexpensive bus services between major cities.

Simplifier Fred Ecks enjoys staying in hostels when he travels:

> A hotel room is just a place to sleep, so I checked into this hostel thing.... basically you just get a bed, and [I] had the best time. You spend $20 bucks a night to get a bed and with that came this community of people. There were people from all over the world in there. ... It used to be mostly younger folks, backpack travelers. But nowadays, quite a few older folks as well. I've met a lot of folks in their 50s and 60's.
>
> [On a trip to Alaska,] I pull on in and meet some other folks in the hostel. [W]e're playing the guitars and hanging out and usually you do this until sunset, right? But this is Fairbanks. In June. And the sun... It never got dark. It kind of turned into this impromptu party. ... It just made it easy to meet some folks to go explore Alaska with.

- You could drive someone's car one-way across the country, or be a courier overseas, or take a berth in a freighter. The International Association of Air Travel Couriers has a website with information on courier travel. Or do a web search for freighter cruises, or vehicle relocation services looking for drivers.
- *Save on lodging by camping.* You may even be able to leave the tent at home: Some states offer yurts (round platform tents) and other semi-permanent structures for overnight stays at campgrounds in their state parks. Many feature cots, and even electricity. These tend to be very popular, so plan ahead and reserve early. Some state parks also have cabins for rent, as do some KOAs (where cabin rental rates will likely be higher than in the state park, so check around).
- Some national forests offer former fire lookout cabins for overnight rentals. These also tend to be very popular, so book ahead. See the U.S. Forest Service website for more information. Some local hiking clubs also offer cabins for overnight stays; stores that specialize in outdoor gear can provide information on how to contact these clubs.
- *Hostelling* is another cheap way to stay. Hostels are not just for college kids: many have private rooms for rent, as well as beds in the dorms. This is a great way to meet other travelers as you go places.
- *Look into a home stay or a home swap.* SERVAS and Travelhoo are two organizations that arrange home stays. Or do an Internet search.
- *Some colleges will rent out dorm rooms inexpensively* between sessions. If you attend alumni functions at a college, a hint of nostalgia can be yours just by renting an empty dorm room for the length of your stay.
- Check web sites for the local convention and visitors bureau for your destination. You may be able to find coupons for food, lodging and attractions.
- Use local transit at your destination instead of renting a car or calling a cab, saving cab fare and parking fees. In Denver, a bus

route called the Cultural Connection Trolley passes many of the city's tourist attractions. San Francisco sells a transportation pass that is good on the city buses, trolleys, cable cars, and some of the trains. Many other cities have similar passes geared to tourists; check web sites before you go. For example, the Washington, DC, Metro system offers a one-day rail pass for $5; the New York City transit system offers a one-day pass, good on both buses and subways, for $4.

- Save the cost of travel and lodging and play tourist in your own hometown. When was the last time you visited all of your local tourist traps and attractions besides the mall?
- *Or travel locally.* Rent a room in a nearby city. Since you can hop in the car and get home in a short time, you need not make all the arrangements that going out of town usually requires, but can still "escape" pretty cheaply.
- *Travel lightly whenever possible.* Not only is there less to lose, there is less to manage and carry while you are traveling. If all else fails, you can usually buy what you need wherever you are.
- *Leave spares there.* If you regularly travel to a particular place, especially if you stay at the same person's house every time, make arrangements to leave "spares" there: spare toiletries, a change of clothes, etc.

Electronic Entertainment

Not everyone is willing to go be a social animal every day, and some days it is simpler just to hang out around your place because of weather, scheduling conflicts, or even just a desire to nest. After a while, even the best book can pall, so if you want something electronic to do, consider some of these:

- *Dig out your old video games* you have stashed three or four layers deep in the closet and see if you can still beat Pac-Man. If you have an older video game console, you can usually find game cartridges you have never played for free or very cheap at second-hand stores or used music stores.

Simplifier Primrose Edmonds related this story about the benefits of traveling light on the Simple Living network discussion boards:

Not that I would recommend the experience to anyone, but my husband and I (no kids) traveled overseas last year for a month and had two large suitcases, two daypacks, and various shopping bags stolen from our car. [We] left it locked but [were only] away for ten minutes!

My point is that, as we both loathe shopping, we decided not to restock our clothes and just enjoy our holiday. It was amazing how liberating it was to only have a choice of one pair of trousers, a t-shirt, one pair of shoes, knickers, and bra to choose from! We just washed them out in the hotel room when needed, and because of the climate, [they] were dry in the morning.

We still met people and went to posh restaurants as their guests, … but all we had to say is we were robbed of our clothes and nobody cared less about what we looked like, and better still, we didn't have to worry about what was the appropriate thing to wear. I just wore my hair in a ponytail, no makeup of course, and looked like a complete hag and didn't care. … We carried [our] things in a plastic shopping bag when checking into hotels and saved lots on tipping! I guess the point of this is to say that we were shocked at how much stuff we take away with us sometimes "just in case". It's not always practical to go with next to nothing, of course, but maybe it might get you thinking about whether you need to take so much away next time.

- Recently, "vintage" video games have shown up as new titles that run on newer computers, so you may not need to find that weird little cable to attach the old console to the TV.
- The same thing applies for old computer games. Jonathan's Apple IIe still runs just fine on the odd day he wants to play a little Choplifter or Zork!
- Your local library can loan you a tape or DVD of some show you have not seen before: anything from an old Ed Wood film to recently popular TV shows might be available. Check out "Attack of the Killer Tomatoes" or "Plan 9 from Outer Space" and invite all your buddies over for a raucous evening of bad special effects and "Mystery Science Theater 3000"-style comments from the assembled peanut gallery.
- In the same way, your library might also have audio tapes or CDs you can check out. You can audition a new artist, or whole new musical genre, without the cost of buying a CD.
- Your library might also loan books on tape. People giving up TV swear by these to "fill the silence" when the radio pales.
- Finally, you can while away an entire day just randomly surfing the Internet. Just be aware that many of the drawbacks of watching television apply to many of the websites available.

Practical To Dos

Pick something from one of the lists above and try it!

Library Guide

Just go and find something interesting! Librarians are always there to help.

Internet Resources

www.cheaptickets.com
www.travelhoo.com
www.travelzoo.com
www.amtrak.com
www.orbitz.com
www.travelocity.com
www.expedia.com
www.courier.org (International Association of Air Travel Couriers)
www.hiayh.org (Hostelling International/American Youth Hostels)
www.hostels.com (a list of hostels, including non-AYH facilities)
www.fs.fed.us/recreation/reservations (for renting campsites and lookout cabins in U.S. national forests)
www.servas.org
www.simpleliving.net
wwwbeakman.com

Search Terms

home stay
volunteer vacation
"freighter cruise"
"vehicle relocation"
hostel
home swap
"city guide" + your city
"visitors' bureau" + your city
"state parks" + your state

CHAPTER 11

SIMPLE POLITICS

You might believe that living simply anywhere means avoiding politics at all costs. No statement could be further from the truth. One of the many reasons Simplifiers give for going down the VS path is to free up time for other interests. Often, building community or volunteering to do something important is a major motivator for Simplifiers. There are no reports of Simplifiers saving for years just so they could watch TV all day.

In his book *Bowling Alone*, Robert Putnam lays out how social capital, the psychic lubricant that keeps the family, civic, and political machinery in motion, has waxed and waned over the last few generations. Social capital is "those tangible substances [that] count for most in the daily lives of people: namely good will, friendship, sympathy, and social intercourse among the individuals and families that make up the social unit."[1]

An easier way to view this is the idea of reciprocity: you do something for me and I'll do something for you. But Putnam says reciprocity must be more generalized if the ideal of "community" is to properly emerge. "A society characterized by generalized reciprocity is more efficient than a distrustful society, for the same reason that money is more efficient than barter. If we don't have to balance each exchange instantly, we can get a lot more accomplished. Trustworthiness lubricates social life. ... Civic engagement and social capital entail mutual obligation and responsibility for actions. ... When economic and politi-

cal dealing is embedded in dense networks of social inter-
action, incentives for opportunism and malfeasance are
reduced."[2]

If everyone is always in strict payback mode (commonly called
"tit for tat"), there is no opportunity to allow your payback to go
to someone else down the road, or for someone else's payback to
come your way. The campaign to perform "random acts of kindness" and the concept of "pay it forward" from Catherine Hyde's
book of the same name (and the movie it inspired) speaks directly
to the heart of the generalized reciprocity idea: do a good turn for
someone else with no intent to elevate yourself in any way, and
eventually someone will do the same for you when you need it.

Putnam's analysis shows, among other things, that the mass
media have changed our definition of participation from actually
doing something to being spectators of events. Just being a spectator does not create or exchange any social capital. Social capital
is created and exchanged by doing with others, not sitting on the
sidelines watching. You cannot create community solely by sitting
in front of your TV. You have to get out and deal successfully
with other people to solve the problems motivating you. Living
together, especially in the city, enhances your opportunity for creating social capital, simply because you can contact, and nurture
relationships among, more people in an urban area.

Politics Small and Large

Politics has been described as "the art of the possible."
Whether it is marital politics, volunteering for the PTA, running
for city council, or taking on the challenge of a higher state or
federal office, the art remains the same: get connected with the
appropriate movers and shakers so you can help move and shake
the situation you want addressed. This is a direct application of
social capital to the challenges facing a marriage or a nation.

Since this is a book about cities, we will leave both ends of the
spectrum for other authors and focus on civic relationships at the

city level. Michael Briand, in his book *Practical Politics: Five Principles for a Community that Works*, defines five practical principles anyone can use as they learn the art of politics and build social capital. They are Inclusion, Comprehension, Deliberation, Cooperation, and Realism.

Inclusion: People want to feel included, even if they do not want to spend any time making public policy. The way to feel included is to volunteer. You need not run for and win a public office, unless you want to. You can volunteer for various task forces that work on issues you feel strongly about. Most cities have a committee or two that needs someone to sit and help with issues. Some cities are even asking for people to sit on temporary Citizens' Wisdom Councils.[3] Council members are selected, meet with a trained facilitator, and disband after a few meetings once a consensus has been reached on the issue at hand.

Comprehension is sometimes used to mean "understanding." But in terms of the political process, comprehension is really a recognition that each of the folks around the table has needs, desires, and convictions. Comprehension means seeing our political opponents as people. Once we understand that our "opponents" are not mindless positions opposed to what we want, but instead are real people with a real desire to see something constructive done about a situation, then we can start to gain the insight each person brings to the issue at hand. If we can respect the convictions and validate the people engaging in the debate, even if not completely fulfilling their needs and desires, it may be possible to arrive at a reasoned solution to the issue before us. Notice that that does not necessarily mean that an *agreement* will be reached. With comprehension, we can work together to find other ways to resolve issues.[4]

Deliberation is the thoughtful consideration of all sides of an issue. Each of the issues facing us politically has a number of good people behind it. Good-hearted people with different viewpoints each see the problem and propose what they feel are reasonable solutions. Ideally, these people will sit down and work through several possible solutions to each problem, examining each solution for fitness against multiple criteria and discarding solutions that have little or no utility given the situation in which the problem exists. For any non-trivial problem, multiple solutions are always possible. We must work together to find the pragmatic answer for today.

Cooperation involves working together for our mutual benefit – in other words, creating more social capital. Cooperation must be distinguished from collaboration: collaboration implies that the participants have an agreed-upon goal. Briand says people involved in a political debate seldom have agreed-upon goals:

> To some degree, in every community – no matter what its size – the public is fragmented. People are divided along lines created by different perceptions of who they are, what the world is like, what goods we should seek and what priorities we should have, and who should do what, when, and how. Whatever the source of our perceptions – cultural, economic, psychological, experiential, generational, sexual, ideological, ethnic – the fact is the community members rarely assign the same priority initially to the same goals.[5]

Practically speaking, there must be cooperation when we work with our nominal adversaries, not because we agree with them but because it is our best interests to do so. We stand to gain more by working with others and accepting a pragmatic (rather than a preferred) solution to some problems. In the long term, we are building social capital by working together, regardless of the outcome of a particular issue. In the short term, we can feel enfranchised by actually helping with issues facing our community.

Realism: It is helpful for all involved to be realistic about solutions reached through the political process. Decisions that seem pragmatic at one time will seem impractical, if not ridiculous, at another time. Issues that would galvanize the nation at one time may receive little or no attention from the citizenry at another time.. Politics is about today's problems being solved by today's people with today's tools within today's milieu; this lends a certain impermanence to the results. We must expect some issues will resurface over time, in different guises, and with different players.

Being realistic also means having a deep understanding that the problems we face politically are, at their root, people problems and emotional problems. Diversity that divides us by creating distrust is a corruption of our greatest political strength: our ability to bring many minds together to seek a good solution.

Finally, Realism means we understand that the public is still largely apolitical, and this lack of social capital in the political arena will have a chilling effect on the decision-making process. Until we can get all the appropriate people around the table to help make decisions, our only choice is to accept poorer decisions than we might otherwise make. This will haunt us for a long time on many, many issues. So the political realist must plan for the general case when engaging in the hurly-burly of the political arcade.

- The political realist expects sinners, not saints. Politics is all about people, with all their personal glories, foibles, and failings. The relentless examination of political candidates' past lives back to babyhood is often pointless and too often degenerates into a smear campaign. The people attracted to politics currently are often those on the extremes—they have an *agenda*. The moderate middle is largely absent from the political process currently.

- The political realist expects size to matter. You cannot always get everyone around a single table. Use multiple tables and multiple meetings, if possible.

- The political realist expects discomfort. Some people want things to happen now; others always want more study. No matter the issue, someone is going to be uncomfortable discussing it or making a decision about the best path forward.

- The political realist expects to benefit from the opposition. We gain knowledge by learning to refute their strongest arguments and vice versa.

- The political realist expects to be painted partisan and verbally attacked. Some people believe that their only goal is to win, by any means necessary, including denigrating all the other people around the table. The realist will not only expect this, but will strive to avoid answering in kind.
- The political realist expects pervasive self-interest. Everyone is looking to achieve some good; use that to further the common good. Use your connections and social capital to understand the "best" solutions and focus on the common good whenever possible.
- The political realist expects intolerance. Practical politics demands that we practice patience, self-control, and restraint. All the people around the table may not understand this.
- The political realist expects to pay your share. There is no ground that is all yours; everyone has access to bits of the truth. Do not sink to your opponent's level and lash out; give and take is a normal part of the process.
- The political realist expects greyness. If there were only black and white questions, no politics would exist.
- The political realist expects chaos. People are involved, so politics is always a slow process with seemingly random movements and false starts. Politics can also be difficult and annoying if you hold the false expectation of a quick resolution to any substantial issue.
- The political realist expects subsurface motivations. The person's true position is almost always different than their stated position. This is often because they are unclear about what they really want, or that they are unaware of possible alternative solutions and the desires of others involved.
- The political realist expects to play hardball. Sometimes your opponent will not let you do anything else.
- The political realist expects to settle for a pragmatic rather than a preferred solution. Some problems are so complex, they can only be tamed, not solved. The time may be right later to reach a lasting solution.

- The political realist expects to be in it for the long term. Nothing gets done overnight. Lasting civic relationships are not built in a day. Good, pragmatic, solutions take time and effort to achieve.

Finally, create and nurture what Briand calls "civic friendships"—ongoing relationships grounded in civic matters with people you would not otherwise associate with regularly. This sets the stage for creating comprehension later; you each have some shared social capital and can use that to your mutual advantage. The people around the table with whom you have shared experiences will have an inkling of where you stand on issues in general and will have learned to trust your judgment, even if they sometimes disagree with your results.

Winston Churchill said it best: "Democracy is the worst form of government, except for all the others." So get out there and make your presence felt. Pick your issue, do any research required, build your social capital, establish long-term civic relationships, and help your representatives as your time, energy, and skills permit to find the best practical solutions to the issues at hand.

Practical To Dos

- Nurture some civic relationships. Build your social capital by volunteering in those areas you are interested in.
- Read the stories about local government in your local newspaper to be better informed about what's going on. The legal notices can be fun, too, and may tip you off to upcoming or planned changes in your neighborhood or city.
- Write well-researched letters and e-mail to your representatives if you cannot meet with them.
- Spend some time understanding your political "opponents" as people. Connect with them somehow, if possible.
- Find evidence to refute your "opponents'" strongest arguments and expect them to do the same for yours.

- Understand that we are all in this for the long term.
- When all else fails, play "tit for tat" before you play political hardball.[6]
- Volunteer. Or run for office if you feel moved to do so.

Library Guide

- *Practical Politics: Five Principles for a Community that Works* by Michael K. Briand
- *Bowling Alone: The Collapse and Revival of American Community* by Robert D. Putnam
- *Nonviolent Communication* by Dr. Marshall Rosenberg
- *Pay It Forward* by Catherine Ryan Hyde
- *Bowling Alone*, by Robert D. Putnam

Internet Resources

pespmc1.vub.ac.be/PRISDIL.html
www.globalideasbank.org/BI/BI-36.HTML
www.bowlingalone.com
www.cnvc.org

Search Terms

"tit for tat" + axelrod
Citizens' Wisdom Councils

CHAPTER 12

RETIREMENT

How many years before you can retire? And when you do, where will you live?

Once you get past the part about telling the boss to take this job and shove it, retirement fantasies pretty much all run along the same couple of tracks, all of which include throwing away the alarm clock, selling the big house, and living comic-strip cat Garfield's philosophy of feline existence: "Eat and sleep. Eat and sleep. There must be more to a cat's life than this—but I hope not."

Books abound on how best to accomplish the variations on the "sell the big house and..." theme. One fellow, John Howells, has made a career for himself in his own retirement by researching and writing books about where other people might like to live after they retire.[1] Howells has looked into diverse options — everything from Costa Rica and Mexico, to small college towns in the United States, to a parking lot in the desert for your RV. One option that he and many others seem never to consider, however, is retiring to an urban area.

But of all the living options you might consider for your golden years, moving to the country might well be the most shortsighted. Your most practical option might be to retire in the city, for three reasons: transportation, health care, and entertainment.

Transportation

In a city you can probably catch a bus at the street corner, or walk to the drug store or supermarket. You can take the subway to the airport or train station and go to visit the grandkids. In a city, you are not completely isolated if you are without a working car or a license to drive.

At some point, if you live long enough, you will have to stop driving. As people age, their reaction times slow, their eyesight worsens, and eventually they have to give up their driver's licenses. Alternatives to driving in the country would be pretty much limited to the county van service, and the kindness of neighbors or nearby relatives.

Health Care

The biggest drawback to retiring to the country is the lack of health care. Chances are pretty good that sometime during your retirement years, you will need health care, and not just the once-a-year once-over by your HMO doctor that you may get now. Options for health care can be limited to nonexistent outside the city. You may have to wait months to see the doctor or dentist of your choice, you may have to drive to the closest big town to see a specialist, and if you need to be hospitalized in an emergency, you will have to hope the doctors there have some experience with your problem; if they are inexperienced with your particular malady, you may be transferred to a hospital in the closest big city.

Lynne has been through this twice, once with each parent. When her father was diagnosed with terminal kidney cancer at the age of 69, he was transferred to a hospital in suburban Chicago, a four-hour round trip from her parents' home. Lynne's mother made this trip daily for several months, sometimes staying overnight. Years later, when Lynne's mother was diagnosed with uterine cancer, she was sent to a surgeon in Chicago, again a four-hour round trip; follow-up treatments involved a weekly visit to a radiologist in South Bend, IN, a two-hour round trip from home.

Lynne's parents were lucky that they lived within a half day's drive of world-class health care. But it would have been much easier for them if the drive had been across town instead of across state lines.

Continuing care, in the form of a visiting nurse or a nursing home, is also easier to find in a city. And in a city, you will very likely have much less trouble locating the hospice care that Simplifier Everette Orr found helpful when his father passed away:

> We had thought about going back to the community [in rural Virginia] where my grandparents were at, and my uncle was at. [But] when he was passing away, they didn't have hospice services. I mean, now you don't think about something like that. But Washington, DC, has a wonderful, extraordinary hospice program...the same as most urban areas.... [W]hen my father was passing away, I didn't know anything about hospices, other than the word. But they came by – Northern Virginia Hospice. They explained the program to me, and at that point, I think I had enough courage to go ahead and bring him to my home, so he could have a nice, pleasant experience with his family and loving people around him, as he made that transition. And those things are not available in rural areas – most rural areas.

Retiring in a city allows you to keep your health care options open.

Entertainment

Howells, and other where-to-live-in-retirement authors, often recommend retiring to a small college town because of the cultural events that colleges attract — lectures, concerts, art shows, etc. — at starving-student prices. But why limit yourself? Your choices for culture that suits your personal taste will be much, much broader in an urban area. And shown in "Entertainment," plenty of cultural events in cities cost next to nothing, too.

Eat and Sleep.   Eat and Sleep.

If you plan to do nothing but catch up on your sleep after you retire, you may be surprised to find out how quickly you reach that goal. Then what? Simplifier Kevin Cornwell, who retired in his 30s by following the steps outlined in *Your Money or Your Life*, says it took some time for him and his wife to get to know one another again:

> There's a heck of a lot more decision making that goes into quite literally every day when you don't have work to go to. What are you going to do today? The classic one with traditional retirees is the husband is going to go golf or fishing every day. Well, you can do that for a week or two weeks. Some guys, or gals for that matter...that is fine with them for an indefinite period. [But] after what I call the vacation part of being retired is over, let's say a month or two, then you get down to the reality, for us anyway, that you need things to keep active and do. And figuring out what that is, when you've been programmed for decades to go to work, and do this and you're successful, and you get a lot of money – going from that complete support system and reassurance model to just a blank canvas – it sounds very romantic, but it takes a fair amount of work and discipline, and I don't think we were quite ready for that. But having gotten through, whatever it is, now almost seven years, I wouldn't go back to the old way. This is so much more fun. And the variety in any given week that I do is a lot more interesting than any job I've ever had.

Even if you continue to do paid work for a more traditional period of time than Kevin and his wife, you need to consider that people now are living longer than ever before. Your "career" in retirement may be as long or longer than your career in the working world. Life expectancy continues to increase; you may well live into your 80s or 90s. That is a long time to just sit and fish.

Staying busy creates a measurable sense of well-being. Robert Kahn of the University of Michigan told *Forbes* magazine,

"People who are productive score higher on tests of functional ability, both cognitive and physical."[2] In short, to be a successful retiree, plan to keep busy. Take your vacation up front, but know what you are going to do next, starting in about month three.

Keeping Busy

You might plan to take the time to live your passion during retirement. As a retiree, your commitment to your art, your inner self, your health, or anything else, can no longer be compromised by having to work from 6 to 6.

That might involve volunteering. Volunteer opportunities exist everywhere, of course, but you have many more such opportunities to choose from in an urban area. You might even have a one-stop Volunteer Connection place available that can match your interests and skills to what is needed in the community. Not only can you help your community by doing volunteer work, but you can also help preserve your mental health. Michael Gordon, vice-president of Medical Service at Baycrest Centre for Geriatric Care in Toronto, and a professor of medicine at the University of Toronto, prescribes volunteer work for some depressed retirees: "I take out my prescription pad and tell them I am going to offer them a treatment that is very effective and has virtually no side-effects. They look at me hopefully, amazed that there is such a treatment. I then write on the pad, "Volunteer, two times a week, mornings only" and give it to them."[3]

Going back to school is another option; you could get that degree you never managed to finish. You could also take continuing education classes at your local high school, community college courses, or classes at a local museum or recreation center. You could even volunteer to teach a class (and possibly make a little money at it, too). Cities are an endless source of ways to keep your mind active, from people watching to fitness trails to live theater to libraries. The "Entertainment" chapter lists plenty of free or nearly free options, most of which are adaptable to any age. In addition, if you are old enough, you could take advantage of services offered by your local senior center: a place where older folks can go to socialize, get their taxes done, find out about volunteer opportunities, and take classes in everything from dancing to surfing the Internet. Many also organize trips by tour bus to nearby destinations. The YMCA or city parks and recreation department often offer fitness classes.

Simplifier Francine Jaskiewicz of Philadelphia loves city living so much that for her and her significant other, it will be a primary activity in retirement: "[O]nce we no longer need to work for a living, we plan to become urban nomads, living in various cities (in the US and around the world), renting apartments for one-year stays."

Retiring Early

Many hard-core Simplifiers plan to retire not just years early, but decades early. They have made it their goal to cut their living expenses to just enough (whatever that means for them) and put away everything else they make. They live by their personal values, most of which have nothing to do with spending: trust, effort, love, and more. With enough money in safe investments so that they can live solely off their interest income, they are financially independent (FI), and can retire from the work force at very early ages. One practical method of doing this is described in *Your Money or Your Life*.

Implausible? Not if your living expenses are $500 per month. At that spending level, you would need just $100,000 invested at a 6 percent annual return to be able to retire. We know several Simplifiers who have done exactly that. Lindi Hulse is one:

> Now retired at the ripe old age of 42, I have been travelling as much as possible with my 2 dogs in a camper van and returning to the L.A. metro area for a few months a year to spend with my family. After I do this for awhile I plan to backpack around the world for a number of years. When I am ready to settle down permanently, I plan to live in a small city in a little studio or one

bedroom condo as close to the city center as possible. I love small city living as I can be car free and walk or bike everywhere. I like the sense of community I feel in a city, as well as easy access to diverse nightlife and entertainment. I also like a small city rather than a large one, as there are usually outdoor recreation areas just a few miles out of town.

I basically just lived well below my means, never got into debt (except a very short mortgage of 4 years), and saved, saved, saved! I made a lot of decisions when I was young that enabled me to save money even on a modest salary. I was in the Coast Guard and chose to live and eat aboard ship and not own a car which allowed me to save most of my tiny salary. I used my VA benefits to pay for college and graduate school so I didn't have student loans. Married someone even more frugal than me ... and lived very, very modestly.

For me the key things to early retirement and FI were:

- to be really aware of all my purchases and activities and their real costs in terms of my life energy as well as the environmental impact.
- to strive to live as low impact and minimally as possible. I'm a naturally uncluttered person so that's easy.
- to save as much as possible while still doing all the things I want to do. I found free or low cost things to be just as pleasurable as costly things; more pleasurable, in fact.
- to not EVER get into debt, except for a mortgage or emergency stuff: not for a car...

The same goes for a house. Ex-hubby and I qualified for a $250K home loan but we chose to buy a small, older, fixer [house] for $120k. [We] put $50k as a down payment and paid the rest off in 4 years. I sold the house a year after I retired at 42 and downsized to a small (900 square foot), inexpensive house in a ski resort town. I later sold this house too, and now call my camper home.

Lindi found *Your Money or Your Life* after a short lifetime of frugality, and realized that selling her house in the city would make her FI. Another early retiree, Fred Ecks, used the same *Your Money or Your Life* tools to retire in downtown San Francisco:

I remember way back when around 1990, I wasn't liking working full time, one night I sat down and said: "How much would I need to save to be able to live off the interest income?" I calculated that I needed to save like $120,000 or something. And I said: "Oh, I'll *Never* Do That!", and I gave up.

> [Later] I read YMOYL again, and by then my ex and I had saved some money. We bought a house ... on a 15 year loan, and we made extra payments to the principal and built some equity, so we had some by the time I read the book. When I reread the book a few times, I saw the light and said "It's going to work." And at that point, over the course of the following years, we continued making progress, and it worked.

By being aware of his spending, and spending within his values, Fred lives a voluntarily simple lifestyle that gets him everything he needs, and enough of what he wants to keep himself happy.

Admittedly, not many people are interested in living on $500 per month. But what about $1,000 per month, or $12,000 per year? $15,000 per year? $20,000 per year? What about just below taxable levels? Here is a table showing how much interest an investment would yield annually.

If your expenses are...	You would need to invest (at 6% annually)...
$12,000 per year	$200,000
$15,000 per year	$250,000
$20,000 per year	$333,333
$25,000 per year	$416,667
$30,000 per year	$500,000

These are hardly the multimillion-dollar figures touted as necessary for retirement by the investment industry. Admittedly, they do not take inflation into account. But as Joe Dominguez and Vicki Robin argue in *Your Money or Your Life*, inflation may not have as big an impact on your wallet as the investment community would like you to believe. For instance, the government's Consumer Price Index (CPI) "market basket" continues to include the price of steak, even after it has gone so high that regular folks have long since switched to hamburger.[6]

Seven years ago, Kevin Cornwell was a company vice-president. Today, he helps his neighbors; he is a Big Brother; and he volunteers with the city of Vancouver, WA, as a neighbor-to-neighbor mediator. He found that he had to reinvent part of his identity after he reached Financial Independence (FI):

> I liked the work I was doing, in fact I really liked it, and I identified quite a bit with it. People would say, "What do you do?" And I'd say, "VP of Human Resources at this company." Then they'd say, after [I retired], "What do you do?" "Well..." It's a tough question. Most people really don't want to know that you're retired. And most people really aren't interested that you're financially independent...
>
> [T]hey all assume you won the lottery and stuff like that....

Kevin says he does not explain to everyone he meets that he is FI. Instead, he evaluates his audience and starts by saying, "Oh, yeah, we're just taking some time off"; if they ask for more details, then he tells them more.

So it is possible to retire early and live in the city—we know lots of people who do it!

Strategies abound for setting up an early-retirement income stream. *Your Money or Your Life* recommended the purchase of 30-year U.S. Treasury bonds, but at this writing, new 30-year Treasury bonds are no longer available. *Your Money or Your Life* co-author Vicki Robin, together with some members of FI Associates, have identified alternatives to the 30-year Treasury bond, including the purchase of other U.S.-backed bonds, as well as the "laddering" of certificates of deposit. The web address for this information is at the end of this chapter. You can also check out the website of FI Associates and the discussion boards at the Simple Living website for more information.

If you are an American and most of your retirement savings is tied up in IRAs and/or 401(k)s, you can tap into that money penalty-free for use as retirement income, even before you turn 60, by taking what the Internal Revenue Service calls "substantially equal periodic payments". John P. Greaney's "Retire Early" website gives an overview of the procedure (as well as a wealth of other information about how to retire early), but you can find the most up-to-date information at the IRS website. (Other countries may have similar provisions in their tax laws; check with your national ministry of finance or taxation.)

(Please note that neither of your authors is an investment professional, and none of the above should be construed as investment advice.)

Practical To Dos

- Do not assume that you have to wait until you are old to retire or that you will never be able to retire. Read *Your Money or Your Life*, practice the nine steps, and do the math for your own unique situation.
- In picking a place to retire, consider how accessible your proposed location is. Would you be stuck without a car? Is health care readily available? Is there enough there to keep you busy?
- Research your retirement plans via the Internet and your local library. Carefully investigate options like assisted living before you commit yourself.
- Enjoy your life while you are saving for retirement. Complete self-denial now to achieve Financial Independence earlier is a gamble on the tenuous future. Living well with enough is truly the best revenge, and only you can define "well" and "enough" for you.

Library Guide

- *Your Money or Your Life* by Joe Dominguez and Vicki Robin
- *Where to Retire: America's Best and Most Affordable Places* (and other titles by John Howells)
- *The Millionaire Next Door* by Thomas Stanley and William Danko

Internet Resources

www.simpleliving.net (the information about alternatives to 30-year bonds can be found at http://www.simpleliving.net/ymoyl/gh-step9revisited.asp)
www.yourmoneyoryourlife.org
www.retireearlyhomepage.com
www.aarp.org
www.scottburns.com
www.irs.gov

Search Terms

financial independence
assisted living
continuing care

CHAPTER 13

TRANSPORTATION

Transportation, or the act of moving yourself, and maybe some amount of stuff, from one place to another, seems to be a basic tenet of modern life. Since the days of Model-T Ford, the landscape of all the countries where the car is king has been relentlessly churned up, flattened out, and paved over in an attempt to fit ever more vehicles onto roadways. We have systematically created and enlarged what many have come to call the concrete desert. Of course, it does not have to be this way.

Getting around in the city can be a breeze or a real hassle. Driving your car through rush hour to the city in the morning, parking it, working all day, and then fighting commuter traffic all the way home in the evening is a way of life for many people. But there are alternatives, both within the city itself, and outside the box, if you are willing to think there. You might even decide to *Divorce Your Car!*[1] as Katie Alvord's book puts it.

Transit to, from, and around the city need not be by a personally owned vehicle. Depending on where you live, you may have access to mass transit that meets some portion of your needs. And even if there is no mass transit available, you might still have a practical and pleasurable life without owning a vehicle. This does not seem possible because the automakers spend $14 billion per year[2] to convince you that a personal vehicle is the only transport you should use. In this chapter, we will try to counter that advertising myth. There is no need for everyone to own a personal vehicle from Detroit or Japan or Germany or ...

Personally Powered Transit

You can choose many ways of getting to your destination without getting in your vehicle if you live close enough. In many cities, walking to many, if not most, of your destinations can be both healthy exercise and the best part of the busy day. A nice walk or run home at the end of the work day can also be a good way to decompress from your job, especially if you can take some time to enjoy the flowers or view the wildlife on your way home. Notice that you never hear about "pedestrian rage" the way you hear about road rage? That is because walking has a calming influence on mood. Your investment, besides breakfast, is a good pair of walking shoes and maybe a backpack. With practice, you will be able to walk or run further than you initially thought you ever could. Anything within one mile is walking distance for most people and anything within two miles is about 30 minutes away.[3]

Many older US cities, such as Boston and New Orleans, that were build before the age of the automobile, were really built as walking cities. This means driving in the older sections of the city is a nightmare. In many older cities, real estate is very expensive precisely because the neighborhoods are walkable: you can walk to school, church, and possibly even the grocery, quite easily and probably faster than driving and parking.

However, not everyone lives within what they perceive as walking distance. There are several alternatives to walking that still rely on your muscle power to get you to your destination. Although relatively new as transportation, inline skates can be used successfully to double or even triple the distance you can go in the same period of time as walking. Skateboards, scooters, and other variations on this theme abound. Each can add variety and fun to your trip. Just be sure you are wearing your protective gear.

Faster than skating, and certainly more recognized in most parts of the world, is biking. Many US cities are recognizing the benefits of bike paths. While some are still on car roads, many bicycles have their own roadways. There is even a "rails to trails" effort in some areas of the country where abandoned railways are being converted to trails for hiking, biking, skating, snowmobiling, and assorted other uses. Simplifier Fred Ecks got into biking as part of living a simpler life:

> I was driving everywhere and I was very overweight...
> Across the road from me was one of my neighbors; he
> didn't have a car and I thought that was the strangest thing.
> He had all these bicycles, but he didn't have a car – he
> didn't drive anywhere. ... And finally one day, I just had
> some time to think for a while and I said "God, you know,
> those guys can do that, I can do that. I could get a bike
> and start riding it around. That sounds kind of nice. I
> remember when I was a kid, I liked riding a bicycle, and
> hey, maybe I could get some of this weight off too." So I
> bought a bicycle and I started riding it to work. At the
> time, work was three miles away and that was *a ride* for me.
> But I noticed over the next number of months that I could
> do it faster, I really enjoyed it, I did start to lose some
> weight, and it was really kind of cool.

Many cities have bicycle clubs. Members are often dedicated bikers, many of whom do not own a car at all or, if they do, seldom drive it. One would think that they would be primarily in the warmer climes, but the largest bicycle chapter is in Minneapolis/St. Paul, MN. In fact, members have been proactive and successfully lobbied the various city boards to build urban bike trails distinct from the city streets wherever possible. In cities where snow is a common occurrence and there is an active biking community, some cities are starting to plow the sidewalks and bike paths.

Many cities have seen the usefulness of upgrading buses to include front-mounted bike racks, thus increasing the useful range of a bicycle and making a personally-owned vehicle even less necessary. This is an example of multi-modal transport: use the bike to get to the bus stop, ride the bus to near where you want to go, and then bike the rest of the way. Some commuter lines, bus or train, will allow cyclists to bring their bikes on only if you have a special pass. Check with your commuter line for details.

And with the advent of more and more people riding bicycles, the types of accessories available have grown. You can buy all kinds of protective gear, bicycles with shock absorbers for a smoother ride, and electric motor kits to help power your bike. Oregon even has a solar-powered bike recharging station! There are also bicycle trailers for hauling stuff or the kiddos around behind you.[4] So if you remember riding a bicycle fondly, you will be in good company when you decide to hit the road on two wheels. Check out your local bike shop or club to get recommendations from all the people who really do this every day. Please remember to wear your helmet!

Mass Transit: Many Forms, Same Idea

Mass transit is what the name implies: moving large numbers of people (with their stuff) from place to place using special vehicles. Usually this means buses or trains.

Regardless of whether you take the bus or the train, the fun thing about mass transit is knowing that each time you get on, you are entering a unique micro-culture. Every route has a different group of people on it, most of whom are really nice. Taken as a whole, each route develops its own personality. Many city commuters find themselves on the same route, at the same time, with the same people, most every day. If you are a gregarious sort of person, you will meet a lot of new people and make a few friends as you travel to and from wherever you always go. Chatting with acquaintances can be a pleasant way to start and end each day. A friendly greeting from the driver first thing in the morning can be a very nice way to start the day.

Not everyone is the life of the train, though, and some days you will just want to be left alone, so many people will wear headphones or read something to signal they want privacy while they commute. So you can be as alone or as social as you want while riding mass transit. Even if you are not the gregarious sort, buses and trains are still great places to people-watch.

Consider what other portions of your morning routine might fit in with your ride. Walk or skate to and from the nearest mass transit stop and make part of your journey into some impromptu exercise as well. One of the fellows Jonathan rides to work with gets off at a stop one mile from his actual work location and walks the remainder of the distance to work on nice days; if it is raining, he gets off right in front of his building. Your morning coffee, made cheaply at home and carried in a commuter cup, might gain you five more minutes in bed. You can plan your day on the way in to work and decompress (nap!) on the way from work if someone else is doing the driving. Or, if you'd rather, you can nap on the way to work and plan your evening on the way home. You can read, do a crossword puzzle, or knit or crochet. Jonathan even changed his car's status from commuter to pleasure vehicle, cutting his insurance costs significantly and making it necessary to put gas in his second car every other month.

Some people avoid mass transit because they fear some event, such as a sick child, will cause them to unexpectedly go home in the middle of the work day. Jonathan's employer offers a free cab ride up to six times per year for such problems. Lynne's area has a similar program you can sign up for in advance and then use as needed[5]. If all else fails and you still need to make an emergency trip from work, a cab can take you where you need to go very cheaply compared to driving every day, especially if you have to pay for parking.

Frequent riders of mass transit often find it cheaper to buy a periodic pass. Jonathan rides the bus to and from work often enough that he just gets an annual pass good for the commuter routes in his burg. In fact, parking is so bad that some employers, including Jonathan's, give out free bus passes just to keep employees from driving to work. Fred Ecks buys a monthly pass and has the use of all the mass transit in San Francisco for around $30. Since he rides to and from various volunteer opportunities most days, he saves at least $30 every month, not to mention the hassle of carrying all the extra cash to pay fares. Some states allow employers to deduct the cost of a transit pass directly from the employee's paycheck before taxes[6] or allow the employer to write off the cost of the pass as a tax credit[7].

If you fear for your personal safety on mass transit, keep in mind that you are far more likely to be in an auto accident than to be attacked on mass transit. The National Center for Statistics and Analysis research for the US DOT/National Highway Traffic Safety Administration shows 1.09 persons injured per million vehicle miles traveled and more than double that for property damage (reported non-fatal crashes). In 2001, there were 6,320,000 vehicle crashes and 41,730 fatalities.[8] According to US Department of Transportation figures, just one personal attack and one property attack occur per million passengers; the rate has been holding steady since 1996[9]. Only 299 riders of US mass transit were killed in 1999.[10] Today's mass transit services pride themselves on cleanliness and safety. In DC, Metro train seats damaged by vandalism are exchanged for brand-new seats nightly. While the rate of vehicle fatalities is falling slightly, you are still 120 times more likely to die while commuting in your car than you are on any form of public transit. The truth is that almost all people riding mass transit are just looking to get one place to another on time and the last thing they have in mind is assaulting someone. Mass transit moves millions of people across the US safely, every day, on time, and usually without incident.

Although you may sometimes run into a scheduling or route problem that makes getting somewhere more of a hassle than usual, these situations can usually be addressed by specific choices. You can choose to use multiple modes of transportation (such as biking to a bus stop with more convenient routes and taking the bus from there). Choosing to live close to a mass transit line that goes directly to your most common destinations can make even more of a difference. [*Editor's note: I chose to live in Seattle's University District in part because 48 different bus lines stop within a mile of my apartment. From here I can reach almost every neighborhood in the county directly or with only one transfer downtown. Very convenient.*]

You can avoid the bus altogether if you can find a group of similarly minded folks all going the same direction at the same time and set up a car or van pool. Your company may have a bulletin board or similar electronic classified ad system that you can use to find others interested in a car pool. Multi-passenger vehicles get preferred lanes in some cities. Your area might even have a "RideShare" services that match riders and drivers. Or you could participate in a spontaneous carpool system like in the Washington, DC, metropolitan area: some parking lots are informally designated as places where would-be "slugs" gather. Drivers hoping to use the high-occupancy vehicle lanes go there to pick up people who are going where they are going.

And if you are really interested in thinking outside the box, you can do what a bunch of workers in California did for a while: band together and rent a bus on a long-term contract that picked up at a location near home and dropped everyone off at work. It helped that these folks all worked at the same place and lived in the same area. A couple of the men were scout leaders and even had scout leader meetings on the bus to eliminate running around to meetings at home.

Mass transit works best when it's full, though the breakeven point for a bus is usually about seven to ten passengers per route. So not only is mass transit often a win for the environment, it can be much cheaper than filling up your vehicle to go anywhere:

Cost per mile of a 15-mile one-way trip		
Driving your car solo		*Taking light rail*
Gas (20mpg @ $1.50/gal):	$1.13	
Car maintenance (IRS estimate):	$0.27	
External costs (taxes, insurance, environmental, social, etc.)[11]:	$0.68-0.98	
Total:	**$2.08-2.38**	**$0.20-0.40**

Powered Personal Transit

If mass transit just will not suit your purposes, and walking or biking is out, there are still alternatives to owning a personal vehicle. For shorter distances, a moped can be quite effective at getting you to and from where you need to go. And if you are really of the high-tech bent, the new Segway by Segway Inc. might just fill your transport needs. (As with most new technology, however, you may find the cost outweighs its benefits.) If you have further to go, or need to carry a passenger, a full sized motorcycle might be a better bet than a moped or a Segway. All these forms of transportation are exposed to the weather, so a little planning ahead will be required, as well as some special clothing. Motorcycles require protective gear and special licenses in all but a few states. Your authors *strongly* recommend proper safety gear, especially helmets, when using these forms of transport.

This leaves us to the most problematic means of personally owned, powered transport: the personally owned automobile (be that a car, a truck, an SUV, or something else).

Operating a vehicle in the city is a hassle. For starters, there are just too many other vehicles on the road, usually at the same time you are on the road. What is your quality of life, really, when your commute is three hours? Or worse, three hours one way? Jonathan spent a year driving three hours round trip to work and absolutely hated the drive. Not because the drive was full of unpleasant scenery or even on overcrowded roads. To the contrary, the drive was through pretty country on a low-traffic, rural highway. But the drive was just another three hours of "work" after an eight, ten, or more hours per day of working.

Because so many vehicles are jammed into such a small area, property crime (car theft or vandalism) is easier to perpetrate in the city, which drives up insurance rates significantly. Even just parking your vehicle near work or home in the city can be an expensive nightmare. The old joke goes that the person finally gets a good parking spot near her apartment, and then refuses to move the vehicle ever again! And with parking costs exceeding $10 per day on long-term contracts in many cities, parking alone can cost more annually than the total worth of the vehicle.

The estimated cost of owning a car in the city, excluding the actual cost of the car itself, is over $3,100 annually[12]. That includes gas, oil, average maintenance costs, parking, and insurance costs. If the average car is driven 15,000 miles annually, that is almost $0.25 per mile just to use the vehicle. And that is just the visible money out of your pocket. The external costs of owning a single car are conservatively estimated at $10,000 or more per car per year[13]. (External costs are costs that you do not pay directly, but do pay for in the form of increased federal taxes, state taxes, health insurance, and other costs.) You can rent a car several times a year for that kind of money, and some of the major rental car companies will even deliver the car to your doorstep! So as an exercise, figure out how much it actually costs you to

---

Hybrid cars are cars that use more than one method of generating motion. The ones on the market at the time of this writing are electric/gasoline hybrids. An electric motor is married to a small gasoline engine by a fancy transmission system. Sometimes the car runs only on the electric motor. Sometimes both motors are active. There are several variations on this theme, so check the description of any hybrid carefully and match the driving style it is optimized for to your driving style for best results.

Hybrid cars can fall into the ULEV, Ultra Low Emission Vehicle, or SULEV, Super Ultra Low Emission Vehicle, categories with respect to total emissions produced while driving. Regardless of which category the vehicle you are considering is in, any steps you take to improve gas mileage and lower emissions are a win for the environment.

drive your car, with and without the cost of ownership, on a "per mile" basis. All of a sudden, mass transit and other forms of getting around will start to look quite cheap!

The Co-op Car

If you have a good driving record and you need a car infrequently or only at odd times of the day, a car co-op could be a good option for you. With a co-op, you buy a share in a fleet of cars. You use the car like a library book: you check it out when you need it, return it clean inside and full of gas when done, and forget about it in the meantime. Like a health club, there is an application fee, as well as a fee for various services the co-op provides to you. However, the co-op pays for the car, maintains the mechanical systems, insures it, pays for parking, and disposes of it when it is past its useful life. There are several car co-ops currently operating around the US. A company called FlexCar is making a dent in private car ownership in the Seattle, WA; Washington, DC; Long Beach, CA; and Portland, OR; and even offers co-op members special parking places at popular destinations. Zipcar in Boston is a similar service, and there are others.

Cities are beginning to get behind the idea of car sharing. In 2002, Alexandria, VA, offered grants to city residents to offset membership and application fees, and to city businesses for membership fees for their employees.[14] Check with your city to see whether something like this is in the works.

If your area is not large enough to support a fleet of cars like the car co-ops, you and your neighbors can do the same thing by sharing the local clunker just like you would share a ladder or a hand tool. If money is going to trade hands, though, you would be well advised to contact a lawyer and an accountant and set up your own business entity with its own insurance, just in case.

Of course, you can take steps to *Divorce Your Car*, or at least, all but one of your cars, which is called going "Car-Lite". But for many people, this just is not a reasonable choice: they choose to live far from mass transit locations or there is more than one driver in the household with conflicting needs. We suggest that, with a little planning and some reliance on alternative transport methods, you might be able to prosper with just one car. The planning can turn out to be pretty simple.

Where Do You Go and How Do You Get There?

Stop and think for a moment how you actually use transportation. Must one single vehicle fulfill all your transportation needs? Perhaps you:

1. Commute to work less than 20 miles one way, with one or two people (this accounts for about 90% of all US driving).
2. Run errands in town with up to four people, round trip 50 miles maximum.
3. Carry children to practice with some amount of sports gear.
4. Occasionally pick up a couple 2x4s or a bulky item at the hardware store.
5. Routinely carry four people somewhere, so that a two-door econobox just is not quite large enough.
6. Carry passengers through six inches of snow or standing water or mud.
7. Occasionally pick up ¼ ton of black dirt to spread on the garden.
8. Drive to the in-laws 500 miles one way twice a year with kids, animals, and luggage.
9. Add your own—what unique uses do you have for your vehicle?

Notice that a personally-owned automobile is not necessary to cover each of these needs. You might discover that you can ride some sort of mass transit to work on most days, share a car to run errands, and have large things delivered, or use rented or borrowed vehicles, to move those things and people the few times per year you need them moved.

So think through the ways you use your personal vehicle across a year. What roles does it play and how often is each role assumed? How many people does it carry? How fast and far must it go? How much stuff must it haul? Is it used as a platform for mounting work tools? Does it sit idle all day while the other car runs errands; would an extra "errand run" to chauffeur someone to work mean a second car is not necessary? When you have identified all the roles your vehicles play, or the transport needs that you have, you can start matching vehicle attributes to those roles. Vehicles might have the following attributes:

- Powered or human powered
- Owned or not owned (rented occasionally, rented regularly by the ride, etc.)
- Seats one, two, four, or more comfortably
- Drives well long distance vs. go around town only
- Electric with "limited" range vs. gasoline with longer range vs. hybrid
- Handles messy payloads easily outside or messily inside the cab
- Easy access to extra gear/luggage via trunk or side door
- Can cruise at expressway speeds, or tops out at "around town" speeds

The trick is to identify all the roles your lifestyle requires of transportation, and then find the simplest, cheapest, and least environmentally damaging way to fill each role. If you live close to work and are an enthusiastic biker, then maybe a bicycle, moped, or even a small motorcycle would take care of your commute. If you choose to live far from work, but near a commuter train station, then walking to the train might cover your job-related transport most days. If you live 15 minutes away from work, and public transport is not a good option (it takes longer than an hour to get from home to work), then maybe an "around town" electric vehicle would be a good choice. Mix and match the attributes; examine several combinations of ways to fulfill all your transportation needs. There is no law that says you must own your own vehicle that is capable of doing everything and therefore gets lousy gas mileage on every mile you drive. You can optimize your transportation strategy to meet your needs more easily in the city.

Even if you choose to own a vehicle, finding ways to drive it as little as possible is a win for you because it will last longer and cost less for fuel and oil; a win for the environment because it will create less pollution, and a win for everyone else sitting in the traffic jam.

Notice that we have scrupulously avoided the discussion of a personally owned vehicle as a "show piece" or an "accessory". We believe that like all fads that come and go, the current fad of a particular kind of vehicle is just that—a fad. There are far better things to buy than a depreciating asset if your real intent is to impress the neighbors. We suggest that you start by paying off all your debts. Getting out from under consumer debt will get their attention, and you will really annoy them if you pay off your mortgage early! If you are intent on buying the trendy vehicle merely because it is trendy, then fine, but at least be honest with yourself about your real motivation. It is your life energy—spend it as you see fit.

Where You Choose to Live

As the section above begins to point out, the place you choose to live has a direct impact on your transportation needs. The closer you live to the places you go all the time, the less likely it is that you need to drive a personally owned, petroleum powered vehicle to get there[15]. You might be able to walk or even ride a bicycle to your common places. This is part of the reason why living in the city is a good idea for so many people: they can live within a short distance of the things they value most.

For Fred Ecks, a condo in downtown San Francisco is the best thing going because living near everything cuts his transportation costs significantly. "I walk to work every day. ... [I can ride the bus to] City College... Also, there are a lot of organizations in the city that aren't in other areas. I volunteer for Greenpeace, for example."

Simplifier Juli Parsons chose to live in a neighborhood near her family, and as a bonus, got reasonable access to mass transit for the whole family:

> We chose our house to be within walking distance of my mom. ... I also like the small business districts within walking distances, we can walk to a few restaurants, video stores, etc., and the proximity to light rail is also great. ... Transportation is much easier in a larger city. ... My husband has begun riding light rail to work and has cut out a 30 mile a day round trip drive to work. He is thrilled with the reading time and now hates to drive anywhere....
>
> ...Not commuting long distances in the car has become a big priority in his considering any job now that he's discovered the difference, and he would certainly choose a company closer to home that he could run, bike, or take light rail to, over another located in the suburbs.
>
> We really enjoy the benefits of a walkable community, although we are certainly not so evolved that we walk everywhere, just to the daily routine places and then to other places as much as we can.

Long Trip Transit

No chapter on transportation would be complete unless we discussed long-trip transit. For many people, this happens infrequently, but living in the city can make it much simpler. Most large cities have easy access to an airport, water port, bus station, or train station, and usually more than one. Getting to your final destination then becomes an exercise in getting to the station or port. This can usually be handled by a taxi or a hired van company for a small fee, and they will often pick up or drop you at your front door. The local mass transit may also have a route that runs past the station or port as well, so check your schedule. Jonathan's city has a van company that picks up anywhere in town and drives to the large airport 90 minutes away and vice versa, all for about $40 round trip. It is a hard service to beat on price and convenience.

Practical To Dos

- The next time you move, consider the availability of mass transit as part of your housing decision.
- Consider your real transport needs and look for other ways to fulfill them than a personally owned vehicle
- Track the number of times, and the reasons, you take your car home early or unexpectedly from work. If it turns out to be less than ten times per year, seriously consider using mass transit.

Library Guide

- *Divorce Your Car* by Katie Alvord
- *Material World: A Global Family Portrait* by Peter Mendel
- *The Consumer's Guide to Effective Environmental Choices* by Michael Brower and Warren Leon

Internet Resources

www.efn.org/~cat (Center For Appropriate Transport)
www.cleancarcampaign.org
www.segway.com
paleale.eecs.berkeley.edu/PATH/CCIT/carlinknew.htm (Shared car test system)
www.eaaev.org/eaalinks.html (electric vehicle links)
www.solectria.com
www.mtn.org/tcbc (Minneapolis bike club)
www.publicpurpose.com/ut-us96-im$pm.htm
www.bikesatwork.com
www.zipcar.com
www.flexcar.com

Search Terms

electric bike
"critical mass" + bike
electrathon
electric shopping-cart racing
"your city" and "FlexCar" (or other transportation options)

Index Words

car
hybrid
electric
gasoline
mass transit
bus
light rail
train
bicycle

CHAPTER 14

BUILDING COMMUNITY

A good bit of talk goes on in the United States today about how we just do not have the same sense of community as we did when we were kids (whenever that was). People used to leave their doors unlocked, we say. Kids were allowed to run wild all over the neighborhood, all summer long. You could still get a week's groceries for under $20. Only wholesome shows were on TV. You could park your car somewhere on a hot summer day and leave the car windows open, and not worry about whether the car would still be there when you got back (although someone may have filled the back seat with baseball-bat-sized zucchini in late August). We trusted one another then. We knew our neighbors. We bowled on Tuesday and had choir practice on Wednesday. People voted. The best man ran for office, and won.

Ah, we say, those were simpler times. Maybe you could still do that if you lived out in the country – leave your doors unlocked and your car windows down on a summer day – but you certainly can't do it in the city. And then we each meditate a bit on whether we should maybe move to a small town, or out to the country.

But why give up on the city? Sure, we will probably never get back to a time when we can leave our car windows down or our doors unlocked. (Sadly, you cannot even do that in the country any more.[1]) But we can certainly get back to knowing our neighbors. We could still bowl on Tuesday and go to choir practice on Wednesday. We can certainly still vote, and if enough of us actually did, the best person might even win.

How We Got Here

In his book *Bowling Alone*,[2] Robert D. Putnam defines all this – club memberships, civic engagement, even inviting over the neighbors to play cards – as *social capital*. He agrees that our stock of social capital has dropped drastically since its peak in the early 1960s. In nearly every way, Americans today are less engaged with one another – and that drop-off accelerated during the 1990s.

Putnam's two chief culprits for our drop in civic engagement are our dependence on electronic entertainment, chiefly television, and the graying of America's population. Putnam blames TV for about 25 percent of the drop-off: among all of the other ills that heavy TV dependence causes (see "Downsize Your TV" for our list of these ills and what to do about them), when we are mesmerized by the boob tube, we are not interacting with one another. He blames fully half of the drop-off in social capital on the aging of what he calls "the long civic generation" – the group of Americans who came of age during World War II. These Americans, Putnam said, joined and organized and voted and ran for office in greater numbers than the generation before them – and certainly in far greater numbers than their children, the self-absorbed Baby Boomers. Putnam found that the Boomers' children are even less involved in civic activities than their parents. Putnam also found that the disintegration of the nuclear family and urban sprawl each account for ten percent.[3]

We cannot do much about our respective ages – no matter how many of us insist that we are going to stay 21 or 29 forever – but we can do something about the other causes. We are not suggesting that women leave the work force in droves; too much good has come from allowing women to work outside the home. What we can do is live closer to our jobs (see "Transportation"), become more aware of our televisions' effects on us, and get to know one another again.

On the Street Where You Live

When was the last time you sat on your front porch and watched the world go by? People-watching is becoming a lost art – we would rather go inside, turn up the air conditioning, and turn on the TV. Yet it is by seeing the same faces pass by our porch, day after day, that we begin to know our neighbors.

You can people-watch anywhere, not just from your yard. It is free, it is endlessly entertaining, and it is much more fun to do in the city. Jane Zeender takes her toddler son out for the day – they sit on the dock and watch the world go by.

Here is a quick and easy way to confuse your friends: have a party just because. Last summer, Lynne hosted an ice cream social in the courtyard of her townhouse complex. She invited neighbors, friends, co-workers, and the families of some of her daughters' friends. At least one person asked her, "So what's the occasion?" Apparently, getting together with friends for ice cream on a late August evening was not reason enough.

Parties do not have to be big, elaborate barbecues, or booze-soaked excuses to gather around somebody's TV. Host your own ice cream social – all you need is the ice cream and toppings. Or invite friends for a potluck, or a picnic, or a game of cards.

Here is an even tougher question: When was the last time you got together with friends for an evening that did not involve somebody trying to get into somebody else's pocket? We are talking about the ubiquitous home party plans for selling everything: jewelry, cosmetics, vitamins, cookware, home décor, candles, lingerie, baskets, crystal, spices, and even laundry soap. Tupperware started the party sales approach in 1948, hoping to capitalize on word-of-mouth among housewives. It worked: Tupperware now sells $1.1 billion in containers, beauty products, and nutritional supplements annually, in more than 100 countries.[4]

The sad thing about these parties is that they almost feel like you are getting together with your friends for an evening of fun.

But make no mistake – very little "fun" is involved. This is business. The Direct Selling Association estimates that 11 million people sold more than $25.5 billion in goods via direct sales in the United States in 2000.[5]

Another sort of non-party is the "virtual community." Some of these are nonprofit, but many were started by somebody trying to sell us something. Promoters of self-help products may include a discussion board on the product's website where folks who are following the prescription of the product's creators can share their successes and urge each other on. Visitors to these discussion boards can find them extremely supportive, particularly if the board's subject is the sort of thing that one normally would not talk about. An advantage of such a virtual community over the home-party-plan party is that once you have found the discussion board, you can bookmark the site and never again have to go through the sales portal. The disadvantage is that such virtual friendships lack the tangibility of a real-life relationship: no matter how many virtual hugs your Internet pals send you, they are just not the same as the real thing.

Social Organizations

Think of things that you like to do – or that you would like to learn to do – and find, or found, a club that does those things. Book clubs are becoming popular, perhaps encouraged by the success of Oprah Winfrey's literary picks on her daytime talk show. You could form one of your own, or join an ongoing one. Check with your local library or bookstore for leads.

You could join a club to learn how to dance, fence, quilt, play bridge, knit, or invest in the stock market. There are clubs focused around a particular issue or certain activities. Groups of die-hards at your company (or your former company) may be looking for someone else to join them in their activities. So keep your eyes peeled: you may find what you are looking for on the local bulletin board or light pole. If not, post a flyer of your own!

Did you play soccer or volleyball or baseball in your younger days? Call your local parks and recreation department – you may find that there is a league for your favorite sport. Get a bit of exercise to go with your socializing!

Salons and Conversation Cafes

In a quest for more ways to socialize, and for more opportunities for a community dialogue about important issues, some people are resurrecting the French tradition of the salon. In 1991, *Utne Reader* published an article about salons, and offered to match readers interested in joining one with like-minded people in their neighborhood; they received more than 8,200 responses.[6]

Since then, the idea has taken off, spawning workplace discussion groups, study circles, book clubs, and other similar gatherings. A more recent type is the Conversation Café. *Your Money or Your Life* co-author, Vicki Robin, created the first Conversation Café in Seattle after the September 11 attacks. She tells how they work:

> By coming, we have followed the first rule of good conversation: we have shown up. In the six weeks we've been meeting at Grateful Bread in Seattle, I've noticed three basic ingredients to the magic of the Conversation Cafés: showing up, "shutting up," and speaking up.
>
> Showing up is not only arriving in time to talk. It's arriving in soul, ready to engage. "Shutting up" is about listening deeply. It's having as much curiosity about what others say as about parading out one's own opinions. "Speaking up" is risking saying what's really real for you. Ah, and there's a fourth rule: "Up." Conversing to enrich everyone. A conversation is like a game of hacky-sack ball. The point is to keep the ball up and in play, not to make the defining move. Good conversation has the quality of an infinite game. You play for play, not for winning. You might come to a natural stopping point, but everyone emerges the victor and the conversation continues with your next encounters.

(Shhh. My secret dream is that Conversation Café-ers will take this philosophical hacky-sack to the streets. Turn to their fellow gloomy bus riders and droopy-lidded latté-line customers and say, "I've been thinking about...")[7]

Conversation Cafés are one way to build community. Washington, Utah, Arizona, and Kentucky all have Conversation Cafés active enough that they post regular meeting times. You can start your own café anywhere, any time. Just spread the word.

Giving Back to Your Community

Lots of organizations would be grateful for your help – and we are not talking about the sort of help involved in just writing them a check. Groups that work with children, such as the Girl Scouts and Boy Scouts, are desperate for people to serve as troop leaders, trainers, and organizers. Lynne has found one perk of being a Girl Scout leader is the free training. Where else can you go camping with a bunch of adults, sing camp songs around a fire, and eat s'mores, all for free? And that does not count the activities she has done with the troop: hiking, skiing, kayaking, and a ropes course with a zipwire (she passed on caving, but she could have done that, too).

Churches and other community groups provide services for the disadvantaged in your community. You could get involved with your local food bank, Habitat for Humanity, or an ecology organization (Eco-Action Alliance is one). You could help sort clothing for a food drive, or books for a used book sale. You could volunteer at your local school; contrary to popular belief, you do not have to have a child in school in order to volunteer. Your local hospital or nursing home may have a use for your time and energy. All these options are available to anyone, no matter where they live, of course, but the sheer diversity of such choices in an urban area is staggering. You should easily be able to find a place for your volunteer skills. Try checking out the library, food co-op, college, or any non-profit near you for volunteer groups focused on particular issues.

You could also get involved politically. Your city or county has numerous boards and commissions that run everything from daycare programs to zoning approvals. Somebody has to serve on them – why not you? If a long-term commitment is not in your plans, you could be an election judge, serve on an ad-hoc committee that meets for a brief period about a single issue, or even represent your neighborhood organization by attending various meetings and reporting back. See "Simple Politics" for more ideas about why this could be important to you and your community—your presence could be more influential than you think.

If none of these ideas strikes your fancy, you could start your own organization. Put up flyers at the library, the grocery store, the food co-op, and the recreation center, and see how many people you can find who are interested in helping you. If you have been practicing the steps of *Your Money or Your Life* for at least six months, you can join the New Road Map Foundation Speakers Bureau, and spread the word about those ideas.

Practical To Dos

- Turn off your TV.
- Sit on your porch and people-watch. Better yet, talk with them as they pass.
- Invite the neighbors over for a party. Don't ask for a present.
- Join a book club, an investment club, or a bowling league.
- Volunteer.
- Start your own organization.

Library Guide

- *Bowling Alone: The Collapse and Revival of American Community* by Robert Putnam
- *Your Money or Your Life* by Joe Dominguez and Vicki Robin

- *Salons: The Joy of Conversation* by Jon Spayde and Jaida N'Ha Sandra
- *Going Local: Creating Self-Reliant Communities in a Global Age* by Michael Shuman

Internet Resources

www.conversationcafe.org
www.yourmoneyoryourlife.org
www.girlscouts.org
www.bsa.scouting.org
www.habitat.org

Local Resources

Your city's volunteer bureau or connection organization
Your local library
Your neighborhood school
Your preferred political group

CHAPTER 15

COMPLICATED RELATIONSHIPS

"I want it. I need it. I've got to have it." Sometimes the biggest obstacles to your success in following the path of Voluntary Simplicity are growing inside your own house: your significant other (SO) or your kids. Indeed, the most commonly asked question by new Simplifiers is, "How do I simplify my family?" There is a whole discussion board on The Simple Living Network website devoted to family and relationships. Some variant of this question is almost always an active topic. Anyone facing this issue is not alone. We have all been there and done it.

Homemade Stumbling Blocks: Adult Family

It should not be surprising that significant others can cause a problem. Opposites often attract. A spendthrift might pair up with a tightwad, subconsciously looking to the tightwad as the parental authority who pays the spendthrift's bills and keeps them both out of bankruptcy. This works, as long as both people in the relationship are willing to go along with the script. But if the tightwad gets tired of the parental role and suddenly expects the spendthrift to parent himself/herself, or if the spendthrift becomes rebellious and refuses to let the tightwad handle the family finances, disaster often follows. More than half of all marriages in the U.S. end in divorce, and the numberone reason cited for marital arguments is money.

But sometimes, like attracts like. What happens when half of a spendthrift couple decides to embark on the Voluntary Simplicity path? Say the wife decides to be more frugal, and begins to hold the husband accountable for his spending decisions. Suddenly, hubby feels as though the fun is over. Both end up frustrated and angry.

This can be especially difficult for couples living in the city. When houses are close together or you rub elbows with lots of people regularly, it is much easier to see the kitchen contractor's truck parked in the Joneses' driveway, next to the gleaming new SUV, right under the new satellite dish, which casts a shadow on the new backyard pool. You might be trying mightily to ignore all that activity on the other side of the fence, knowing the Joneses are maxing out their credit cards, mortgaging their property to the hilt, and living paycheck to paycheck, to get all this shiny new stuff. While you are resisting the urge to do the same, your SO is hanging over the fence, drooling, and asking, "Can we have one?" This usually makes for some tense "discussions".

This happens a lot. In fact, it might well be the norm that one partner in a relationship jumps on the VS bandwagon while the other is still stuck in the Consumer Culture. The best advice we can suggest is this: give them time and show them that this simplicity stuff really does work. Your SO might just be a little behind the learning curve; your good example might draw them into the movement. There really is truth to the saying, "Actions speak louder than words". If you are walking the talk, your SO will begin paying attention. At the very least, we hope, your SO will view your newfound frugality as a charming personality quirk, and will not actively undermine your efforts to simplify. Usually, though, after some lag time and grousing, they come around to some degree.

Our experience is that two people who are willing to work together to make a relationship can weather this storm if they are both willing to communicate. Although it is a profound error to go into a relationship expecting to change your spouse, it is equally erroneous to assume that your spouse (and you!) will never change. People change all the time, but they usually will not change on your command. So find some area where simplifying your life appeals to your partner, and work from there. Play to your respective strengths; for instance, one of you might love creating and using a price book, which is a list of items you regularly purchase and the price of those items at each store where you usually shop.[1] Your price book can be used to evaluate whether sale prices are really good deals. Control freaks will love this exercise, but the laid back, creative type will balk every time.

Money is often thought of as taboo, and many couples have difficulty breaking through the taboo to discuss money effectively. Embracing VS may finally break this taboo. All relationships have to distribute power to some degree. Since money is the preferred way to express power in our society, it is not surprising that this topic is really very sticky for most couples. Calling in air strikes on your neighbors or SO really is bad form. So put on your best empathic listening skills and dig in for an education in how your SO's mind, and your own mind, work with money. It truly is worth the effort.

M is for Myth: A Compatible Spouse

There are many myths surrounding money in our society: "Money is the root of all evil." "I have to protect my assets first." "We will make an equitable division of the expenses." "More money will make us happier." And like all myths, there is an element of truth in each one. But that does not mean they are all true all, or even some, of the time.

First, the accurate Bible quote is "The *love of* money is the root of all evils."[2] So as long as money is not being loved for its own sake, you are fine, right? Maybe, maybe not. Money is the means by which just about everything is acquired in our society. We trade huge blocks of our life energy for money. Naturally, we want to trade that money for something that we perceive will enhance our life, be that food, water, basic clothing, and shelter, or a mansion with closets stuffed with food and clothes and a five-car garage with a different classic car in every one. So, do we love money if we are trading the money for assets we love? Well, maybe, but only if we value the assets we are purchasing more highly than our relationships with the people around us. There is nothing wrong with owning a thing, taking pride in owning it, getting good use out of it, and maintaining it so that it will be useful a long time. But if you "have to wax the car" instead of dealing with a delicate issue with your spouse, then the car maintenance is getting in the way of something much more valuable.

Many people come to a relationship with the assumption that they must, at all costs, protect their assets from the SO. It is a good idea to talk with your potential spouse about his or her monetary life before committing to a long-term relationship. Getting your respective philosophies of money on the table is just part of finding the "right" mate. But that does not mean you have to pull a credit report on all your dates, or force your betrothed to sign a prenuptial agreement[3]. If you are paying reasonable attention during the early stages of your relationship, you will begin to understand your date's spending style and can find an opening to discuss money after you know that the relationship is getting serious. If you find your intended partner will not discuss money, then the warning flags are up: proceed at your own risk.

Another myth that pervades modern society is that each spouse must contribute money to the household equally or in proportion to the amount they actually make at work. What utter rubbish! If your relationship is all about who paid for what, open up a business with your partner and terminate the personal relationship. Money in this case is a divider, not a reconciler, for you and your spouse. We state categorically that if you and your spouse agree on how to handle money, your personal relationship is flourishing, and your bills are paid on time (usually), then the method by which you handle money is completely irrelevant to anyone except you two. We are pragmatists at heart: if it works for you, then it works.

The last myth that seems to drive people apart in our society is this odd idea that having more money will make us happier and our relationship stronger[4]. This flies completely in the face of all the research to date, which shows conclusively that the amount of money earned by a household has no correlation whatsoever to the amount of happiness in the couple's relationships[5]. You can be dreadfully unhappy in a mansion and deliriously happy in a cardboard box[6]. Once you have enough money to keep food in your stomach, basic clothes on your back, and a place to spend the next night, the value of money ceases to have much intrinsic meaning to your relationship; the relationship starts to hinge on your internalized values instead.

So, hopefully, you find yourself in a situation where you and your spouse can find common ground about spending, even if you have to agree to disagree on some spending. But what if you cannot?

M is for Miserable: The Antagonistic Spouse

If you find yourself in a situation where your SO does actively undermine your efforts to simplify, you may want to consider counseling. Even if your SO does not go with you, you may be able to gain a perspective that will allow you to accept, and maybe counteract, your SO's actions peacefully. If counseling does not work, or is out of your financial reach, here are some other ideas:

- Keep walking the walk. If you are consistently relaxed when money comes up in discussion, your SO will eventually notice. When they comment on it, there is your opening to ask: "Would you like to know why? And how you can help?"
- Let the spendthrift SO stew in their own debacle for a while, and then bail them out *after* having a gentle talk about how the current debacle was not all that bright. We suggest you choose your words wisely.

- Find a different way to reach your SO. There are tape courses[7] available if your SO is constantly in traffic. Or you could rent a cabin, drop the kids off somewhere, and "kidnap" your SO for a long weekend of listening to tapes and working through your finances together.
- Finally, if all else fails, you might be wise to separate your finances from your SO's. This can get sticky in community property states (see a lawyer), but it can be done. This might be a mandatory step in your financial self defense if your SO has a drug problem or a personality disorder. This means more than just having separate accounts. This means deliberately having accounts that only one of you can legally access. Your real or personal property, and perhaps your insurance policies, may have to be adjusted as to owners and beneficiaries as well. This may sound like a lot of work, and it is. But if you are living with an alcoholic or someone afflicted with bipolar personality disorder, or any of the other afflictions that can cause erratic spending behavior, the only way you may be able to keep your family's finances intact is to respect these rules. If you are in this situation, please see a counselor and a lawyer to assess what the best plan is for your situation. The world is littered with the wreckage of joint accounts that one spouse cleaned out to support their habit while the other was not looking.

It has also happened that one of the couple adopting VS principles has been the straw that broke the couple's back: the things driving the couple apart were exacerbated by the money issue. Some couples really do divorce because of disagreements about how to handle money. We do not want that to ever happen, but if divorce is the only way to be true to yourself and stop the war, then that is what you have to do. As Simplifier Katherine Carter says:

> When you got married, you and your spouse ran a small family farm and you had dreams of converting it to organic. Now, ten years later your spouse will not discuss the possibility of conversion to organic, you have become

vegetarian, and the primary money making part of the farm is a mega hog operation. ... Ultimately, you cannot control or change your spouse if they don't want to change. It may be time to let go of what the relationship used to be and move on. Only the two of you will know if this is the thing to do.

M is for Me Want: Young Family

The kings and queens of "Can we have one too?" syndrome are kids. Many of the people you have met in these pages are childless, or their children are grown. But a significant portion of those following the VS path have children, and they acknowledge that it is difficult to raise a child in this consumer culture. Difficult, but not impossible: Simplifier Juli Parsons has found one way to stem the tide of consumerism among her children. She writes, "My kindergartner tends to want everything advertised on TV and anything she's seen at her friends' houses. We have a policy that they can make lists of things they want and either save their allowances to buy them or ask for them for birthday or Christmas presents. 99% of the items are never mentioned again, and I try to help them make the connection that these are clearly things they don't really want or need since they never remember them."

All parents on the VS path agree on one thing: we are giving our children a healthier upbringing than those parents who are still enmeshed in the consumer culture. Not buying your children every toy they see is good for them. Refusing to allow your children to be mesmerized by the TV or the computer or the game console, insisting that they read instead, is good parenting. Turning off your television or canceling cable is not child abuse, even if the little sharpies do try to turn you in to the police. As Katherine Carter puts it:

> What kids *need* is food, shelter, love, and discipline, and not necessarily in that order. They may prefer food from McDonalds, and designer clothes, but I am [in no way] obligated to provide it to them. I don't think it dam-

ages their psyches. ... I gave the TV away. This simplified my life so much that it would be hard for the average American to understand. Benefits of not having a TV with children:

1)   They are not exposed to as many commercials for things they don't need: G.I. Joes, Pudding Pops, and Disney World.

2)   I can't use the TV as a babysitter and must interact with them more—something that is a "need" under the love and discipline categories.

3)   Because they are not passively entertained, they must seek active entertainment: drawing, building forts with the couch cushions, playing the piano, annoying their siblings. These activities increase their creativity and their independence.

4)   All of my kids have learned to read ahead of their peers. Ask any teacher what an advantage this is.

On the other hand, scheduling your children's every waking minute with expensive, programmed, group activities is the best way ever found to stifle their individual creativity and will. The easy way to resolve this is to take away a child's video games and day planner for several days. Doing this without consent or as a punishment is not a good idea, but if you can get the kiddos to go along as part of an experiment, then go to it. Observe their behavior during this period—do they readily turn to imaginative play and use whatever objects are at hand? Or are they oblivious to all the possibilities around them and sulk the entire time? Your kids may say they hate you when you force them upon the VS path, but in the end, they will bless you.

M is for Mooch: Extended Family

Like it or not, when two people make a relationship commitment, some people called "family" come along . And there are always some family members who just do not quite have a handle on this "money" thing. You know this because all they ever talk about is being in debt and the eternal quest for yet another loan or credit approval to buy a (fill in the blank). Likely as not, one spouse will get hit up by "family" for some money and the other spouse will object, sometimes violently, because of the proposed use the beggar has for the cash. So, the poor, hapless spouse in the middle is faced with annoying *family*, with whom they have nurtured a life-long relationship, or this *other person* with whom they have a newer relationship. Whomever they decide to appease, they are going to be perceived as having done the wrong thing by the other.

It is no one's business how much your immediate family takes home, unless you make it everyone's business. So, open your yap at your own risk. "Brag and be depleted" is the operative sentence in some extended families. You can engage in a little intentional camouflage and misdirection though: complain about your credit card interest rate just like everyone else, even if you pay your card off every month and never pay any interest. You can also whine about your mortgage, even if you are prepaying. After you are debt-free, things like college tuition and car payments are always fair game if you appear to be paying them. Whining about the things you "want," even if you do not really want them, can be effective as well. If you think it is in your best interest to lie outright,[8] and your immediate family is in on the game, then you can invent debts that do not exist to "brag" about when you are swimming among your extended leeches.

Now, are all these ideas comfortable? Probably not. On the other hand, Jonathan knows a woman who had to move two hours away from her extended family in order to avoid being bled dry every time she managed to get a little bit ahead. The standard mode of money management among her siblings and cousins was to live it up until the next crisis, then call around to see who could bail them out that week. Although she was assertive, her family was insistent, and her only defense was to get out of the situation completely. She did what she had to do in order to achieve her financial goals.

Practical To Dos

- Organize a TV turn-off week or participate in National TV Turn-Off Week in April.
- Cancel cable.
- Make your children buy their own toys with money they have earned. Of course, give them opportunities to earn.
- Make time to read with your children: you read to them and they read to you.
- Take an assertiveness training course.
- Take steps to bolster your financial self-defense.
- Do not tell anyone except your spouse about your finances.
- Track your expenses and your spouse's expenses separately. Have a talk when you have enough data to draw meaningful conclusions. This might take one month or six months, depending on your situation.

Library Guide

- *Unplugging the Plug-In Drug* by Marie Winn
- *Women, Men and Money* by William Frances Devine, Jr.
- *The Millionaire Next Door* by Thomas Stanley and William Danko
- *Co-Dependant No More* by Melodie Beattie
- *Nonviolent Communication* by Marshall Rosenberg
- *The Complete Tightwad Gazette* by Amy Dacyzyn

Internet Resources

www.simpleliving.net
www.adbusters.org
www.newdream.org
www.cnvc.org

Search Words

"plug-in drug"
assertiveness training

CHAPTER 16

SIMPLE CITY PETS

Having a pet makes it more fun to come home. Nothing beats having someone who is glad to see you when you walk in the door. A pet can entertain you, urge you out the door for some exercise, and comfort you when you are feeling down.

But not all pets are suited to city life. Small spaces and close neighbors can all cause problems for the potential pet owner beyond the usual problems of allergies, proper housing, and finding time to exercise your pet that every pet owner already faces. By proper selection of your companion animal, however, you can own a pet relatively simply in the city.

There are places to live with your pet in every city. You can find out which buildings and landlords are pet friendly by calling your local humane society or veterinarian. If they do not know the answer, a web search can usually find rental listings that allow pets. Whatever you do, play by the rules. Trying to hide your pet from an unsympathetic landlord is a fast way to lose your peace of mind and your living space, and maybe find yourself embroiled in a lawsuit. Be sure to read through the contract for your living space carefully and discuss any potential problems with your landlord before signing the lease. Your landlord may require that you show proof of pet insurance before you can rent, or he or she may require you to pay extra for each animal to defray their insurance cost. Many places also charge various fees when you have a pet. Some of these fees will be refundable and some will not, so read the fine print carefully.

Pet insurance is available from many providers and a policy may be enough to put your landlord at ease. A web search can help you find insurance for several types of pets. There is even insurance available based on breed. In a similar fashion, pet health insurance is available if you feel the need and your breed of pet is known for health problems.

There are also alternatives to your pet living with you. You can kennel your pet near your residence in some cases. Family or friends can take your pet. You might even find someone with a better living situation for your pet to take the animal.

What is never appropriate is for you to abandon your pet. Releasing your animal outdoors is cruel and inhumane, regardless of the reason. No matter how you acquired your pet, when you acquired it, you became responsible for its welfare for the rest of its natural life. You owe it to yourself to see that your pet finds a proper home or is put down humanely if you can no longer house it appropriately.

Pets released into the wild can survive, turn "feral" and drive out other valuable species that compete in the same ecological niche. Areas where foxes live often lose the foxes when feral cats arrive. While it is speculative at best to suggest that alligators and crocodiles can live in northern city sewers, it is quite possible in the lower latitudes. Worse yet, some exotic species imported as pets from other continents can do serious economic damage. In mid 2002, a man from Hong Kong who now lives in Maryland imported a couple of northern snakeheads, an exotic fish, from China in order to make soup for an ailing relative. By the time the fish arrived, the relative had recovered. Instead of humanely killing the fish, the man instead released them into a nearby pond. Unfortunately, snakeheads tend to eat all the other fish in their pond, and when the food source in their neighborhood runs out, they can "walk" on their fins to another pond. Maryland Department of Natural Wildlife officials had to poison the entire pond in order to get rid of the threat.[1] This is another case of an invasive, exotic species turned loose by Man where it should not be.

Dogs

Many good breeds of dogs can live comfortably in small spaces. Some larger breeds, like the French bulldog, do just fine in apartments. Dog breeds worth investigating for the owner with a small place are: miniature and toy poodles, some Corgis, Yorkshire terrier, chihuahua, dachsund, borzoi, shih tzu, pug, and Pekingese. Many people think that any small dog is suitable and end up with breeds like the Jack Russell terrier. Jack Russell terriers are small dogs, but they are also completely incompatible with a small living space. They are bred as working dogs and have way too much energy to be kept confined to an apartment. Many breeds of small dogs, especially the terriers, were bred as working animals and therefore are much more suited to rural or suburban areas.

Each individual dog's personality is also a factor. If you find a mellow bulldog, whippet, or Irish wolfhound (you better have the space for this dog to stretch out, though), they might adapt to your small space quite well even though they are bigger dogs. But your chihuahua that barks all the time and annoys the neighbors might not. You may have to try a dog or three before you find one that will work in your living space. Your local animal shelter may let you do a trial adoption. However, the local pet store may not take returns after a few days, so research carefully and have a humane back-up plan in case your new dog does not work out. Turning that cute puppy that turned into the small pony loose to fend for itself on the streets is not a humane option. If your dog does not adapt well to being alone while the head of the pack is off earning money to keep you both in kibble, consider keeping Fido in a crate while you are at work (or school), look into hiring a dog walker, or personally finding Fido a new owner.

Cats

Cats are often thought of as the perfect small-space pet: they sleep a lot, they don't bark, and they come already litter box trained.

Many people let their cats out routinely, but we consider this to be a dangerous practice, especially in a city. Cats that run wild can be killed by cars, injured in fights, or contract fatal diseases such as feline leukemia or FIV from feral cats. Most cats do *not* have to have the run of the neighborhood to be happy; plenty of cats live out their lives indoors in contentment. Two of Lynne's cats have been indoor kitties from day one, and are actually scared to go outside. If your cat insists on going outside, however, you can try training it to walk on a leash. Neutering can reduce your tomcat's drive to get outdoors, and it has the added benefit of ensuring that Mr. Kitty will not be contributing to the pet overpopulation problem if he does get out (more on this below).

Unlike dogs, cats inhabit 3-D space; they are not limited to just the floor and the first level of the furniture. Consider attaching a "ladder" of shelves to the wall, with the longest shelf near the ceiling; the entertainment value of such a "kitty run" for both you and your cat is endless. Position your sofa under the long shelf for the inevitable day when your cat falls asleep up there and rolls over into empty space.

You will have to decide whether to have your cat declawed. If Tabby likes to shred your carpet, or prefers your sofa to the cat condo you bought her, declawing[2] might be a wise investment. Renters especially will want to leave with the wall-to-wall carpet intact. However, your local humane society will likely advise you against it. If you decide not to declaw, you can find deterrent sprays at a pet store. They work with varying degrees of success. Another option, if you do not want to declaw, is to purchase tiny latex caps that you glue onto the tips of your cat's claws. This also works with varying degrees of success, depending on how well you can get the cat to sit still during the gluing process. Yet another idea is to cover furniture with a plastic cover; whether that is a specially made cover or just a used store bag wrapped around the vulnerable area is up to you. Jonathan's cats resent the bagged chair cushions, but they did adapt to the scratching posts well.

Cats can be great pets, and we have recorded evidence of cats and humans living together as far back as 2500 B.C.E. in ancient Egypt. So when a *felis catus* (domestic house cat) decides you are its servant, you probably ought to just give in. Just try to get one that does not drool when it purrs.

And no matter whether you end up with a dog or a cat, please have your pet spayed or neutered. If you are waffling on this, perhaps out of the belief that your kids should "experience the miracle of birth," please call your local animal shelter and ask how many unwanted dogs and cats the shelter puts to sleep each year. We have more than enough unwanted pets. Please do your part to make sure that number does not increase.

Birds

If you get a bird that can live in your space, you may find yourself with a delightful companion. Parakeets, conures, canaries (and other members of the finch family), adapt to cage or small room life quite well. Just be sure to train a speaking bird to say clean words. The papers have published enough stories of cursing birds. Like dogs, not all birds are suited to living in small spaces. Larger birds, like the cockatoo and its relatives, die if left in cages for long periods. Some birds, parrots especially, will gnaw on exposed woodwork or make a mess of cut flowers or houseplants if let out of their cages unsupervised. Choose your breed of bird quite carefully.

Fish

Fish are often a good choice for small spaces, as long as you can fit the tank in your space in the first place. That said, there are breeds of fish that require larger tanks and some fish that will outgrow any tank if fed too much. Since a large tank can easily weigh several hundred pounds, care should be taken in older buildings not to overload the floor. However, the burbling of the oxygenator can be quite soothing.

Fish can be quite expensive, depending on the choices you make. To set up an aquarium to be self-sustaining requires several different species of animals and plants. Saltwater aquariums are generally more expensive than freshwater by the time you get all the denizens properly placed. Before you get involved in this science experiment, consider carefully whether a good screen saver for your computer might not be a better buy. After all, you cannot pet your fish, whether they are real or virtual. At the very least, you do not have to clean the inside of your monitor!

Rodents

Rabbits, like cats, can sometimes be taught to use a litter box and can be socialized as good pets. Be sure you read up on the rabbit varieties before you get one, though. Most fit well into small spaces, but some are gnawers and may destroy woodwork.

Rats, guinea pigs, mice, gerbils, and hamsters are all examples of small rodents that can be raised as pets. The major appeal of these pets is not the animal itself, but all the toys you can buy for them. Gerbils and hamsters will often run through those looping, twisting, plastic cage tubes, run in the wheel, or otherwise endear themselves to you by their antics. As long as you do not go bananas buying the gear, these kinds of pets will fit nicely even in tiny spaces.

Exotics

"Exotic" animals are not exotic so much as they are unusual to have as pets. That is not to say, however, that they are bad as pets or incompatible with city living.

Turtles and iguanas can have long life spans and they eat a lot. If you choose to get a turtle that lives to 120+, make sure your will is up to date; most zoos will not take former pets. Smaller reptiles like lizards and salamanders tend to escape all but the most secure cages. A gecko loose in the communal bathroom will probably cause an uproar the first couple of times it happens.

Hedgehogs, ferrets, pigs, and other exotic mammals can be fun pets as long as you can provide the environment they need to thrive. Snakes can also be fun pets, especially if you are willing to socialize them. The biggest problem with these animals is that many buildings will only allow "normal pets". Trying to pass a ferret off as a starving stray cat will only fool the most ignorant of landlords.

Practical To Dos

- Volunteer at your local animal shelter or humane society to help take care of the animals instead of owning a personal pet.
- Verify your pet is welcome in your building.
- Check into pet insurance, if you cannot afford to pay for new carpets or other damage your pet may cause.
- Select the right kind of pet for your personality and space.
- Train your pet to ensure appropriate behavior.
- Consider getting a virtual pet, one that only runs while your computer is idling or runs on batteries.
- When traveling, you can rent a pet if taking your own is not realistic.

Library Guide

- *Paws to Consider* by Brian Kilcommons and Sarah Wilson
- *You & Your Cat* by David Taylor

Internet Resources

www.akc.org
www.cyberpet.com
www.canismajor.com
www.avma.org
birdsnways.com
www.petinsurance.com

Search terms

"pet" + whatever kind of animal you are considering
crate training
virtual pet
pet insurance

CHAPTER 17

CONSUMER CULTURE

We have all heard it hundreds of times: Living is expensive today, and living in a city is especially expensive. This idea has been repeated so often, in fact, that almost nobody questions it any more.

We are here to question it. In fact, we are here to tell you that it is an urban myth. Living in a city can be downright cheap — and environmentally responsible, and socially responsible, too. All it requires is a little adjustment in your thinking.

Magazines: Information or Insecurity?

Many folks consider reading a magazine to be a relaxing way to while away an afternoon or evening. The pages are glossy, the pictures are big and bright, and the articles often do not require a lot of thought.

There is a reason for that. Many magazines are designed to be nothing more than showcases for the products manufactured and/or sold by their advertisers. Former magazine staffers will tell you that when you see an ad next to an article about the product, it is no accident: it is called product placement.

If you have read the chapter on advertising already, you already know that advertising is designed to make us feel inadequate in some way. With the reader off-balance emotionally, the product is shown as the answer to her discomfort. This, hopefully, convinces her that the item being sold is just the thing to make her newly induced feelings of inadequacy go away. (The choice of the pronoun is deliberate; most ads are aimed at women.)

So we rush out to buy sugar blivit drops to cure our halitosis, when all we really need to do is brush our teeth. Why should you succumb to this kind of rank manipulation? Why give your money to someone who makes you feel lousy in the name of "business" or "commerce"? Cancel your subscriptions.

Of course, sometimes you might want to read a magazine to gather actual information. Rhett, a Simplifier in Portland, OR, loves his city library for that purpose. "The Portland Library...is almost a holy place to me. I think of all the knowledge there and I'm simply awed and comforted by the incredible energy and potential in the people just within two square miles of me."

Your local library might have a giveaway case where magazines are placed for free pickup on a regular basis. Or ask local companies if you could help clean their offices by taking the copies you want. You could borrow a friend's copy, or look up articles on the magazine's web site.

Not only does giving up the magazine habit unjunk your mind, it also unjunks the landfill of the subscriptions you have bought and saves you money in the process – a win-win situation for everyone. Plus, you will never again have to keep a pile of magazines by the bed that you mean to read someday, if you ever have the time. Who needs that kind of self-induced guilt?

Newspapers

Newspapers are nowhere near as egregious as magazines in pandering to their advertisers. And reading a newspaper is certainly a better way to get information than watching a TV newscast.

But newspaper reading can have its own downside. Right after September 11, 2001, Lynne agreed to take a daily newspaper subscription on a trial basis. But when she found herself getting angry with one of her daughters for constantly interrupting her while she was trying to get through the paper, Lynne realized that reading the newspaper every day had turned into a chore—a chore that she felt she had to accomplish at the expense of her family time. The trial subscription ran out shortly thereafter and she did not sign up to pay for the daily paper.

Instead, she tried reading the paper online, thereby saving paper, production, and recycling costs of the print version. Now, she scans the headlines from the newspaper box on the way to work to see if it is worth her time to surf to the newspaper's web site on her coffee break.Other good alternative sources for newspapers include libraries, or leftover copies on the bus or train.

Newspapers in some cities allow you to subscribe to the paper only on Sunday, or only on the weekend. Taking a Sunday-only or weekend-only subscription would save you some time during the week and you will still get most of the coupons.

Internet Pros and Cons

Yes, we did just suggest that you read newspapers and magazines online. But we still suggest that you look at the amount of time you spend on the Internet.

Surfing the net can be a gigantic time-suck in its own right, and can be dangerous to your pocketbook. Companies spent $5.8 billion on Internet advertising in 2001, according to Ad Age; by comparison, corporate spending on advertising on broadcast TV totaled $38.9 billion during the same period.[1] Do you routinely close those banner ads and pop-up ads, or do you stop to read them, click on them, and think about buying? How many times have you gone to eBay "just to look" and ended up bidding on something?

The Internet is wonderful for many purposes, but beware the ads and the commercial sites. You can stuff your junk drawers full of useless thingums by browsing online just as easily as you can by browsing at the mall.

> Like most Simplifiers, alex glenlee is happy to avoid the Consumer Culture because he considers consumerism to be "a form of slavery." He says, "We talk about what the Soviet citizens went through, not being able to speak their minds, but they did not have twenty- or thirty-year mortgages, and they did not have credit card debt, and personal lines of credit that they were paying off every month. [In Consumer Society] your only worth is your net worth."

Recreational Shopping

Have you ever visited a shopping center after a quiet, contemplative period — perhaps after a church service — and felt vaguely uncomfortable in the store? Many Simplifiers find today's retail spaces, with their bright lighting, canned music, and visually noisy product displays, too jarring. You may also have noticed that prices are higher at the mall; mall stores often charge more for a given item than a store in a different venue would, because mall rents are so much higher.

Despite this, many people still consider shopping a form of recreation. If you are interested in breaking this habit, see the "Entertainment" chapter for many, many ideas for other things to do in your free time. All are free or extremely inexpensive. There really is more to life than raking up more charges on your plastic at the store.

Big Box Stores and Warehouse Stores vs. The Little Guys

Many Simplifiers object to big-box stores because they have killed their competition. Mom-and-Pop retailers across the country have had to close their doors because the big chains offer so much more of a selection for less money. That may be the price of a capitalist economy, but it comes at a cost. Service in the big-box stores just cannot compare with the neighborhood store where everybody knows your name, or the druggist who will fill your prescription today because he knows you will get paid two days from now and you are good for the loan.

That said, shop carefully in these big stores. Take a list and stick to it. If you do not have room in your apartment for a 15-roll package of paper towels, split the cost and storage space with a friend. Not only does this save money and space, but helps build community connections with those who share your values.

Where you can, consider patronizing small, local retailers. Look into a membership in a Community Supported Agriculture program or join a food co-op. As a member of a CSA, you contract with a local organic farmer, who delivers fresh produce to you on a set schedule throughout the growing season. You may be able to cut your cost by volunteering some time in the fields. CSAs exist even near large urban areas; Local Harvest is just one of several groups with a listing of CSAs on their websites. Food co-ops feature "bulk" sections, where you can bring your own container and buy just what you need out of the 25 pound bag or 50 gallon drum; Jonathan has been doing this at his food co-op for years. The price is usually cheaper than the same pre-packaged item. Some store chains allow this too, so you have to check around.

Organic produce is becoming easier to find, especially in urban areas. Simplifier Souix Fox of Vancouver, BC, says she has found "lots of organic veggie stores" in her area and that the organic veggies are not as expensive as they used to be. Also check out local farmers' markets for fresh produce – most cities have at least one, and you may find several close by. Marilyn, a Simplifier who lives in Baltimore Co., MD, loves the seasonal farmers' market in downtown Baltimore. "It is a friendly place to start my Sunday mornings before we go to church and there are several farmers whom I make sure I patronize because of the quality of their produce and their service."

Shop in markets in ethnic areas of your city; most are locally owned, and if you are an adventurous cook, you can find many foods there that you cannot find at your local grocery store. Simplifier Doug Carroll does this occasionally in St. Louis. "There's two meat markets down in Soulard Market, and I'll buy some specialty meats there once in a while, with produce. Specifically bratwurst. I've bought a couple other things ethnic that they have that you can't get...anyplace else."

Saving Money on Food

One of the great things about urban living is that the choice of supermarkets is much larger than it would be in a rural area. The larger choice means that one or two stores are bound to be cheaper on most things, more often. You may already know who the local cheap player is; if not, do a little homework. Amy Dacyzyn, who edited *The Tightwad Gazette* newsletter for many years, suggests creating a price book.[2] Get a small notebook and write in it the products you use most often. Then take the notebook with you when you go shopping, and jot down the price of each item at each of the stores you go to. You may find that in your area, one store is cheap on some things but not others, or you may find that one store is cheap on just about everything. Some stores specialize in just a few categories of items and make those items as cheap as possible, relying on volume sales to make their money, not a wide variety of products.

We hear more and more that obesity is becoming a major health problem in the United States. Advertising continually parades past us thin, healthy-looking models eating like there is no consequence at all to a few thousand extra calories. Of course, those models do not really eat that food during the photo shoots.[3] Even if they did, a one-time overindulgence on the set is not going to blow their diet to smithereens. It is when we practice the same behavior every day that those calories add up to excess tonnage fast. Add in the merciless way advertising uses body images to upset the viewer, and it becomes quite clear that the less advertising you are exposed to, the more likely you are to have a simpler, healthier, and lighter life.

Yard Sales, Flea Markets, and Thrift Stores

Yard sales, flea markets, and thrift stores can be cheap. The merchandise selection is unreliable, but that adds to the fun. You are also helping the environment by keeping other people's stuff out of the landfill, and your purchase of perfectly good, already-manufactured items saves natural resources. At a non-profit thrift store and some yard sales, you have the added advantage of contributing to a good cause. "Most Simplifiers buy at least some things used. Many are veteran yard salers who regularly spend their Saturday mornings browsing through other people's junk. But do not go unarmed, or you are liable to take home a bunch of stuff that you did not need."

Amy Dacyzyn would go to yard sales armed with a list of clothing sizes and items that her family needed for several years into the future. If the people holding the sale did not have clothing in the sizes she was looking for, she would go on to the next sale.[4]

The best kind of yard sale might be the "Free Sale". You take out an ad in the paper for your "free" sale, and then place all the stuff on the curb. Depending on the weather and what you have out there, it may all be gone within a couple of hours—and without you having to dicker or make change.

Some communities have Treasure Hunting Days, a similar concept to the "Free Sale", but done on a community-wide basis. Anything not picked up by someone else is picked up by the local garbage company the next pickup day or week. Among other benefits, the communities that do this seldom have "junk piles" behind people's houses that harbor pests and cause the neighbors to complain. If your community does not have one of these, maybe you should try to get one started.

Barter Systems

Another way to avoid spending money is to get involved in a barter system. Barter is the direct exchange of goods and services with someone else. Many cities have locations, events, newsletters, or other resources for connecting with others who wish to do this kind of exchange. Also, see the chapter entitled "Local Alternatives to Money" for more information about community money systems, a related, but more sophisticated, way to make exchanges without the usual Federal Reserve money.

Sustainable Products

Sustainable products are kind to the environment and, therefore, to the public's health and general welfare. In theory, sustainable products cause no harm to the environment in their manufacture, nor do they cause damage to the users of the product in any way. Also, sustainable products are ideally sustainable across their full lifecycle: from extracting the raw materials from the Earth, through all the manufacturing and sales steps, to the use of the product and the final return to the Earth of the product or its residue. And, of course, sustainable products are ones that the buyer really needs—they provide real value.

In practice, this can be a tall order. But it is not impossible. Nor is it hideously more expensive, though some industries would have you believe that. There is a limited supply of raw materials, but with sustainable production practices, that limited supply is carefully managed so that future generations can use the same amount of the resource. So if you are in the tree business, you harvest trees in ways that do not injure the forest as a whole, plant at least as many trees as are removed from the forest annually, and maintain the natural balance within the forest's wildlife community.

As a consumer, the best way to deal with the sustainability issue is to buy responsibly.

Responsible Buying

The best way to buy responsibly is to reject the idea that you must buy to be happy, to have a place in life or uphold it, or to fill your inner emptiness. Buying for any of those reasons alone is a waste of money. As they say on Madison Avenue: "You don't drink the beer; you drink the advertising." What sells is the illusion of happiness, but you're smarter than that.

Finding inner peace and happiness, if you have your basics already taken care of, is just not going to happen in the store no matter what the mass media and your junk mail tell you. Buying just to uphold your place in life quickly becomes a shallow ritual, and not a pleasurable experience at all. So reject the consumeristic messages you see and hear; buy only those things you need and those that you know will repay your life energy many times over in enjoyment. Stop allowing yourself to be used up.

Once you make the decision to buy, consider your purchase carefully, and from many angles:

- Can you just buy the minimum? Buying enough for what you need now, and for the foreseeable future, is usually a better strategy for things that decay or wear out.
- If a product is made from paper, plastic, glass, metal, or rubber, does it contain at least some recycled content? Even some carpets do.
- Is the item multi-use? One way to avoid buying unnecessary things is to visualize multiple ways you will actually use the thing before you put your money down.
- Is the item well-made? A pot you can use for 30 years is more sustainable and cheaper than three pots that have a useful life of ten years each. Reconsider your use of disposables wherever you can.
- Is the item easy to maintain? Taking good care of the things you choose to own is part of making a good purchase.
- Find items that are organically grown or sustainably harvested.
- Look for items that are made or grown locally, so the energy used to transport them from their origin to your place is lower.
- Look for items that do not generate hazardous waste when you are done with them. Nearly all toxic cleaning supplies have safe—and cheaper—counterparts.

- Look for items that have less packaging, or at least less environmentally hazardous packaging. Let your merchant know you want things shipped without foam peanuts, if possible. Buy in bulk when you can, using your own container whenever possible.

- Look for low energy-usage machines. Appliances with the highest Energy Star ratings and vehicles with the highest mileage cost less to run and use less energy in the long run, even if they cost a bit more up front.

- All these assume you even need to buy at all. What if you could make, rent, or borrow the thing you need instead? One company leases carpet made from sustainable materials; they manage the carpet's entire lifecycle in ways that reduce waste to an absolute minimum, and at prices similar to other carpet companies[5].

Once something is no longer useful for its intended purpose, can it be reused, by you or someone else, for another purpose? By reusing things, we eliminate the need to have more items generated from the Earth's limited resources. By reusing things, we are valuing the life energy we have spent acquiring and maintaining them.

Recycling is Not the Final Solution

Recycling is an extremely important component of Simplifiers' effort to live more lightly on the land. Recycling aluminum, for example, results in 95 percent less air pollution and 97 percent less water pollution compared to producing new aluminum products from ore. The amount of energy needed and the volume of the planet dug up to mine aluminum ore are correspondingly reduced. Recycling aluminum is common across the United States now, but we still manage to throw away enough aluminum every year to replace the entire U.S. commercial airplane fleet four times[6].

But in society's emphasis on recycling, we tend to forget that the recycling symbol has three corners, and that recycling is only one of them. The others, of course, are *reusing*, which we touched on in the last section, and *reducing* the products we consume. Underlying the entire symbol is *rejecting* the artificially created needs that advertising seeks to induce within us.

Think about an inexpensive toaster, sitting on a shelf at your local big-box store. This toaster is made of steel, plastic, and electrical (and probably electronic) components. It is packed in a cardboard box, surrounded by more cardboard and other packaging materials — perhaps styrofoam or bubble wrap, or some other type of cushioning material.

Where do all these materials come from? The steel is made from iron ore and coke, which is a form of coal. Both iron and coal must be mined. Energy is used to move aside the rock and soil covering the iron. In the case of coal, energy is used to tunnel into the earth (or strip-mine) to get to the coal seam. Both iron ore and coal must then be transported to the mill to be refined, combined, and rolled. The resulting long roll of steel is then shipped to a factory, where the toaster parts are cut and assembled.

The toaster's other components require similar processing. Plastic is a petroleum byproduct. Electronic components require special clean-room manufacturing. Wires and coils — the electrical parts of the toaster — are also made of metal, which must be mined, refined, rolled, cut and assembled in the much same way as steel. And the packaging is more of the same: cardboard comes from paper, which is chemically-processed wood fiber; styrofoam is another petroleum byproduct; bubble wrap is made from plastic. Even the ink used to print the brand name on the box must be manufactured somewhere.

Once the toaster is assembled and packaged, it must be packed in yet another container and shipped, probably twice, to the store, where it lands on the shelf. Think of the energy expended for all that manufacturing and shipping. Think of the environmental damage from the mining, petroleum refining, logging and paper-making. Communities and ecosystems may be damaged or destroyed; lives may be lost in accidents. That does not even address the research and development money that went into designing this consumer product that could have been spent on something to really benefit mankind.

And when the toaster is thrown out? Steel will rust away, but plastic is practically forever. Any electronic components in the toaster contain some lead and other heavy metals; the heating element is also a source of chromium that can leach into the environment.

How to stop the madness? Don't buy the toaster! Repair the one you have, or buy a used one at a yard sale. Or buy a really good toaster in the first place, so that you don't have to spend $20 every couple of years for a new one. Then write the manufacturer, or fill out a comment card at the store to complain about this wasteful manufacturing and shipping system. If enough of us complain about the waste in making and selling throwaway toasters (and computers and inkjet printers and...), and stop buying the junk, manufacturers and retailers would have to change the way they do business.

If you are buying something for your organization, and not just for yourself, look into the latest "Green Procurement" strategies that are starting to appear. The Center for the New Ameri-

---

Do you still think of frugality as deprivation? Simplifier named Florence from the simpleliving.net discussion boards knows better:

Frugality has meant that I am deprived of:
- being in debt,
- sleepless nights worried about how to pay bills,
- having fights with [my husband] over money,
- being tied to my job.
- Frugality has enabled me to look at my wants and needs realistically and be creative in meeting needs and enough wants. And frugality helps me feel in control of my time and money.

can Dream distributes a guideline for faith communities. There are also guidelines available at the federal government level, and several states are getting on board as well. These are sound buying strategies that can be used by even the most conservative agencies to make better buying decisions.

Practical To Dos

- Cancel your magazine subscriptions. Instead, investigate free alternatives. Read issues at the library. Or borrow them from your company's waiting room. Or rescue gently read copies from the recycling bin when you drop off your newspapers.
- Read newspaper and magazine articles online.
- Subscribe to the newspaper only on weekends. Or "borrow" a paper left behind on the bus or subway. Do not think of it as being too cheap to part with a couple of quarters; think of it as keeping another newspaper out of the waste stream.
- Watch the time you spend on the Internet. Consider online purchases as carefully as you would any other type.
- If you are a recreational shopper, look for alternative activities for your free time.
- Watch your spending at big-box and warehouse stores; if you routinely walk out with a lot more than you went in for, consider limiting the number of times you go. Or go with a list and stick to it.
- Check out locally-owned sources for groceries: CSAs, co-ops, ethnic markets.
- Make a price book for grocery purchases.
- Look for bargains at yard sales, thrift stores and flea markets – but be careful that you do not come home with more than you planned to buy.
- Investigate joining a barter program.
- Buy or rent sustainable products.

- Think about the impact of the purchases you make, not only on your wallet, but on the environment and on the quality of life of everyone else on the planet.
- Reject, Reduce, Reuse, Recycle.

Library Guide

- *The Complete Tightwad Gazette* by Amy Dacyzyn
- *Going Local: Creating Self Reliant Communities in a Global Age* by Michael Shuman

Internet Resources

www.newdream.org/buygreen/index.html
www.newdream.org/procure/
www.sustainableproducts.com/
www.worldwise.com/
www.organicconsumers.org
www.localharvest.org
www.ecosustainable.com.au/exchange.htm
www.eacnyc.org/html/recycling.html
www.energystar.gov/default.shtml

Search Terms

sustainable product
green procurement
externality
"barter" and <your city>

CHAPTER 18

GARDENING

Every city household seems to have at least one plant. Plants are good for the environment because they take in carbon dioxide and produce oxygen. Plants, regardless of whether they are flowering or produce vegetables, give us something to care for and to look at and admire their beauty.

Benefits of a Garden

Many Simplifiers have successfully had a garden in limited space while living in the city.Wendy Carroll knows this first hand:

> There's tons of gardening opportunities around here. People have this idea, "Oh, I have to move to the country so I can garden". You can do that right here. Absolutely. It's all over the place, it really is. … This quadrant of the neighborhood is plain skinny little houses and they're not very expensive, but they all have big yards, and so there's a lot of gardeners just in this little area, so we're all real close. We share plants and chores and that sort of thing.

There are about as many reasons why people garden as there are gardeners. Some garden for the purpose of growing their own food (in whatever quantity they can) or to know where a portion of their food came from. Seeds are relatively inexpensive and can last several years. It can be very surprising how many tomatoes one plant will produce in a season or how many salads you can make from just a couple of lettuce plants. Unless you buy certified organic foods from a local farmer, you just do not know where that food was grown, or what type of chemicals were used to stimulate its growth, artificially ripen it, or preserve it on the trip to your local market. When you grow your own food, you know where it came from and the conditions under which it was grown.

Others garden as a hobby or a way to relax after a stressful day at work. Since many of us have desk jobs that keep us inside a good portion of the day, gardening is a way to get outside and spend some time with nature. It may sound funny, but it can be very relaxing to go outside to the garden and pick weeds or push the tomatoes back into their cages or train the cucumbers or peas to grow up a trellis. It can even be nice to just walk through the garden and see what new fruit has started or how much a plant has grown since the day before. The digging that is involved in gardening is a great way to release some of the stress of the day. Digging is a much better stress buster than road rage or yelling at your family members.

Still others garden to grow specific crops that bring them pleasure or that they use heavily and would like to not have to purchase as much. Many people have just herb gardens where they grow the herbs that they use frequently. These herbs can be for cooking such as parsley, sage, rosemary, thyme, dill, oregano, basil; or for drying to make tea, such as chamomile, spearmint, and peppermint.

Flowers bring joy for their beauty and their variety. Cut flowers can be quite expensive if bought from the local florist or the farmer's market, so why not grow your own? Then you can enjoy them both indoors and out. A flower garden can also be a way to attract birds and butterflies, bringing another kind of beauty into your life.

What is a Garden?

A garden, as defined by Webster, is a plot of ground where herbs, fruits, flowers, or vegetables are cultivated. Gardening then, is cultivating this plot of ground.

At a bare minimum, to garden you need some dirt, a place to put this dirt, something to plant in the dirt, and water and sunlight to allow the plant to grow. The dirt can be a bag of the appropriate potting soil from the nursery, or a pile of dirt from an already established garden that has the right mix of necessary nutrients.

Your potting soil can be put into a large flower pot, or a deck planter or whiskey barrel purchased from the local home and garden store. Your dirt might also be put into a raised bed or other type of garden plot in the yard. The truly adventurous can even try a simple plastic bag.

The next ingredients for a garden are items to plant. A garden can be started using seed or plants. You can obtain seeds most easily from a local store or a mail order catalog. Plants can be obtained from a variety of places, the easiest being the local nursery or garden center. You can also talk to neighbors about your plant needs. They may have extras or can give you new plants that they have after dividing theirs. (Plants that are divided tend to be perennials, not vegetables.)

Last, your garden needs to have sunshine and water. Most plants do not need to be in full sun all day and do quite nicely with just several hours a day. Your garden should be situated so that it does get some southern or western exposure. If Mother Nature cooperates and brings plenty of rain to water your garden, you are all set. If not, you will need to make sure that the plants receive an adequate amount of moisture to continue growing.

As with anything, you can either go for the basic and simple garden or the larger and more complex garden. Whichever type of garden you choose, these minimums still apply. For those choosing the larger garden, there are a few additional tools that you will want to have to make the job easier: a spade, garden fork, rake, trowel, pruners, watering can, and gloves.

The Apartment Garden

You can certainly garden in a city apartment or similar space. Many apartments have patios or decks that can be used as mini-gardens. The best way to accomplish this is by using many large flower pots now available at home and garden centers. Since plants in pots require richer soil than those in a garden, use a professional potting mix. Plants grown in pots tend to dry out quicker than those in a garden and thus will need more attention. As in a garden, mulching can help keep the plant in your "container garden" from drying out too much. Mulch is simply a surface covering that is applied to the soil — usually chipped or shredded pine or hardwood — and can be purchased at any garden center.

Just about any kind of container can be used for planting as long as proper drainage is provided. The traditional pot does not just come in the old, standard, orange-clay type any more. There are now many sizes, shapes, colors and designs to choose from. If you will need to move your pots around to provide the best sunlight, you would be better off using plastic containers. They weigh considerably less than the clay or ceramic ones, and you will need that weight savings once it is filled with dirt. One of the recent fads is the strawberry pot. This is a clay type pot with numerous holes running up the sides; the plants are tucked into the holes. If you want to go with something more unique than the standard pot, try something like an old washtub, a half whiskey barrel, an old birdbath, or a portable wooden tray. The possibilities are unlimited.[1]

Before you run out and purchase various containers and plants, you need to determine what types of plants you want to grow. Different types have different needs; for example, some plants will need to have a larger container that will allow sufficient space for the roots, whereas other plants can be grown in much smaller pots since they do not have as large a root system. Use the books referenced at the end of this chapter and other books from your local library to get an idea of what you want to grow and the needs of each plant.

Annuals are the perfect flowering plant for the deck or patio. These plants produce bright flowers all summer long and need very little care. Once planted, they need only sufficient water and some deadheading to keep the plants blooming to their maximum. Deadheading means simply that the dead flower is removed from the plant. This is not a necessity, but your plants will have more blooms if you do.

Many herbs are also well suited to container gardening. Kitchen herbs such as oregano, thyme, parsley, dill, and basil do very well growing in pots in a sunny location. Some of the more invasive herbs, such as those in the mint family and oregano, are best planted in their own containers. Your herbs can be grouped in combinations that complement each other or are used for the same purpose. For example, you could combine pasta sauce ingredients such as oregano, basil, and thyme together. Many of the perennial herbs can be wintered over inside your dwelling in front of a sunny window. Check a reference book for the best way to keep your herbs from year to year.

Most people think of growing vegetables in a garden rather than in containers, but many of the most popular vegetables can be grown in containers as well. The same principle of good quality soil and plenty of water apply here. You will also want to make sure you have the appropriate sized container for the vegetable you are growing. Vegetables with larger or extensive root systems will need larger pots. Those with more shallow root systems can be placed in smaller or shallower containers. Tomatoes and peppers do better in larger, heavier pots that can accommodate the root system and the weight of the plant on top. The container also has to be large enough to allow for staking or caging, if needed. Similarly, vegetables such as radishes or carrots will need a deeper container to allow the root to grow. Many people have had success growing all sorts of vegetables in containers: everything from lettuce, spinach, and cabbage to peppers, tomatoes, and even peas. The main thing to remember is to provide the plant what it needs in terms of temperature, sunlight, water, space and support. Another thing to think about is the amount of produce you get for the amount of space the plant takes up. Since your space will be limited, you may not want to invest the valuable real estate in large plants such as broccoli and cauliflower that yield only one head per plant.

When putting together your container garden, also think about layering. Tall plants should be placed so they do not shade other sun loving plants. You can also use layering or positioning to allow more shade tolerant plants to grow in an otherwise very sunny spot. Place the tall plant so that the shade loving plant receives the cooler morning sun and is shaded from the hotter afternoon sun. A layered garden is also gives a more pleasant view of the garden for the owner. One pot can be turned upside down to make a pedestal for another pot. Deck planters can be used to bring plants up off the ground; this is especially useful for vine-like plants. Garden centers have all sorts of wrought iron planter pedestals that can also be used to raise a plant off the ground. If your space permits, hanging planters might also be an option.

The Very Small Garden

City dwellers may not have much yard space to work with. That's OK. There are many space saving gardening techniques out there that can be adopted. You will still be able to grow quite of bit in the limited space. Homeowners with small lots can find many ways to have a garden in a small space.[2]

Mel Bartholomew's space-saving method is explained in his book, *Square Foot Gardening*. Bartholomew developed his simple but versatile system after seeing the demoralizing effects traditional gardening brought to those he worked with on a community garden project. This method not only works for gardeners who need to limit the amount of garden space they have for manageability, but also for those with limited space available for gardening. The square foot gardening idea is based on squares instead of rows. You only plant as many seeds as the number of plants that this space will support. For a one-person garden, a four foot by four foot square plot is recommended. With this small space, a person can grow two tomatoes, four cucumbers, two peppers, two cabbages, two broccoli, two cauliflower and four square-foot spaces of smaller plants such as lettuce, radishes, spinach, and carrots. By carefully planning the plants by season and replanting immediately after harvesting one crop, as described in Bartholomew's book, you can get even more out of this small space in just a single season.

Another space-saving method is known as intensive gardening. With this method, spacing is crucial because you are trying to grown the greatest number of plants at once in a given space. The idea here is to not plant all one type of plant together. The individual plants are spaced out over the entire space and interplanted with others. For example, a radish needs two inches of space between plants. But when planted with another crop such as lettuce, radishes need more space but the lettuce needs less. The general rule is to take the sum of the number of inches needed for both crops and divide by two. So if radish plants must be two inches apart and lettuce plants must be eight inches apart, you should plant each radish seedling five inches from the lettuce seedling next to it (2 + 8 = 10; 10 divided by 2 equals 5). Using this concept, you can get the following into a four foot by five foot space: twelve radish, thirteen carrot, four beet, seven lettuce, four garlic, seven onion, nine peas, six spinach, two turnip, two parsnip, one celery, one cabbage, two Brussels sprout, two potato, one Swiss chard, and one marigold. After these early season plants are done, they can be replaced by late season ones.[3]

Another idea that can be implemented in a small yard space is that of the edible landscape. Use a combination of perennial flowering plants along with the vegetables to create a varied and interesting landscape. Red cabbage, leaf lettuce, broccoli, cauliflower, garlic and others can be an interesting addition to the traditional bushes that surround most houses. This idea works too if you would like to have more of a flower or herb garden. Use the space either between or in front of those traditional bushes for some perennial and annual flowers. Or insert some of your favorite herbs amongst the flowers and bushes. By including edibles, flowers, and herbs within the traditional landscaping, you can have a different looking house every year.

The practice of vertical gardening is one way to have fruit and vegetables that grow on space consuming vines. Instead of having the melon or cucumber patch, you have the melon or cucumber trellis. There are many ways to create a trellis on which to grow your vines. Some are as simple as stock lattice sections and some as complicated as custom hand-made wooden trellis, complete with platforms for the fruit to rest on.[4] It is important to remember that the larger fruits such as melon will need some support, but it need not be fancy. Simply using old nylons or similar flexible material works great to support the growing fruit.

The Backyard Garden

Just about all of the previously mentioned gardening ideas can also be used by those who have a more spacious yard in which to garden. To achieve more of a variety, you can try combining some of these methods. Space-saving methods can be used to maximize the amount of yield you get from the space allotted. The portion of the yard receiving the most sun can be used for the main garden to grow the sun-loving plants. Shadier spots can be used for shade loving flowers such as hostas, astilbe, lilly-of-the-valley and others. Containers could be used closer to the house so they are easier to move around as needed for use of the outdoor space. Many people will grow their herbs in containers close to the house just so they are handier for cooking. Plus many herbs have nice fragrances that can be enjoyed while sitting outside.

Borrowed-Land Garden

What if you have absolutely no space in which to garden? Such may be the case for someone living in a basement apartment or a high-rise apartment where there are no decks or patios. Do not despair, you can still have a garden. You could ask a friend or co-worker who lives in the suburbs or outside the city who has a

garden if they would mind letting you help them with their garden in return for a portion of the produce. This often happens in
families where one family member has the acreage and the rest are
required to help with the chores if they are to get any of the benefits.

Your friend or co-worker who lives outside the city may not
garden themselves but would be willing to rent you a portion of
their land on which you could garden. Anyone you know with
some extra land could be a potential landlord for your garden
space. Instead of renting garden space for money, you could barter for it by giving them a portion of your produce.

Another idea is to see if your city has community gardens.
These are typically plots of a certain size on city land that are
rented out to individuals for the gardening season. The size and
cost of the plots varies by city. Many times good friendships come
from those working garden plots next to each other. You can also
gain gardening advice from these fellow gardeners. Try to get a
plot towards the center of the area, so the deer will eat someone
else's food first.

Many large cities have community gardens that have grown
out of vacant lots that were once dumping grounds. These types
of gardens are typically sponsored by some organization. Contact the sponsoring organization for information on getting in on
the action. Your city parks department might even allow you to
maintain a flower garden in a local park, if you follow their rules.
Doug and Wendy Carroll's neighborhood association works closely
with their parks department. Doug noted, "There's a pergola,
and they have grape vines and several people do that that aren't
into the vegetable gardening end of it. And then we have entry
gardens: there's little plots all around, some urns in various locations, a lot of little theme gardens in the park itself. We have an
elderly woman that's retired that takes care of a lot the little beds
around the park."

Compost for the Garden

Many gardeners include compost as an essential ingredient for their gardens. A good compost pile recycles waste from the yard and garden, as well as kitchen scraps, thus reducing the amount of garbage that the community must deal with. Compost is an ideal material to improve your soil and boost plant nutrition. Composting saves money and lessens the need for outside fertilizers. Just about everyone can have access to this rich, soil-building material.

Some neighborhoods and communities have laws or covenants against composting. For these people, there is still the "worm farm" that can be used for kitchen scraps without offending the neighbors. They may not even know you are composting unless you tell them. A "worm farm" consists of a container about 1 foot by 2 feet by 3 feet, filled with a bedding of shredded newspapers or leaf mold to which special red "compost" worms are added.[5] Simply feed the worms your food garbage (after it has been ground up in a blender) daily. Worm castings, which look much like coffee grounds, are five times richer than most fertile soil and loaded with microorganisms.[6] Another option for the gardener is to get your compost free from a municipal compost project.

The most traditional composting method is the "pile out back". These piles usually consist of a combination of leaves, grass clippings, hay, straw, kitchen scraps (no rat-attracting fats or meat scraps, though), and garden residues. The compost pile can be simply an unrestrained pile or it can be collected in some type of bin or container. The "hot" compost methods such as layering are more difficult and time consuming, but they also produce compost much faster. There are other methods such as bag composting, ventilating stacks, or prefabricated compost barrels that are slower but much easier.

Take into account the amount of fodder you have for your pile as well as the amount of space you can devote to composting

Some states require that wooden pallets be treated for bugs before use to avoid transporting noxious insects around. If you get your pallets from a supplier of chemicals, you might get a pallet that has had something toxic spilled on the pallet. As much as you can, you want to know where a wooden pallet has been before you compost in it. If you get a pallet and are unsure about its pedigree, you can take it apart and leave the boards in a sunny spot for a couple of seasons. Rainwater will remove water-soluable chemicals, and sunshine will break down many others. Stay away from pallets which have oily residue on them.

when thinking about where to locate your compost pile or constructing a bin. The advantage of using a compost bin is that your materials are confined to specific space and can keep animals such as dogs or cats from rummaging through it. Compost bins can be any size, shape or material that you desire. Some materials for making compost bins include concrete blocks, scrap wood such as pallets, and used fencing or wire mesh.

If you lack materials and space to compost, check with local community gardens or local government to find out how to get good, locally-produced compost.

Budget Gardening

Gardening can be a very expensive hobby, but it does not have to be. *Budget Gardener* author Maureen Gilmer suggests creative thinking for those who would like to garden on the cheap. "Budget gardening is a mindset. The key is to shift from the consumer mentality to that of the hunter-gatherer. In countries where people live off the land, a tremendous amount of thought and creativity goes into how best to use each resource at hand."[7]

Gilmer's book suggests numerous creative ways for reusing household items in the garden.

Saving money gardening is like saving money in any other activity. Make sure that you always shop with a list and buy quality when it counts. One area in which quality is very important is in the tools you use. A quality tool may cost more initially than the cheaper one, but after buying several replacements for the poor-quality tool, you will have spent more than on the one quality tool that would have outlasted all the others. Look for things like a good handle that fits your hand, a thick sturdy blade and well-formed, strong connections: e.g., where the blade meets the hand grip. Highly respected tool manufacturers include Felco, True Temper, Ames, and Razor-Back; and quality mail-order supply companies include Gardener's Eden, Gardener's Supply Company, A.M. Leonard, Inc., and Smith & Hawken.

Always take proper care of your tools to make them last as long as possible. But when something does break, try to repair the item before buying a new one. Many a gardener has replaced broken handles either with spares from other tools or with a replacement handle purchased at a store at a fraction of the cost of a new tool.

Home solutions abound for such things as fertilizer, weed killers, fungicide, and pest control.[8] Most of these are made from household items or relatively inexpensive ingredients. And quite often these are environmentally friendly solutions compared to the expensive, harsh chemicals found in the stores.

Mulch can be a problem for the city dweller. Those who have a yard that has not been sprayed for weeds can use the grass clippings as a mulch under their vegetables or add them to the compost bin. Another money saver is to use your lawn mower to chop leaves in the fall instead of purchasing a separate chipper/shredder. These shredded leaves can then be used as either mulch around perennials or, again, added to the compost bin to make more of that black gold. But in some cities, like St. Louis where Simplifier Wendy Carroll lives, even the supplies can be cheap or better: "Beautiful compost that the city just provides it for you. Free! You just have to go pick it up. Or we can point to a place in the park or in the community garden and say 'drop it here'. Put a big giant load here; it's wonderful. And it's all free!"

In Alexandria, VA, where Lynne lives, the city collects Christmas trees from residents during regular trash pickups in January and chips them into mulch, which is then given away free.

Plants can be one of the more expensive items needed for any garden. There are cheap ways of obtaining plants. Many horticultural societies or nature centers have plant sales as fund-raisers. These can be a great source of plants that are native to the area in which you live. These plants may be small to start, but given the right environment and a little time, they will grow to their full potential. Many garden centers will sell plants in various sized containers. The larger the container, the more expensive the plant. Granted, you get a larger plant to start your garden with, but by the next year you will not be able to tell the difference. Vegetables are often sold in four- or six-packs for smaller plants for the same price as a larger one in a single pot. Again, once these are transplanted to the garden and allowed to establish themselves, the smaller ones will produce just as nicely as the larger ones. If you do not need all four or six of the plants, find a friend and share.

Sharing with friends is a great way to get free plants as well as give away those new plantlets, roots, and bulbs that result from dividing. Some flower gardens consist entirely of plants that the gardener obtained from others after they divided their plants.

Seedlings need some type of protection in the spring when there is still a chance of a cold snap. One of the most popular methods of protection is to construct some type of greenhouse. These greenhouses come in all varieties, from the plastic-covered frames available at the local nursery or hardware store to the custom-built buildings. Cold frames serve this same purpose, but take up less space and cheaper to construct. Cold frames can vary from the wide-mouth canning jar to an old piece of glass that is propped up over the seedlings to heat the area beneath. Another option is to use the commercially available row cover material.

This can be draped over the plant with enough slack for the plant to continue to grow. Row cover can also be draped over some type of frame. These frames can be just about anything that you might have around the house or can easily and cheaply obtain: twigs, stakes, chicken wire, concrete reinforcing wire, tomato cages (as found at the garden center), old milk crates (either the old metal ones or the newer plastic ones), and wire baskets turned over, can all be used. Ideally, your prop would be something that is not needed until later on in the season when the row cover is no longer needed. That way you get multiple uses out of that one item.

Common items normally considered waste, such as pruned twigs, have many uses in the garden, so do not throw them away. Straight twigs can be used as plant and flower stakes that blend in much better than the artificially colored or metal ones purchased at the garden center. Bind the ends of several long twigs together to make a teepee for pole beans; or add some baling wire or string and use them for peas or other vine plants. If you have enough twigs, lash or nail them together into a lattice to support vines such as morning glory of other flowering vine.

Another common household item that can be used for many things in the garden is the plastic jug. You can make a seedling cover simply by cutting the bottom off and unscrewing the lid to allow the plant more air and moisture while still protecting it. Once the top has been cut off and holes poked in the bottom for drainage, another use for plastic jugs can be as planters for starting your seeds. A handy scoop can be made by keeping just the handle part along with a portion of the jug. Two-liter soft drink bottles can be used to provide drip irrigation to plants. Plastic jugs make good containers for hauling water for your plants if you do not have access to a hose or other water source (as in the case of a community garden).

Indoor Gardening

For those who would like to have a garden, but are not ready to tackle an outdoor garden, the indoor garden provides a good alternative. Whether you live in a tiny apartment or a house, live plants can add beauty and color to any room.

Plant stands are great space savers, as are hanging plants. Many plants of varying sizes can be grouped in this single space. Stands to hold your plants can be made of wood, metal, glass, or wrought iron. One popular stand is the baker's rack. Your stand could even be a small ladder with plants arranged on the steps. You could construct your own stand from whatever materials you have available. Pedestals can be used to highlight a certain plant instead of including it on a stand with many others. One advantage of a pedestal is that it and the plant can be moved to a different location if you choose. Larger plants can be placed on the floor and work especially well at filling those empty corners of the room.

Just about any room in your apartment or house is suitable for plants, even the bathroom. You just need to make sure they receive enough light, either natural or electric. The living room seems to be the most popular room in which to include plants. This tends to be the room with the most space and the one in which most people spend the majority of their time. A large, sunny window also contributes to the popularity of the living room for plants. A couple of plants placed in the entry hall can make a good first impression for visitors. If your entry also includes a stairway, think about cascading the plants. If your entry does not have very good light, you could alternately move plants between the entry and another room with better light like the living room. Plants in the bedroom can provide a relaxing atmosphere, especially when the more graceful palms and ferns are used. Ferns are also a good plant to consider for the bathroom. The bathroom is usually the most humid of all rooms and the perfect place for ferns or orchids. The kitchen is another popular room for plants. Kitchen plants tend to be herbs, but they don't have to be. Cabinet-tops make excellent spaces for vines or creeping plants.

To have success with indoor gardening, you need to provide each plant with sufficient lighting and growing conditions. For the south or east window, try vegetables like carrots, cucumbers, Japanese eggplant, radishes, and midget varieties of green peppers or tomatoes. Most herbs also like south or east windows. Flowering plants such as gardenia, geranium, poinsettia, waxplant, spider plant, bougainvillea, jasmine, or fernleaf lavender also work in these spaces, if you do not want to grow edibles.

For the west window, try these vegetables: lettuce, spinach or tomatoes. Most foliage plants do well in this location. Include flowering plants such as begonias, bromeliads, calamondin, chenille plant, fuchsia, gloxinia, orchids, cape primrose, spathiphylum, or zebra plant. Northern exposures should not be ruled out as unfit for plants. Foliage plants such as dieffenbachia, dracaena, and philodendron do well in these locations. A north window can be an excellent place for several flowering plants: Chinese evergreen, Christmas cactus, begonias, bromeliads, spider plant, and African violets.

Specialty or Theme Gardens

If your interest in gardening is more for the visual pleasure or artistic value of the garden, there are many specialty or theme gardens that you can create. You can create a garden with just about any theme that you can imagine. If you have some unpleasant views, you can create an urban retreat by surrounding a space with the types of plants and flowers that you enjoy while sitting outside. Sitting in a secluded retreat can make you forget about the world outside.

Water gardens can encompass many things: a simple, small fountain with marine colored accessories; a water garden in a barrel; or a more extensive fish pond. Or you can just go for the nautical theme and decorate as if your space was part of a cruise ship or lighthouse island—whatever floats your boat.

Other theme ideas can be taken from areas of the country or the world. Try an Eastern tranquillity garden or a classical garden with statues and garden ornaments. Creating a garden in a hacienda style, a West coast style, or a colonial style could be fun and exciting.

The cottage garden has been around for many years and continues to retain its popularity. This is one of the simpler types of gardens because it is unstructured, yet is always stunning. A large variety of flowers confined to a small space, usually close to the house and surrounded by a low picket-style fence, are characteristic of the cottage garden.

Another more traditional style garden is that of the romance garden consisting of roses, cool white flowers and white painted iron furniture.

The kitchen and herb garden may not be what a person thinks of when talking about a theme garden, but it is just that. There is no reason why you could not create a kitchen garden that upon first glance does not look like a vegetable garden at all. Many herbs are very fragrant and produce beautiful flowers.

Your garden could be done in all one color. Many people have a favorite flower color and select plants that produce flowers in only that one color or various shades of a color. The selection of plants producing white, blue, pink, red, yellow or even black flowers is so numerous, you may have a hard time limiting yourself to what will fit in your space.

When all is said and done, there is great satisfaction in knowing that you are capable of growing something edible, or as beautiful as a flower, from something as tiny as a seed.

Practical To Dos

- Think about what type of garden you would like to have.
- Assess the amount of space you can devote to gardening.
- Check out lots of books for ideas.
- Design your garden space.
- Start gardening.

- See your local parks & recreation department for how to sign up for a community plot.
- Check for local university agriculture departments in your region.
- Check your county agriculture office.

Library Guide

- *Square Foot Gardening* by Mel Bartholomew
- *The Budget Gardener* by Maureen Gilmer
- *Hyponex Handbook of House Plants* by Elvin McDonald
- *Green Places in Small Spaces* by Kerwin Fischer
- *The Able Gardener by* Kathleen Yeomans
- *The Contained Garden* by Kenneth Beckett, David Carr, and David Stevens
- *Balcony and Roof Gardens* by Jenny Hendy
- *Gardening in Small Spaces* by Jack Kramer
- *The American Horticultural Society Illustrated Encyclopedia of Gardening: Container Gardening*

Internet Resources

www.garden.org
www.gardenweb.com
gardening.about.com

Search Terms

container gardening
houseplants
vegetable
worm tea
composting
vermicomposting

CHAPTER 19

SIMPLIFYING WITH KIDS

Raising kids in our consumer culture is hard enough. Raising them while walking the path of Voluntary Simplicity can be really tough. Early on in her book, *Living Simply with Children*, Marie Sherlock lists the hurdles that face every parent trying to live simply with his or her children in America today:

- Marketing aimed at kids and parents, indoctrinating them with the belief that happiness can be purchased
- Age-inappropriate and violent media
- The peer pressure of a society that believes more is better
- Overscheduling of children and adults
- Practices that harm the environment and, consequently, children's futures
- The commercialization of schools
- The sheer excess that has become the norm in America.[1]

Jumping those hurdles is particularly hard when living in a city. Your kids' friends may wear trendy clothing, or brag (or complain) about their enrichment classes and sports practices every day after school, or expect to get brand-new urban assault vehicles for their 16th birthdays. You know that the friends' parents are stuck on the work-and-spend treadmill, barely squeaking by, and charging their credit cards to the hilt while they live it up, but all your child can see is that their friends have a lot of stuff that they don't.

That is why educating your kids about our consumer culture is one of the most important things that you, as a parent, can do.

Teaching them to manage their money wisely and giving them the tools to resist the urge to spend it on command is a major accomplishment. Your kids need to hear from you that pinpointing their values, and then making choices according to those values, will make them happier than will acquiring more stuff.

Why Is It So Tough?

Simple. Advertising.

All of the statistics we cited in the chapters "Downsize Your TV" and "Advertising" are true again when it comes to marketing to children, and then some. Marketers target your kids because it makes good business sense.

Some 79 million kids were born between 1977 and 1997, and 30 million or so of them were teenagers in 2000. Teens spend more than $150 billion of their own money each year on consumer goods and services.[2] That is a pretty good chunk of change all on its own, but it does not take into account the amount of money parents spend on their kids because the kids pester them into it. Younger children, those aged four to twelve, influenced an estimated $188 billion of their parents' spending decisions in 1997. That figure is more than triple the amount of consumer spending attributed to the "nag factor" 15 years earlier.[3] The older kids get, the better they get at nagging: In 2002, the Center for a New American Dream surveyed American kids between the ages of 12 and 17 and found that the average teen will ask a parent for something *nine times* before accepting "no" as an answer. Some 12- and 13-year-olds will ask up to 50 times before giving up.[4]

With so much money at stake, marketers are busy thinking up new angles to influence young people. TV advertising is the most familiar of these, but it is just the start. Toy manufacturers routinely develop toys and then design cartoon shows to create a demand for them (remember "Strawberry Shortcake" and "The Smurfs"?). Product placement occurs in children's programming and movies as well as in adult fare. Cross-promotion puts a Batman figurine in your child's fast-food meal, even though most parents feel the "Batman" movies are too violent for their child to see. And schools have gotten into the act: bringing McDonald's and Pizza Hut into their cafeterias; placing vending machines where students can get to them (and getting a piece of the action from the machines in the process); distributing paper book covers and stickers featuring corporate names and logos; and exposing kids to programs like Channel One, a daily TV "news" program that comes prepackaged with two minutes of ads. Contrast this with Sweden, which bans TV advertising aimed at kids under the age of 12 and prohibits characters from kids' TV shows from appearing in ads. The Swedish government enacted the bans after several studies showed that children cannot tell the difference between the ads and the programming. Sweden also bans direct advertising to children younger than 16.[5] See below for a more thorough discussion of the commercialization of our schools.

By making it easier for kids to spend money, marketers can increase the amount they can spend. In 2000, Visa U.S.A. introduced the VISA Buxx card, sold to parents as a "parent controlled, reloadable payment card" for teenagers.[6] Though it was marketed as a way to teach kids about managing money, what was the message that kids got? If you want something, pull out the plastic. Seven percent of high school students had their own credit cards in 1999[7]; now we're cultivating the plastic habit in their younger siblings.

Robert D. Manning, the author of *Credit Card Nation: The Consequences of America's Addiction to Credit*, says the average American undergraduate student carries $2,000 in credit card debt. Usually, college kids get their cards at freshman registration, from banks who strike deals with the schools to offer cards with the college's mascot on it. Manning says, "There are people in Delaware [where many credit card issuers are incorporated, due to the state's active efforts to lure banks by offering tax breaks and other incentives] who think it's okay for college students to have $5,000 or $10,000 in credit card debt by the time they graduate, on top of their college loans. They say, 'It's good for them to have debt. They're at the beginning of their earning cycle.'"[8] This is on top of average student loan amounts of $17,100 for public school and $21,200 for private school students.[9]

It is not just the teens that marketers are after; they are aiming their message at younger and younger audiences. They call it KAGOY: Kids Are Getting Older Younger. It is not unheard of for marketers to talk about the "age zero" demographic.[10] In this atmosphere, it should not surprise you that babies are already recognizing images of corporate logos at the age of six months, and children begin asking for brand name products at the age of three years.[11]

Our advice for teaching your children about money management is to skip the Visa Buxx card and other products that teach kids questionable spending habits, and instead have your kids surf to the Zillions.org web site (which is affiliated with *Consumer Reports* magazine), the PBSkids.org "Don't Buy It" media awareness program, or the kids' section of the Center for a New American Dream's web site. Each of these sites has materials that will help you give your child a responsible financial education. In addition, in conjunction with the New Road Map Foundation and FI Associates, Lynne has written a study guide for middle schoolers based on *Your Money or Your Life* by Joe Dominguez and Vicki Robin, which is available online at no cost from the Simple Living Network.

The Role of Television

In 1985, author Marie Winn published her book, *The Plug-In Drug*, about the effects of television viewing on children. Winn's observations, groundbreaking then, are well accepted now: kids who watch a great deal of TV are more aggressive and less able to entertain themselves. This is partly because a lot of TV shows are action-packed, and because shows with a lot going on get the best ratings. Winn has a theory for why that is: "By choosing the most active programs possible, viewers are able to approximate a *feeling* of activity, with all the sensations of involvement, while enjoying the safety and security of total passivity. They are enjoying a *simulation* of activity in the hope that it will compensate for the actuality that they are involved in a passive, one-way experience."[12]

We mentioned in our TV chapter that television encourages passivity while also engaging the body's fight-or-flight response. Kalle Lasn describes in his book *Culture Jam: The Uncooling of America* that TV programming includes many more "jolts" now than it did ten or 15 years ago. Lasn describes a "jolt" as a technical event that interrupts the flow of the program — anything from a shift in camera angle to a gunshot to a commercial. Lasn says television programming featured about ten jolts per minute in 1978. In 1998, the number had doubled, with some programs such as music videos delivering up to 60 events per minute.[13] Marie Sherlock quotes one parent who wonders whether the increase in ADD and ADHD among children today might not be traced back, at least in part, to this rapid-fire aspect of TV.[14]

Kids have a lot of built-in energy; they learn best by doing. The last thing they need to do is spend a lot of time "involved in a passive, one-way experience." As convenient as it may be to plop the kids in front of the TV while you get something done, TV is a terrible sitter. One of the biggest favors you can do for your children is to turn off the set and allow them to tune up their imaginations. Kids' TV is presented as a learning opportunity, and certainly, TV can present facts and kids can learn those facts. But is that *useful* learning? Robert Keeshan, better known as Captain Kangaroo, believes that it is not:

> When you are spending time in front of the television, you are not doing other things. The young child of three or four years old is in a stage of the greatest emotional development that human beings undergo. And we only develop when we experience things, real-life things: a conversation with Mother, touching Father, going places, doing things, relating to others. This kind of experience is critical to a young child, and when the child spends thirty-

five hours per week in front of the TV set, it is impossible to have the full range of real-life experience that a young child must have. Even if we had an overabundance of good television programs, it wouldn't solve the problem.[15]

School is Not an Ad-Free Zone

Children have not been safe from advertising in school for many, many years. Since at least the 1960s, children have learned about what makes a "good breakfast" from a colorful chart provided by a cereal manufacturer, and about proper tooth brushing techniques from a company that makes toothpaste.

These types of corporate intrusions into the school day still occur, and they are accompanied now by even more aggressive product placements in school corridors and classrooms. The Center for the Analysis of Commercialism in Education at the University of Wisconsin-Milwaukee collected media references to the commercialization of education from 1990 through 1997.[16] Their sources included the popular press, business publications, advertising or marketing publications, and publications aimed at educators. They documented seven types of commercialization occurring in schools:

- Sponsorship of programs and activities, including contests and athletic tournaments.
- Exclusive agreements, most notably "pouring rights" agreements, in which schools contract with a specific soft drink bottler to feature only that bottler's products in soft drink machines at the school.
- Incentive programs, such as programs in which schools encourage students to collect cash register receipts from certain stores. The schools redeem the receipts for a fraction of their value for merchandise such as computer equipment.
- Appropriation of space, which ranges from providing free textbook covers featuring a product logo to putting a corporation's logo on a scoreboard or even the school roof.

- Sponsored educational materials, such as the toothbrush training in days of yore.
- Electronic marketing, including Channel One and corporate-sponsored Internet access.
- Privatization of the schools themselves, in which a corporation either owns or manages the school.

What most troubled the authors of this report is that commercialization in schools was, by and large, not mentioned at all in the publications aimed at educators. It appears that, at least in the 1990s, educators considered such deals with corporations to be a good thing. In fact, school officials actively seek advertising partnerships in order to bolster their budgets. But it is not clear that the schools benefit all that much. One report indicates that an effort by Colorado Springs, CO, schools to sell ad space on buses and in hallways netted just $338,680 between 1993 and 1997, or about $2.50 per student, per year. Another report, on a "labels for education" program, showed that a school had to collect $131,747 in soup can labels (assuming each can of soup cost 59 cents) in order to earn a single computer, and $649,000 in labels to earn a 15-passenger van.[17]

Some incentive programs cause more trouble for the participants than they provide in benefits. Lynne's children participated for a couple of years in Pizza Hut's BOOK IT! program. The program encourages kids to read a certain number of books. Children who reach their goals are given a certificate for a free personal pan pizza, and the classroom with the most students reaching their goals receive a free pizza party. Lynne found that the pizza certificates were a lousy deal. Normally, her family gets pizza by delivery, but the certificates had to be redeemed at the restaurant. That meant eating at the restaurant and paying for overpriced drinks for everyone, as well as shelling out a larger tip. Then the child without the certificate would want her own personal pan pizza, too, but that meant buying her a kid's meal, which of course included a toy; then the kid with the certificate was disappointed because she did not get a toy, so the parents had to spend another couple of bucks to keep everybody happy. Getting kids to read more is a worthy goal, but it is Pizza Hut, not the kids or the schools, that benefits most from the BOOK IT! program.

There are indications that the pendulum is swinging back. The Los Angeles School Board voted in August 2002 to end the sale of soft drinks in its schools by January 2004, despite arguments from school administrators that the decision would cut into the budget. The sponsor of the resolution, board member Marlene Canter, said, "I find it appalling that we are discussing economics at the risk of our children's health."[18] The health risk Canter referred to was not the effect of advertising on students, but the effect of the availability of junk food in schools on students' weight. We were disappointed that the pernicious effects of advertising in schools was not even part of the discussion.

Seeing How the Other Half Lives

One of the best ways to get your children to appreciate what they have is to give them an opportunity to meet others who have very little. Traveling is one way to accomplish that. A staff writer for the *Washington Post* took her materialistic seven-year-old to Guatemala for a month.[19] Such a trip is not an option for most of us, but certainly alternatives exist closer to home. Take your child with you to volunteer at a soup kitchen or food bank, or volunteer to deliver gift baskets at holiday time. Your local scout troop or Habitat for Humanity might be a good place to get involved with others of different backgrounds. Check out *Material World: A Global Family Portrait* by Peter Mendel, Charles C. Mann and Peter Kennedy at your local library to see how people around the world use their stuff.

Make sure, too, that your children respect the non-human creatures of this earth. Give them an appreciation for the outdoors. Scouting, again, is a great place for city kids to learn how to get along in the out-of-doors, but it is by no means the only alternative. Your city's parks and recreation department may offer nature walks and craft classes for children (and adults!), or just check out a field guide to birds or trees from the library and take the kids on a hike yourself. Parks, zoos and nature preserves may also have nature programs for kids. The National Park Service offers a Junior Ranger program at many national parks; call the ranger station or check out the NPS website for details. Another possibility for older kids is to volunteer at your city's animal shelter. Most shelters will not allow elementary-school-age children to work with the animals, but younger kids can collect old towels and blankets, then visit the animals when they deliver the fruits of their collection effort. Be sure to check with your local shelter to see what they might need before starting a collection drive. In addition, shelters are usually happy to give tours, together with a talk on the problem of pet overpopulation. Call your local shelter to schedule a tour.

Get your kids involved in recycling and community clean-up efforts. More than one youth group has earned its way to camp or a trip by collecting recyclables. We're not just talking newspapers; Lynne's daughters' Girl Scout troop helped fund a trip to New York City by collecting old cell phones through the Donate-a-Phone program administered by the Wireless Foundation. Your city or neighborhood may sponsor a clean-up day for a local park; watch for fliers posted in the neighborhood or notices in the newspaper. Your older child's favorite group might sponsor a section of roadway to keep clean for a year. Clean-up days are an especially good opportunity to talk to your kids about how overpackaging hurts the environment, as well as adding to the cost of an item. Explain to them that the choices your family makes along the VS path are good not just for the family bank account, but for the environment, too.

Mom, When Do I Get a Day Off?

You might be tempted to simply add some of these activities to your kids' current schedules, but please think twice about this.

Many children today are already overwhelmed with enrichment activities, after-school classes, and sports practices and games. As parents, we sign our kids up for things with the best of intentions. Sometimes, parents need to park their kids somewhere between the end of school and the time that Mom or Dad gets home from work. Sometimes, the child wants to play soccer (or another sport) with his or her buddies. Sometimes, the parent sees Junior's latest art project and envisions a Junior Rembrandt, or Junior expresses a passing fancy for horses and the parent signs him up for riding lessons. Or, perhaps worst of all, Mom or Dad always wanted to try puppeteering but never got the chance, and sign up Junior for puppeteering so that he will not have the same supposedly bleak childhood as the parent did. Regardless of the motivation, your child can end up with after-school activities every night of the week, and most weekend days, too. No wonder many schools are handing out day planners to kids as young as elementary school age.

Not only do all these activities cut into your child's time to just be a kid, but the constant chauffering, supply purchasing, and expectations for parental involvement (from coaching to fundraising) might also be adding to *your* stress level. Consider limiting your kids to a certain number of extracurricular activities at a time. Lynne's rule of thumb has always been two activities per child; some families limit their children to three. You may have to experiment to find the right number for each kid.

The corollary to limiting extracurricular activity is to allow your kid time to be a kid. Give him time to just swing on a swing; give her time to look for polliwogs at the creek. And, most importantly of all, give your child the gift of *your* time. As one parent interviewed by Marie Sherlock said, "Toys break and get boring, even books tear and go the way of all things. Give [your children] yourself. They don't really need a whole lot more than that."[20]

Get out the board games and have a family games night. Tell each other stories. Play catch. Go outside and dig in the dirt together. Turn off the lights and spend the evening like the pioneers did.[21] Laugh together a lot. Your child will remember these experiences forever.

The Earlier You Start, the Better

The younger your kids are when you start on the VS path, the easier it is for you. In fact, you can start before your kids are born. Marketeers target prospective parents relentlessly, with everything from coupons to free issues of magazines to samples of disposable diapers. Resist the urge to make preparing for Baby's arrival into a shopping event. In most cases, umbrella strollers work just as well as the ones with antilock brakes and three-digit price tags (and are a whole lot easier to wrestle into the trunk of the car or onto the bus). Thrift stores are full of designer baby-wear that has seen little or no wear because the kid outgrew the size before it was hot enough or cold enough to wear it. Really and truly, you do not need a changing table; Lynne rigged up a pad and belt atop a three-drawer dresser she already owned, and used it as a changing table for both of her daughters. When the girls outgrew diapers, the belt and pad came off easily. Her 15-year-old is still using the dresser today.

Simplifier Katherine Carter feels as though she is under constant pressure to "do more, spend more": from her kids, her family, and from the Consumer Culture. One of the ways she has coped with it is to give away their TV. She says that her kids do understand that not everybody lives this way: "[W]hen the kids go to their dad's house, they get TV and McDonald's and doughnuts, which is okay. They understand that they do different things at Dad's house than they do at mine."

Everette Orr's family traveled with him all over the world while he was in the Foreign Service, but they settled in McLean, VA, outside Washington, DC. He says that bucking the Consumer Culture is tough. They live just a few miles from Tysons Corner Center, one of the largest shopping malls in the region. "But," he says, "you don't have to get caught into the Tysons mall experience." He says today, his children appreciate being able to take friends into downtown Washington on the Metro and attend a free performance at the Kennedy Center.

Lynne began practicing VS when her oldest daughter was already in middle school. She had set the stage by encouraging her daughters to read practically from birth, and by restricting their TV viewing all along. It also helps that she does not live in a neighborhood where kids expect a Porsche for their 16th birthday. Still, she feels plenty of pressure from her kids to spend, spend, spend. Yet every now and then, she sees a glimmer of hope; not only does Lynne set aside part of the girls' allowance every month and put it in savings for them, but her younger daughter is learning from Mom's example of not spending every penny, and is saving another chunk of her allowance, all on her own.

Buddhist Simplifier alex glenlee thinks just getting together and talking with your children is a great way to start:

> You know, sometimes it would be healthy to talk to or look into the eyes of another human being. i try to encourage people to talk: "Guys, let's get together. Heck, c'mon over to my place we'll have a cup of coffee. This place, our house, the door is always open, it's like 1950 here." People don't believe it. i encourage the kids to bring their friends over [and] we sit in on the conversations. You always get, "Really?!? You do that with your parents?" Sure. You can, too. Why not?

Practical To Dos

The following list originated from the Center for a New American Dream web site. The original list has 115 tips for fighting commercialism aimed at kids. We do not have room to print the whole list, but you can get the address of the whole list from the Internet Resources section on page 218.

- Get rid of the TV.
- Do not get rid of the TV. Rather, teach your kids why and how to control their use of this plug-in drug. Set a good example. Watch occasional programs that you choose with good reason. Always be willing to explain your decisions and compromise if possible. Talk about the commercialism.
- Don't just turn off the TV, but instead show them something better to do.
- When confronted by TV hype, call it by its name.
- Exercise freedom of choice; support "Turn Off TV Week" and "Buy Nothing Day" (sponsored by the media awareness organization, AdBusters).
- If you have a radio, be highly selective about when you listen and to what you listen.
- Unsubscribe from your newspaper.
- Weed your magazine subscriptions.
- Give kids time, give them the gift of music and art, both as enjoyers and makers.
- Attend high school drama productions.
- Take them to local games and let them see sports without the commercial trappings.
- Take them outside for hikes and camping trips.
- Take them traveling if you can afford it.
- Give them chores but also unscheduled time to exercise their imaginations and play with other kids.
- Give children a big box of crayons and rolls of shelf paper.
- Play Legos, talk, play badminton, dance to records, go canoeing, hang out and talk science and history.
- Go for walks, cycle, kick the ball around the yard, garden, play table tennis, read together, play cards and games, do crafts, wrestle around on the living room floor.
- Read them bedtime stories.
- Take an active part in schools.
- Get schools to adopt fund raiser policies that (1) provide an educational experience for kids, and (2) contribute to some social good.

- Home school or alternative school your children.
- Arrange for them to spend lots of time with their grandparents.
- Don't buy when you can borrow, do without, or make do. Buy things used whenever possible. Buy local whenever possible. Look above all for quality and durability.
- Remove the logos from clothes, theirs and yours. Talk with kids about why you're doing this. Suggest that they design their own personal logos.
- Let them make their own choices in the marketplace by giving them money and guidance, then let them live with their choices.
- Illustrate to children that we each have gifts and talents that are inherent in each of us and cannot be bought and that every living thing has dignity and deserves respect.
- Church attendance—give them a spiritual basis for resisting the messages from the popular culture.
- Make children responsible for age-appropriate chores around the house.
- Do voluntary community service with your kids.
- Have a no-electric night once a week or weekend once a month, when the family will do without electricity and even plumbing.
- Tell your children what you think. About everything. Tell them while they are very young because when they get to be 14 or so, they think you're nuts.
- Teach by example and conviction a set of values that allow kids to make their own choices.
- Feel free to say no.

Library Guide

- *The Plug-In Drug: Television, Children and the Family* by Marie Winn
- *Material World: A Global Family Portrait* by Peter Mendel, Charles Mann and Peter Kennedy

- *Simplify Your Life with Kids* by Elaine St. James
- *Living Simply with Children* by Marie Sherlock

Internet Resources

www.zillions.org
www.adbusters.org
www.newdream.org (see the full list of parenting tips at:
   http://www.newdream.org/campaign/kids/115tips.html)
www.pbskids.org/dontbuyit/
Your Money or Your Life Middle School Study Guide:
   (www.simpleliving.net/resource.asp?sku=BSG4)
www.nps.gov (U.S. National Park Service)
www.girlscouts.org
www.scouting.org
www.wirelessfoundation.org/DonateaPhone/index.cfm

Search Terms

KAGOY
Channel One
product placement

CHAPTER 20

ENERGY

After taxes, shelter, vehicles, and food, energy to keep our homes comfortable and our appliances running is likely to be your next largest expense. This is not surprising, since energy costs have been rising, often substantially, year to year for the last two decades. That rise represents increased spending that is easy to dismiss as small stuff; but it's really not. Substantial savings in energy costs can often be yours, regardless of whether you own or rent. Like all other forms of consumption, energy usage is another choice we make on a daily basis. Using the minimum required to keep you reasonably comfortable is the best strategy for everyone, unless you want to generate your own.

When You Own

When you own your home, and can make internal structural changes to it without having to notify someone else, then you have the most opportunities to save energy.

Every time you tackle the next part of the renovation plan for your building, you can build in the costs of retrofitting it for energy efficiency. Every time a wall, ceiling, or floor is opened up for work, you can install or replace insulation. Proper vapor barriers will also help in the walls, attic, and crawl spaces and are easy to install as part of normal renovation tasks and may be required to pass inspections if you had to get permits for your work.

Proper insulation saves far more than its cost over the life of the building in avoided utility bills. The reason insulation works is that it traps air and keeps the heat in it from moving quickly to a lower temperature area. By carefully installing insulation to ensure there are no voids or gaps—that is, no place where heat can move through quickly—you are maximizing your insulations value. Too often, insulation is an afterthought and may be hastily and incorrectly installed. Do not succumb to this temptation; take the time to do your insulation right. If you hire this kind of work out, inspect the insulation thoroughly before allowing it to be sealed away from sight.

Weatherproofing, in the form of gaskets, seals, and caulk, works in much the same way as insulation. It slows the movement of air from hot to cold places. Properly caulking doors, windows, and other intentional holes in your building's shell (the outer walls, ceilings, and floors) is something you should do any time you do renovations inside, and on an annual basis outside. Get into the habit of checking your caulk annually on a pleasant day before your big energy use season. Properly maintained, caulking is easy to touch up on most one-story structures. If your doors and windows are ancient and leaky, seriously consider replacing them with new energy efficient units.[1] There are even energy efficient window options for historic buildings. Also, awnings, shades, shutters, and window films can help control the amount of heat entering your space. Be careful to check with the manufacturer of your windows before applying window films or using window quilts, however, since these can void your window's warranty.

Appliances are the next largest area of energy savings. Especially for built-in appliances, look for the lowest energy usage rating you can get. Most appliances come with tags outlining expected energy costs and many have an Energy Star label. While Energy Star units often cost a bit more up front, the cost payback can be as short as a few months. Do not let the higher price tag fool you into buying a cheaper, energy-hogging appliance; you will pay the difference in initial cost several times over in wasted energy. Buying the most energy efficient appliances you can afford is especially important for the major energy hogs in most people's houses: air conditioners, furnaces, refrigerators, dishwashers, water heaters, electric dryers, and electric ovens. Once installed, proper maintenance on these appliances will not only extend their lives, it will also cut your energy costs, sometimes dramatically. Keeping the coils on the back of the fridge clean[2] and changing furnace filters as often as monthly will improve their efficiency and decrease your energy bills.

According to *The Consumer's Guide to Effective Environmental Choices* by Michael Brower and Warren Leon, differences between high-efficiency refrigerators and low-efficiency refrigerators can be as much as 40%—a far larger improvement than simple maintenance can provide. Over time, too, efficiency has increased thanks to U.S. Department of Energy standards. If your refrigerator was manufactured before 1989, you may be able to increase efficiency by over 50% simply by buying *any* new refrigerator. The Union of Concerned Scientists, who did the research used in the book, found that refrigerators and freezers represent about a quarter of the energy use in the average American household.

When it comes time to replace water-using devices, consider getting Energy Star water heaters and dishwashers. Many water heaters now come with built-in insulation, but if your does not have any, a water heater blanket can help keep the heat in. Anywhere you have access to your water pipes, figure out which is the hot water pipe and insulate it with an appropriately sized pipe wrap. Pipe wraps can be found in your local hardware store and are basically an insulating tube with a slit down the side; just slip them over the pipe and you're saving both energy (and thus minimizing environmental damage) and money. You may want to wrap the cold water line too, to help prevent water damage in the wall due to sweating. When using the dishwasher and washing machine, do full loads whenever possible. Not only will it save you time and energy, you will also save water. Note that there is a dependency between the dishwasher and the temperature setting on your water heater. Check the owners' manual for the dishwasher and see what incoming water temperature is required, and set your water heater for that. Many dishwashers now use 120°F water, instead of 140°F, so you can lower the water heater thermostat and save even more money. If you can do it, hang your clothes outside to dry or use a drying rack instead of using the dryer.

When You Rent

For many people, opening up the walls is a job best left to the actual building owner. Many house- or apartment-renters and condo owners only own from the paint inwards, and are simply not allowed to make many of the changes listed in the previous section. But there are still a myriad of things they can do to save energy! And all these apply to owners as well.

Consider carefully when appliances are used. A timer on your electric water heater may be a reasonable way to cut your electric costs. Likewise, lots of cooking, especially with the oven, during the peak cooling period of the day is not a frugal idea either. Restricting cooking to cooler times (early morning or later in the evening) and doing all the oven cooking at one time can save enormous amount of energy. If you plan carefully, you can do all or most of you oven cooking at one time and therefore heat the building only minimally, or in ways you want it heated. By varying cooking times and carefully considering appropriate coverings, dishes that require different cooking temperatures can all be cooked at once, saving even more energy.

Also consider using the microwave or a toaster oven instead of your range oven. A microwave is *much* more effective at turning electricity into hot food than a conventional oven,[3] and the smaller size of a toaster oven means it takes less energy to heat the space inside the oven. Both also end up radiating less heat into your living space, decreasing the energy needed to cool it. The *Consumer's Guide to Effective Environmental Choices* says, "The

American Council for an Energy-Efficient Economy has estimated the relative costs and energy use of different methods for cooking the same casserole. What would take an hour in a 350-degree electric oven takes only one-quarter of that, or fifteen minutes, in a microwave. The difference in energy used and expense is even greater—2.0 kilowatt-hours and 16 cents versus 0.36 kilowatt-hours and 3 cents. Other options—a crockpot, a toaster oven, a frying pan, a gas oven, and an electric convection oven—are also better than the large electric oven, but they are all two to nearly four times worse than a microwave."

Turn off the auto-defrost on the refrigerator to save even more money (though you will need to defrost the freezer when the ice gets more than $\frac{1}{4}$ inch thick).

Various coverings for windows and doors can be used to great effect on your utility bill. If your landlord permits and the windows allow, a window quilt or clear window plastic can block an enormous amount of air leakage and heat transfer. Doors can be "weatherstripped" by runners, carpeting, or even hanging blankets designed for that purpose. Keeping doors to seldom used rooms shut can cut your heating and cooling bills as well. Adding extra blankets, and if you have a water bed, extra foam insulation, can make your sleeping space even cozier yet still allow you to keep the door closed the majority of the day. For each single degree below 68°F you reduce your thermostat temperature in the winter, you will typically save between 3% and 5%. Similar air conditioning savings can be achieved in the summer for every degree above 78°F. And if you use ceiling, higher temperatures in the summer may be even more pleasant inside than outside!

Proper settings on blinds and shades will allow most of the light in but bounce most of the heat back out. Using compact fluorescent bulbs in fixtures you normally turn on and leave on for more than $\frac{1}{2}$ hour at a time will help trim your electric usage. (While you may not have to leave the lights on for 30 minutes to save electricity, there is evidence that compact fluorescent bulbs last longer if they are not flipped on and off constantly.) Lynne's dining room fixture uses five chandelier-base bulbs; she replaced the 25-watt incandescent bulbs that were there when she moved in with five-watt chandelier-base fluorescent bulbs, cutting the total energy output for the fixture from 125 watts to 25. Likewise, there is no need to put the maximum rated bulb in every socket. Jonathan's bathroom mirror has spaces for five 40-watt bulbs. He put in 25-watt bulbs instead, providing plenty of light for the bathroom, and saving an extra 75 watt-hours every day,[4] or $2.74/year.

If you have access to a few tools (pipe wrench or large slip lock pliers, an old rag, Teflon pipe-joint tape, and any other tools the installation instructions suggest), a low-flow shower head can easily be attached to most showers, saving significant quantities of water. Similarly, aerators can be added to most faucets, simultaneously restricting the amount of water and partially oxygenating it. Keep the old parts around so you can swap them back before you move out. Or better yet, call the owner and have them install the head and aerator in all their units. Finally, if there is a running toilet or leaky faucet, call and get that fixed too. Toilets with even a small leak can waste over 50 gallons of water a day!

Power Procurement Options

Although there has been much discussion in recent years about deregulation of the electrical generation and distribution systems, there have been few, if any, choices open to the retail electrical consumer. The closest you can come to getting green electricity in your home, short of installing your own solar panels, is to join a "green power" program through your electrical utility or provider if they have one.

Many of the so-called "green power" programs look good on paper. You pay a premium price per kilowatt-hour (KWH) of electricity and the utility supposedly buys your energy from a "green energy provider," or supposedly uses your premium payment to help build sources of green power (hydro, wind, etc.). However, the actual electrons flowing through your building may still come from a nearby coal, natural gas, or nuclear generation plant, even though you are paying extra. So is your utility ripping you off?

Yes and no. If you join a program that collects a premium to help your utility finance building green power sources, then at least you can guess where some of your money is going. If your utility has a contract with a green energy provider, then from an accounting standpoint, you are getting "green electrons". The "electrical grid" in North America is administered the same way as the natural gas pipelines: generators put so much electricity on the wires, and users take so much off. The amounts generated and used are subject to contracts.

Practically speaking, however, there is this little problem called Kirchoff's Law getting in the way. Kirchoff's Law says, basically, that electricity travels the shortest route possible from generator to user, so the farther away you are from a power plant, as the power lines run, the less likely you are to be using electrons from it. So even if you are paying for electrons from a green provider three states away, you may still be using electrons generated at the nearby nuclear plant. However, by participating in these green power programs, you *will* be increasing the amount of renewable energy in the system, even if your household is not necessarily the one using it specifically.

Besides the truly green power alternatives, which are all recent comers with respect to utility-scale applications, one pseudo-green electrical generation power source has been in use for decades: waste to energy facilities have burned garbage for at least 30 years in the United States. There has been substantial debate about calling incinerators sources of "green" power. It is true that trash will be landfilled somewhere if it is not burned, and trash sure appears to be a renewable resource.

Burning garbage releases many different kinds of pollutants. Like most fossil fuels, incinerators emit nitrogen and sulfur oxide compounds into the atmosphere. These combine with ozone and water to create acid rain and smog. Like coal plants, incinerators also release toxic metals as airborne particulate waste. Mercury, nickel, and other metals are poisonous to most animals, including humans, when ingested via respiration. Finally, there is a certain amount of energy needed to acquire, transport, sort the garbage before it is burned, and that is not free either. So calling waste incinerators producers of "green" energy is problematic. If your city has a waste to energy facility, do what you can to ensure it is operating at or better than the acceptable pollution levels for the cleanest utility plants. If it is not among the cleanest and cannot be fixed, then campaign either to get it replaced with a newer model or to shut it down.

Solar Power in the City

Many people think that solar power and off-the-grid living requires a secluded rural paradise to experience. However, solar power enthusiasts live deep in the heart of many cities. Solar electricity and solar heated domestic hot water (DHW) are done in the city as well, but without the huge wood lot, the sprained back, and the blisters from chopping your winter heating fuel.

More and more infill construction is being seen in older city neighborhoods.[5] And as these new buildings are constructed, the opportunity exists to build buildings with more solar attributes. Simple architectural details, like where the windows are placed, can radically effect the amount of energy a house uses. Solar design principles suggest that if heating the building is generally more important than cooling it over the course of the year, large glass areas (windows and some doors) should be oriented towards the Equator—that's south for those living in the northern hemisphere. This allows the building to soak up the maximum amount of heat in the winter just by leaving the curtains open., which can substantially reduce the heating bill for the structure. This kind of design, where overhangs, curtains, and the sun do all of the work, is referred to as "passive solar" (as opposed to "active solar" which means there is a machine with moving parts involved: motors, pumps, etc.).

Not everyone pays attention to these details, however, as David Boyce, a solar power enthusiast in Minneapolis, MN, puts it so well:

> I think that the hard part of solar in the city, and I'm working on this with some other folks, is that a lot of streets and the way cities are set up are not conducive to putting solar on your house. You get mature trees, and everybody likes to have mature trees, they have a lot of goods things going for them, but you run into shading problems. I know a guy who has a house in Minneapolis and he has solar hot air on his house and solar hot water. He had to look for months because in Minneapolis all the streets are set out north-south, so your house is either facing east or west; your house is not facing south. He finally found one where there was a cemetery across the street to the south. The house is on the corner so he could use the whole south side of his house to do these things on and he was confident that there wasn't any building going to be built across the street.

> So that consciousness hasn't seeped into people: city planning, architecture in general, you know, all these plats. You drive around and see all these huge McMansions that could, with just a little bit of moving the glass panes from one side of the house to the other, could be great [passive solar buildings]. But I see a whole wall of glass facing [the wrong way for passive solar input] because they don't care which way they are sitting on the lot. They want [the windows] to face the street. That's it. They don't care which way the street is.

David is also working on a plan with a local business to set up a power cooperative using the roof of the business as the mounting place for the solar panels. Part of the incentive to the cooperative members is discounted or free merchandise from the business based on the amount of energy generated. So even if your lot and structures are oriented such that solar power is impractical for you, this neighborhood version of the utility companies' Green

Power program makes economic sense and allows you to directly participate.

Unless your lot is in a registered architectural conservation district or the neighborhood association is active in enforcing the neighborhood covenants, you are often free to build a structure that suits you as long as it conforms to current building code. Even if you face covenant or historic restrictions, however, you have significant solar possibilities. Many styles of older homes had significant solar designs built in because heating and cooling systems from that architectural period were either unavailable or too expensive.

For the real solar enthusiast interested in a historic buildings, there are slate roof tiles with built-in photovoltaic (PV) panels.[6] For more modern buildings that use three-tab, asphalt shingles (in black or very dark blue), there are PV panels that have the same form factor and mechanical function as a conventional asphalt or organic-mat three-tab shingle and generate electricity when the sun shines on them.[7] Some historic buildings have crimped, galvanized, sheet-metal roofs: trimmable-to-length PV panels can now be laid in the channels of the roof.[8] For buildings with flat roofs, PV and domestic hot water panels can be bolted to commercially available racks called skid pans,[9] eliminating the need to penetrate the roofing membrane and invite water leaks. These "temporary" panels are often hidden behind the building façade. Since they are invisible from street level, historic building codes and strict covenants can often be successfully navigated.

Many solar options are available to the urban dweller. A note of caution, however: many people find the various sorts of solar panels to be "ugly". Some will make wildly inaccurate health claims they think will help prevent construction. Yet others will fret about panels, racks, or other objects self-destructing, spreading chaos and damage in the disintegrating piece's paths.[10] So you have to get your neighbors involved early. Sit down with your architect, builder, or installer and come up with some concept drawings. With a decent computer graphics package, you might even be able to patch together some photo-realistic graphics that show your proposed design's final "look." Then go chat with all the neighbors, and we do mean *all* the neighbors. Get them to sign off on your project This may mean you have to modify your design to answer your neighbor's fears about property values or whatever. Make reasonable changes or drop the project; going to court just is not worth it unless you have money to burn. With all your neighbors in agreement, if someone raises some far-fetched objection when you are getting your project approved by the appropriate city authorities, you will have the local neighborhood on your side and their signatures to prove it.

Of course, you do not have to own your own building as long as your landlord is cooperative. There are cases where renters have installed PV panels with the building owner's approval. A couple of students at the University of Wisconsin-Madison even made their own winter-only passive refrigeration unit out of an open window and a storage chest. They also created a bicycle-powered electric generator to power their TV, and used PV panels mounted temporarily on an awning and on the roof of the apartment, with the landlady's approval.[11] Other renters have made small and inexpensive PV systems that are easy to put up and take down, with minimal change to the landlord's building[12]. You just have to convince your landlord that you will not damage the building in any way before you embark on your solar project. Whether you live in an apartment downtown or own your own plot on the city fringes, you can still participate in the solar economy if you want to! There is absolutely no need to move to rural anywhere to benefit from solar energy.

How much you benefit from solar energy depends mostly on how much energy you use. If you can reduce your energy needs below the amount a reasonably sized system for your space can generate and store, then there is no need to be plugged into the electrical grid at all. You can call the power company up and get them to disconnect you, and therefore not pay a monthly bill. Most city dwellers will not have enough space to put in a large enough system to do this though, so they install a "peak shaving" system. The system is sized to fit the purchaser's budget, not their actual usage. The system is connected to the electrical grid[13] and the owner sells any excess power back to their utility.[14]

At the time of this writing, peak shaving systems are not financially feasible from a strict money perspective except in the few states that offer large subsidies. However, most people wanting to do solar power are not looking at accounting for every last penny: they want to do it to lighten their footprint on the earth[15] or it is their hobby. Also, most solar equipment is falling in price and improving in ease of installation as more and more people get interested in the technology. The quality problems that plagued these systems in the 1970s have been solved; the "true believers" have kept at it until they got it right. Most equipment now sold new is backed by multi-year warranties from the manufacturer or installer and is certified for safety.

A reputable installer will not only train you to use your system, but they will help you select the best quality gear your budget will allow. Just about every state has a cadre of installation companies that size, sell, and support solar electrical and DHW systems. If you are thinking seriously about installing a solar system, find a local installer. They can tell you what works in your area and what does not. They will also have established a working relationship with all the appropriate authorities in most cases: they can help you navigate the city, county, and possibly state and federal, rules you have to comply with as well.

Practical To Dos

- Install low-flow shower heads and faucet aerators and fix any drips or running toilets to save water and money.
- Install ceiling fans and turn up your thermostat in the summer a few degrees.
- Wear more clothes in the winter, and turn down the heat a few degrees.

- Check your water heater temperature and see if you can turn the temperature down.
- Perform proper maintenance on your appliances so they can run as efficiently as possible.
- When replacing appliances, consider Energy Star rated appliances first.
- Check your library for *Home Power* magazine or donate a subscription if they don't have it.
- Look for and attend a solar home tour in your area; there are more than you think.
- Research passive and active solar building techniques and see what you can use in your existing or planned building.
- Contact your local chapter of the American Solar Energy Society or Solar Energy Industries Association (or the equivalents for your area) for a list of nearby contractors.
- Consider your electrical utility's green power program carefully.
- Check out the nearest solar energy fair (MREF, SOLWEST, etc.) for a great time, good information, and tons of renewable energy equipment (toys).

Library Guide

- *Home Power* magazine
- *Practical Photovoltaics: Electricity from Solar Cells* by Richard J. Komp
- *Consumer's Guide to Effective Environmental Choices* by Michael Brower and Warren Leon
- *The Complete Guide to Remodeling Your Basement* by Gary D. Branson
- *A Consumer's Guide to Home Improvement, Renovation, and Repair* , Robert M. Santucci, et. al.
- *Superhouse: The Next Generation of Passive Solar Energy Saving Houses* by Don Metz
- *Consumer Guide to Home Energy Savings*, published by the American Council for an Energy-Efficient Economy

Internet Resources

www.doe.gov
www.hud.gov/owning/index.cfm
www.homepower.com (includes a list of active installers of solar
     energy systems)
www.the-mrea.org
www.nrel.edu
www.solarwall.com
www.realgoods.com
www.energystar.gov
www.gridlesshome.com/index.html

Search Terms

net metering
green energy providers
green energy programs
Million Solar Roofs
R-value
energy saving
water saving
home repair
compact fluorescents

CHAPTER 21

HOUSING

In the introduction section of the book, we talked about how you don't need five acres of land to live a voluntarily simple life. In fact, living in an apartment in a city can allow you to leave less of an impact on the earth than you would by living on a small farm in the middle of nowhere.

Living in a city can also be cost-effective. We are not going to pretend that urban real estate is cheap. Home prices and rents (unless rent-controlled) are higher, in general, in bigger metropolitan areas, and have skyrocketed in many parts of the country in recent years. But when considering where to live, you should weigh your cost in life energy of an urban home vs. a McMansion at the end of a long commute. See our chapter, "More Money," for instructions from *Your Money or Your Life* on how to measure your life energy by calculating your real hourly wage. In many cases, even though your real estate costs are higher in a city, your other costs will be cheaper, and could, in fact, completely offset your higher housing costs.

Much of this book is designed to give you ideas for lowering these other expenditures. If you live in a city, you can get rid of your car and take public transportation nearly everywhere; if you want to change careers or take a second job, your opportunities are far greater. Living in the city means a culturally diverse world of entertainment is just down the street; this makes it easier to avoid the shopping-as-hobby trap and the boob tube trap. See related chapters for more on all of these.

But even in a city, you can find cheap housing alternatives. These alternatives are almost as numerous as there are city-dwelling Simplifiers. We have listed some of the most common below. Consider our list a jumping-off place; with a little brainstorming, you can find the alternative that is exactly right for you.

Living Spaces of the Frugal and Unknown

In general, to save money on housing in the city, think small. *Rent, do not buy.* Lynne has owned two houses, and now chooses to rent a 1,500-square-foot townhouse. She was never able to own a house long enough to recoup her investment; every time she sold, she lost thousands. Also, it seemed that every time she turned around, something needed to be fixed, and as the saying goes, when something goes wrong with your house, all you have to do is throw $100 bills at the problem until it goes away. The constant repair costs ate up the tax break she got from owning her own place. As a single mother, Lynne finds renting simpler. Yes, her housing costs can go up every year, but they did with her adjustable-rate mortgage too; and now when something breaks, she calls maintenance to get it fixed. The end-unit townhouse she now rents gives her the feel of having her own home. The management company allows tenants to plant flowers, which gives Lynne an outlet when the urge to garden strikes. She and her family live in a stable, single-family neighborhood where she could never afford to buy.

Apartments do offer less space, but that can be a good thing. Jane Zeender lives in an apartment in Arlington, VA, with her husband and toddler son. She says they get less criticism from family members for their frugal lifestyle because their living space is small: "[W]e have a 940 square foot apartment … because it costs a lot of money to live in a small place in the middle of the city. So that we don't have to feel sucked in, to have to buy a lot of furniture or do all those things, because there's no space to put anything."

Fred Ecks is also comfortable in his small space, a 307-square-foot studio apartment in San Francisco: "I picked my home for its price and location. It's a perfect size for me, which helps me to avoid accumulating stuff I don't need, and the price was lower than anything else in San Francisco. The location is ideal, right in the civic center, so I can walk everywhere. I stay fit, and don't need a car at all...."

Buy an older place and fix it up. Existing housing is usually cheaper initially than new construction because the developers' costs have long since been recouped. Judge your renovation prospects carefully, however. Gutting a building and renovating it up to current building codes may be more expensive than just demolishing it and starting over, even if you do all the work yourself.

Older places are smaller, which can help you keep your inventory of personal stuff down. In 1950, an average single family home measured just over 1,000 square feet, a far cry from today's average of 2,200 square feet. This same period saw the average family size shrink from 3.4 to 2.6 per household.

Simplifiers Doug and Wendy Carroll bought an old house in their St. Louis neighborhood. The house is in a constant state of renovation, but Wendy says they love the place and their city neighborhood. "[W]e ended up in this neighborhood because we kept coming back to it again and again and again. And because it's so beautiful; I've always liked Victorian architecture...."

Buy, but rent out part. Many people find this is a great way to afford the higher housing prices in a city. You could buy a small apartment building or a big, old house that has been subdivided into apartments, and live in one flat while renting out the rest. Of course, you should think twice about this alternative if you have no desire to be a landlord, or if you are not handy at home repairs.

Work as an apartment caretaker or rental agent. If you *are* handy but do not want the hassle of being the landlord, or if you enjoy customer service, you could get a job with an apartment management company. Free or reduced rent is usually one of the benefits.

Other types of businesses also sometimes hire on-site care-takers. Funeral homes, for example, need to have someone there twenty-four hours a day, and so may hire a caretaker to live there. Kevin Cornwell says one of his brothers did this for a while. We would understand if you do not want to live in a funeral home, but you could think about other types of businesses that also need a twenty-four-hour presence and see whether you could live on-site in exchange for a free place to stay.

Work as a house sitter. People who will be living away from home for several months — on a job assignment out of the coun-try, on sabbatical, or flown south for the winter — often look for someone to live in their house while they are gone. The house sitter's job is to keep the place clean and keep an eye on the owner's belongings. The down side to this is that you have to move fre-quently (which could also be a plus, if it keeps you from accumu-lating too much stuff of your own!). As the population ages, we may start seeing more people with health care skills "working from home". Although financially independent, Kevin Cornwell has a plan if housing just does not work out: "There are two widows who live by themselves in 1500-2000 square foot houses across the street. I have said a whole bunch of times that I would move in with them and help take care of them rather than go back to work full time."

Take a room in a group home. Gretchen Kinder moved into an eight-person co-op just outside Boston more than two years ago in order to spend more time with her significant other. "[W]e are in a three-story house nestled on top of a small hill. We have eight bedrooms, two living rooms (one of which we use for our biweekly potluck and folk sings, the other is more of a catchall room), a large kitchen with seating for up to about 18, an enclosed second floor porch, and three additional open porches, three full bathrooms, garage, basement, and a pantry/larder."

Gretchen enjoys the atmosphere and the activities. Her co-op shares power tools, transportation, and a bulk buying program with another co-op nearby, and the two co-ops together are organizing a nonprofit corporation that will serve as a property manager for co-op homes in their area.

Gretchen says noise is not a problem in her house because all of the residents are either graduate students or professionals and so appreciate their peace and quiet. The house also has a formal system for airing gripes among housemates. But do not think that co-ops are just for college kids. Gretchen says one of her housemates is a 77-year-old writer.

Move into an intentional community, or start one of your own. Group homes can be a kind of intentional community, with members meeting regularly for meals and sharing house chores equally. But the term "intentional community" usually means something more elaborate: several families agree to buy a plot of land together, building their houses around a community center or meeting house. Each family helps to maintain the community center. Often, residents commit to eating some meals together in the community center. The intentional community becomes an extended family for its residents.

Because most cities are already pretty well developed, it is sometimes difficult to locate an intentional community within a city. However, it has been done. Hearthstone in Denver is a case in point. Community members there redeveloped part of a former amusement park site for their intentional community. If you are interested in forming your own intentional community, it may be easier for you to recruit like-minded people in a larger, urban area. For example, alex glenlee would prefer a city-based intentional community:

> I'd rather do that in the city. No, i'm not [one of the] commune-type guys: that is, going to go out into the country, and let's break the land, and let's build our own isolated community. i think there's some really good things that go on with things like cooperative housing, where people share and help each other. They have a common kitchen and they have some common recreation areas and that sort of thing. Along the lines of the sort of things that

are being done in Denmark and Scandinavia. They do
this in major centers and urban areas.

Look for housing alternatives, such as houseboats. Lindi Hulse and
her now ex-husband lived full-time on a thirty-foot sailboat in
Long Beach, CA: "It was right in downtown Long Beach, cheap
(under $300 per month dock fee including utilities), and easy to
maintain. Lots of fun, too!" Her ex continued to live on the boat
after they split. Those who have lived aboard a boat say it is a
great boot camp for divorcing you from your stuff: there is so
little storage space aboard a boat that you cannot own more stuff
than you really need.

Live in a city-within-a-city. Arlington County, VA, just across the
Potomac River from Washington, DC, has concentrated on devel-
oping neighborhoods around subway stops, with jobs, retail options, housing and transportation all within walking distance. Jane
Zeender lives in Crystal City, one of the first such developments
in Arlington. Her husband walks to work, and a network of tun-
nels connects their high-rise apartment building to shops, the post
office, and the Metro. A short walk takes them to the Potomac
River. A bike path leads to Ronald Reagan National Airport, or
they can take the Metro one stop to get there.

Other new neighborhoods in Arlington, such as Pentagon Row
in Pentagon City, are patterned after European city spaces. Retail
space is on the ground floor, apartments or condos are above,
and public transit is nearby.

New Housing in Old Neighborhoods

You may be considering buying one of the new townhouses
or condos springing up on small parcels of urban land in your
city. We suggest that you consider this move carefully.

The practice of building new housing on city lots, sometimes
by "scraping off" a small, existing house to make way for a bigger
house or a row of townhouses, is known as "in-fill development."
It is supposed to be a panacea for urban sprawl. No new infra-

structure is needed: streets, sewer and water pipes, and school buildings are already in place. New buildings create a bigger tax base for the city, with more townhouse owners per square yard to pay property taxes, shop at local stores, etc. Construction jobs are created.

But the construction disrupts traffic and neighborhood tranquility. Streets and schools may already be overloaded. Putting fifty families where once one, or none, lived is going to create a need for road improvements and maybe temporary classrooms at the neighborhood school. Water and sewer systems will also feel pressure from increased usage. City bureaucrats, police, firefighters, housing inspectors, dogcatchers, and all the other public servants will have more work to do. All this costs money — maybe more money than the city will collect in new property taxes.

Even with in-fill development, there is still an environmental cost. New houses require the cutting of trees to make lumber, and the manufacture of other construction materials, and most developers are unlikely to use green products.

You may also find that your quality of life suffers. You may find that so many housing units have been built on a single parcel that your windows are just a few feet from your neighbor's.

There is another human cost, too. The buildings that are scraped off are often older housing stock – aging apartment complexes or small houses. The people who live in such places are often there because they cannot afford anything else. Now they must find new homes. As their neighborhood gentrifies, they may very well not be able to afford another place near their old home. In other words, poor people are the ones who pay the real price for in-fill development.

In response to complaints from residents near such in-fill development sites, cities and state legislatures have begun imposing restrictions on in-fill developments, including restrictions on housing density and style, inclusion of affordable housing, maximum size of house relative to lot size, etc. While these rules can help mitigate the negative effects of in-fill development, it is likely that they will not get rid of all of them. If you have an interest in social justice or in helping the environment, consider buying or renting existing housing stock, rather than something brand new.

You may see the term "smart growth" used by some developers doing in-fill development. Ill-planned in-fill development is not the same as smart growth. Smart growth is about designing a community, not a block.

The Downside

City living does have its drawbacks. Housing is more expensive, as we have said, and the quality of public education in inner-city school districts can range from fair to battle zone.

But solutions exist, as we have outlined above. Do not forget that the idyllic McMansion in the far-flung exurbs comes with what could easily be a long, nightmarish commute. Do the math. You might well find that the cost of commuting (having to own one or more cars, buying gas and oil, wear and tear devaluing the car, wasting your life energy while parked on the expressway twice a day, having to make special appointments to get your car maintained, etc.) quickly eats up your housing savings. At that point, it becomes a quality-of-life question: Is your life better for spending hours parked on the expressway while owning a big house? Or would you be better off paying more for housing closer in, walking to work, and spending your new-found free time with family, friends and hobbies you do not have time for now?

The education problem is a tougher nut to crack for your school aged kids. Private schools are an option, albeit an expensive one. Home schooling has its own pluses and minuses. You could also compromise: live in the city before you have kids, move to a better school district for raising the kids, then move back to the city when the kids have moved out. Or you could search for the holy grail: a decently-priced home in a good urban school district. A close-in suburb may be your best bet for this strategy. This is, in fact, what Lynne chose to do: Alexandria, VA, is less than 20 miles from Washington, DC, with a good school system, reasonable rents, and an easy commute to her job.

In sum, do not fall into the trap of believing that the city living has to be expensive, and the only way to afford it is to move to the exurbs. Alternatives do exist.

Practical To Dos

- Do the math. Living in a city might well be cheaper in terms of your life energy than living in the exurbs.
- Consider whether renting would be better for you than buying.
- Winnow your stuff so that you can live in a smaller space.
- Think about getting a job that includes a free place to live: apartment caretaker, house sitter, etc.
- Take in a boarder.
- Look into moving into a group home.
- Consider joining an intentional community, or starting one of your own.
- If you must buy, buy existing housing stock.

Library Guide

- *Your Money or Your Life* by Joe Dominguez and Vicki Robin
- *Divorce Your Car* by Katie Alvord
- *Suburban Nation: The Rise of Sprawl and the Decline of the American Dream* by Andres Duany, Elizabeth Plater-Zyberk, and Jeff Speck
- *Caretaker Gazette*

Internet Resources

www.ic.org (provides a list of intentional communities throughout the world)
www.caretaker.org
www.epa.gov (includes more information on smart growth)

Search Terms

intentional community
house sitting
in-fill development
caretaker
"community land trust"
"smart growth"

CHAPTER 22

FINDING TIME

Time is the most precious of the "commodities" we have. We cannot buy any for our personal use, though we sell our personal time regularly. We cannot put any in the bank. Indeed, we do not even know exactly how much we have left in our lives. So in our daily lives you would think that we would spend a little time to pause and reflect on our time and how well we are using it. Self-reflection of this sort ensures that we are doing what we want to be doing, and helps us enjoy each moment of activity.

No matter where we live—city or small town or out in the country—it seems like we all struggle to find the time to do what we want to do.

Finding Time to Get the Important Stuff Done

If you are like the vast majority of U.S. consumers, you are in warp drive most of the day. Snag some breakfast, if any, on the way to the car. Drop the kids off at school or daycare and screech into work at the last possible instant. Run errands at lunch or eat at your desk while you dig through e-mail. After work, more errands, grab dinner from somewhere, and run the kids around. Go back home, tuck in the children after homework is done, clean a bit or vegetate in front of the boob tube. Then crash for six hours or so, dreaming about tomorrow's schedule all night and wondering how things ever got this crazy (to quote the Eagles) as you drift off to sleep. Get up tomorrow and repeat until the weekend rolls around. And nowhere in there is there time to re-ally think through why you are flying through all these activities.

Sound familiar? If so, you are not alone. In survey after sur-vey, study after study, Americans in particular are expressing a feeling of "time famine" — so much so that they say they would give up pay at work for a less time-consuming job. In *The Over-worked American*, Juliet Schor quotes a 1987 U.S. Department of Labor study in which 84 percent of respondents said they would trade part or all of a raise for more free time, and 47 percent said they would trade a whole 10-percent raise for more free time.[1] Americans feel as if there are not enough hours in the day to do all the things that must be done. Many feel like they are on the work-and-spend treadmill or they are a rat in the rat race. The majority of people have consistently overloaded their lives. The result is a feeling of constantly being rushed. Juli Parsons knows the feeling:

> I worked for a national chain of copy centers for eleven years. The last position I held was regional operations manager, which entailed air travel two to three times per month and daily driving of an hour or more to visit the branches I supervised to ensure they met revenue and profit objectives. … I was working 80-plus hours per week with two little kids at home, making piles of money but incred-ibly stressed out and miserable. I used all my wretched insomnia hours in the dead of night to read all the books on Voluntary Simplicity that I could find… The last few months [of work] were so unbelievably stressful and hor-rible that I was able to quit when my third child was born and *never look back*.

Juli's job experience is the same agony as many others experi-ence today, every working day. The sad part is that it does not have to be this way. Millions of people have "downshifted" to a saner life. Gretchen Kinder of Boston is one of them. She also gave up a job that involved a lot of travel: "After three and a half years, [I] realized that I felt horrible about what I was doing. I hated the driving – I drove all over the state…. Driving made me

anxious. I was biting my nails all the time and eating a lot. And I
realized that it just wasn't healthy for me to be driving around so
much, nor was it good for the environment. But for me personally, it just wasn't a useful way of spending my time. It wasn't
making me happy. And I also realized that I wanted to be...working
closer to home..."

Gretchen now works for a non-profit company in Boston that
counsels wealthy people on how they can live in accordance with
their values. By spending less time on the road, she has freed up
time in her life to get to know her co-op housemates and her
neighborhood, and to spend more time with her significant other.

Jef Murray and his wife, Lorraine, were living the classic American version of the Good Life in Atlanta, GA: two high-stress careers, two incomes, two houses, two cars, and a lot of dissatisfaction and doubts about the future:

> I was an engineer. I did electrical engineering ... inte-
> grated circuit design and software design and all this other
> stuff. Lorraine was an editor – she was in charge of all the
> publications that came out of Kennesaw University in
> Marietta... And we were both working the 40-, 50-, 60-
> hour sorts of workweeks, very high stress, lots of com-
> mute time – particularly for Lorraine – and we were mak-
> ing an awful lot of money. ... And I kind of looked for-
> ward ... and I was thinking: "You know, by the time I'm
> 40, I'm going to hate this job. I'm going to absolutely hate
> what I'm doing." And right around that time, a friend
> gave us a copy of *Your Money or Your Life*. It had just been
> published. And I kind of tore through it; didn't sleep for
> a couple of weeks. I recognized all of the worst symp-
> toms of being caught on the earn-and-spend treadmill ...
> in Lorraine and me, and in our situation.

That was in 1992. By 1997, the couple had sold their vacation
home, and both had quit their high-stress jobs. If it were not for
their need for health insurance, the Murrays could have both quit
paid work entirely. Instead, they now both work half-time at Emory
University, a mile and a half from their home, for health insurance

benefits. In their spare time, Lorraine is a writer — her first book, a collection of theological essays, is due out in the spring of 2002 — and Jef is a wildlife artist who has donated his work to organizations such as the Nature Conservancy and Zoo Atlanta.

You do not have to be financially independent or quit your job completely, though being "rich" certainly makes this easier. Katherine Carter is a single parent of three small children and works as a hospice nurse in a smaller city. Her actions demonstrate that having knowledge of your real needs and wants and, truth be told, a certain amount of raw grit, can get you what you most value. She went to part-time work so she could ensure what was most important to her: "I see that my kids need more time with me and less in the company of professional caregivers, no matter how good they are. This choice [part time work] is *only* possible because I have been on the path of Voluntary Simplicity for awhile, and I know what our 'real' expenses are."

Gain Control of Your Life

You can do a number of things to gain control over your life. The first thing you need to do is make a log of what you do with your time. For many of us, this is as simple as opening our planner or turning on our electronic organizer and filling in a few blanks. If you do not use a planning tool, then keep a small notebook or note card with you for a week or month and record the time whenever you change tasks. Then tally the amount of time you spent on each activity. Be careful to consider the preparation and travel time for each of the activities you see listed in your notes. You may find that you are spending more time traveling to and from an activity than you spend actually doing the activity! You may even find that you end up with more than 24 hours of work in your day, as a result of multitasking. No wonder we are so tired.

Many of us are so caught up in the hustle that we cannot find ten minutes to think about priorities. So give yourself a time out.

Take a day off, unplug all the electronics (especially the phone and the pager), and think about what is really important to. You could even take a monastery retreat for a few days of silence and reflection.[2]

In other words, unplug yourself as much as you can from the warp drive for a time and consider your deepest values. Now sit down with a pen and paper and list your dearest priorities and goals. What, if it does not happen, will make you ask to stop the world and get off? What, if it looks like it will not happen, will make you stop everything until it does happen? What else is important to you? What are the relative rankings of all these things you consider important? Write them down on a piece of paper in some kind of priority order. Be honest; this is just for you, not your mate or boss or kids.

Now you have a grip on where you are *really* spending your time, and on your real priorities. Look at your schedule. Which activities really represent your values in action, and which return little or no value to you? In his book *Managing Management Time*, William Oncken, Jr., calls these "monkeys" on your back: tasks that require management action to complete.[3] We like to think of them as "time sucks": tasks that leach away your life energy with no payback. Obviously, you cannot escape some time sucks. Would you be able to rearrange your life to minimize their suction? Or can you turn them from time sucks into windows of opportunity? For example, can changing your commute from car to bus give you time to read all those books and magazines you have been accumulating to read "someday"?

Look again at the time sucks on your schedule. How did those leeches get stuck on you anyway? What will it take to get them off? How many of these time sucks can you give away? Which leeches can you just say no to and ignore until they die from lack of attention? The trouble with many of our activities is that they seemed like a good idea at the time, but turn out to be enormous time wasters later. The faster you can cut these time sucks loose, the faster your time will free up for the things that are important to you. Even better is not collecting the time sucks in the first place; pleasantly saying "no" when appropriate will save you a lot of grief in the long run.[4]

Look at your work needs carefully. Can you change your scheduled shift, work flextime, work part time, or work from home? One of Jonathan's neighbors gave up a supervisor position on second shift, thereby giving up a better paying position as well as shift differential, for a regular welding job on first shift. The benefit to him was staying married and being able to help raise his kids, something the extra money could not buy.

Do you truly need to carry a pager or cell phone, or is it just a convenient vehicle for someone else to use in order to drop time sucks on you at all hours? What would you miss by not having it? Is there a way to mitigate that loss and come out with more freedom?

Make these time sinks understand that "no" means "no", and if they do not agree, eliminate them from your life. That might be a tall order in some cases, but if these people or activities are conflicting with your values, elimination from your life is not too high a penalty for you to pay, and it will not hurt them any. Changing jobs is not the end of the world in today's society, and neither is taking time off from a cause you believe in to do something more important to you. Juli Parsons experienced this in the political arena:

> I became involved in local politics last year and found causes worth fighting for, friends I enjoyed, and a sense of being good at something beyond wiping noses and bottoms. Unfortunately, it's all too easy to get sucked into spending all waking moments, as well as some moments while you should be sleeping, thinking about or working on political causes, and the result was a miserable family. I reverted to the convenience foods, filthy house, and lack of patience with my kids that I so disliked when I worked. I started to hate my day-to-day life and was having the insomnia at night that had plagued me during my working years. I finished my work on the committee I'd volunteered for and then backed off.

Even with the best of intentions, time sucks can multiply before you are aware there is a problem. The rest of the ideas below may or may not fit your specific situation. Take what you can and discard the rest.

Look at your hobbies. Do you really want to play golf (or any other hobby activity really, but we will pick on golf here) that badly? Or are you just escaping from your frenzied schedule? Or is it even an escape? How often have you decided to take a Saturday and "work on your golf game"? Is there any intrinsic value to whacking a bucket of balls when the same tension release could be achieved by splitting wood or any of the other things you need to hammer on around the house? And if this really is an escape from your frenzied work life, why are your cell phone and pager with you? If all you really wanted is some exercise, and a good long stroll is just the thing, why make a competition of it? It was Mark Twain who said, "Golf is a good walk spoiled." Save your greens fees and stroll the local parks for the same amount of time, and probably for free.

Look at your "incompletions" – all those things you have not managed to finish yet. Do you even care anymore? If you really do mean to get back to it "real soon now", is it still necessary for you to do it or can someone else finish the job you have started? The finisher in the project might well be someone completely unrelated to you; you could sell or donate that half-completed craft project to someone else who might be delighted to finish what you started.

Or you could just forget about the idea altogether. Jonathan keeps a to-do list of things that need to get done eventually. Some of the items on the list have been there, literally, for a decade or more. These are items that have value, but less value than anything else he needs to do. After this list got to be three pages long, he reviewed it and threw away over half the items as no longer important.

Lynne takes a different tack. She has several lists: quick things to do today, things that have to be done this weekend, and longer-term goals. If an item gets on a list, she makes a point to do it. Very few items get carried over from one list to another. This keeps the size of her to-do list manageable, which keeps her from feeling overwhelmed at the amount of stuff left to do. It also helps her recognize time sucks: if a leech has been carried over on several lists, she knows that she never intended to do it anyway, and it's time to either forget about it or get somebody else to do it.

Perhaps the biggest time sucks today are electronic ones: primarily watching TV (playing video or computer games counts as TV time in this respect) and surfing the Internet. Television is a big, if not the biggest, time waster. TV is also bad for both you and your wallet. Free your mind *and time*; kill your TV. See the "Downsizing Your TV" chapter for reasons why reducing or eliminating TV watching is an all-around good thing to do.

Some of those reasons would also apply to those of us who have traded our TV watching time for Internet surfing time. The Internet is not ad-free, any more than TV is ad-free. While the 'Net can be a time saver, it can also be a giant time suck. Who has not looked up from the monitor, bleary-eyed, to find that two or three hours have disappeared? Of course, you do not have to be online to waste time on the computer: just ask your favorite game addict, if you can pry him away from his joystick. Ultimately, you have to be the judge of whether the hours you spend on your computer are in accordance with your values, or whether you could be sleeping, exercising, or relating to your family instead.

Practical To Dos

- Think about your real values; write them down.
- Figure out what you are spending your time on.
- Eliminate activities that don't fit your values.
- Identify your time sucks and dump them.
- Review your to-do list(s) with an eye toward delegating or eliminating some items.
- Reduce or eliminate TV time.

Library Guide

- *The Overspent American* by Juliet Schor
- *Downshifting: How to Work Less and Enjoy Life More* by John Drake
- *The Seven Habits of Highly Effective People* by Stephen Covey
- *Your Money Or Your Life* by Joe Dominguez and Vicki Robin

Internet Resources

www.newdream.org
www.simpleliving.net (especially the discussion boards)
www.barberasher.com

Search Terms

downshifting
voluntary simplicity
time management

CHAPTER 23

YOUR HOME AS ART

Putting the terms Voluntary Simplicity and home decorating in the same sentence would seem to make for an oxymoron. But everyone expresses their own taste with décor, and Simplifiers do decorate their homes—not all of them in the "early flea market" style.

Shabby Chic

Some time back, "shabby chic" was all the rage in decorating. The idea was to haunt yard sales, flea markets and junk shops to find furniture that required rehabbing, as well as old quilts that one could turn into drapes, tablecloths, and so forth. The result was supposed to be a living room that resembled a Victorian parlor. The practical result was a huge increase in the price of old quilts and the upscaling of many junk stores to "antique shops" so that the owners could double their prices.

Since the trendsetters have now moved on, it is once again possible to find cheap used home décor. Living in a city gives you a wide selection of sources for cheap furnishings. Check out yard sales, thrift stores, consignment shops and, yes, even flea markets, for furniture and accessories that have some life left in them. "Free" piles left on front lawns or curbs and Dumpster diving can be an amazing source of stuff, too. Many times people throw or give away perfectly good stuff.

If you prefer shopping online, Goodwill has an online auction site that features all kinds of used stuff, including clothing, furniture, electronics, and the celebrated bric-a-brac. Think a smaller, quirkier eBay, without the featured retailers. At least if you are spending money at Goodwill, you know that your dollars are going to a good cause. And nobody needs to know that you got your new wall plaques at the Goodwill unless you choose to tell them. Jonathan uses Goodwill for picture frames, work clothes, and the odd kitchen gadget he cannot live without.

Sometimes, all that is needed is a good stripping and refinishing for a wooden piece, or some new cushions or fabric for an upholstered piece. Living in a city gives you access to classes where you can learn furniture rehabilitation skills. Your local community college may offer classes in furniture making or refinishing and upholstery; fabric stores offer classes in sewing and quilting. The Simple Living Network offers a series of free-for-the-downloading pamphlets that give instructions for such "lost arts" as chair caning and seat weaving.

While it is nice to know how to sew, upholster a chair, or refinish furniture, it is not always necessary. Flea market finds can be spruced up with slip covers, cushions, and other inexpensive aesthetic improvements. Lynne picked up a sofa at a flea market in Denver for $30 and has spent only $60 over the last four years to keep it serviceable and looking nice. It's hard to beat a $90 sofa, especially if you only use it in a basement room or other low-traffic area.

It is not just rampant "cheapskateitis" that pushes Simplifiers toward rehabbing rather than buying new. It is certainly cheaper to buy used, but there is also an environmental cost to buying new furniture. Trees must be cut; fabric must be woven, dyed, and otherwise processed. This takes energy, creates waste, and causes pollution. Some of the exotic woods used in today's furniture are harvested from rainforests, which have already suffered from clear-cutting for food production. In addition, the materials used in some of today's upholstered furniture can give off toxic gases when new or when burned

A New Lease

A technique most often used when remodeling a home, but could be used for interior decorating as well, is the idea of rescuing old items from the junkyard and recycling them into your home. One California couple did just that. They spent weekends rescuing old cars and incorporating them into their home remodeling project. A 924 Porsche windshield serves as roof over the door. Hatchbacks from a couple Volvos were used as the railing at the top of the stairs. The porch railings were made from old truck tailgates.[1]

Not many of us would use old car parts, but plenty of other discarded objects could be made into home decorations or furnishings, as well. The idea is to recycle the items into something useful for your home.

House as Self

Denise Linn, author of *Sacred Space*,[2] views your home (whether it is a house, an apartment, or something else) as an extension of yourself, a reflection of your personality and spirit. For example, if the way you commonly enter your home is cluttered and visually unattractive, she contends that this is a reflection of the way you present yourself to the world. In the same fashion, she sees your bedroom as a sanctuary, the place you recharge. So if you are the life of the party, maybe your bedroom should be a little darker and more nest-like. In sum, you need to create a space that nurtures your inner peace and rebuilds the energy you need to face each day.

Linn also suggests that you surround yourself with special objects:
• Sacred objects, or those that come from your loved ones or spiritual guides.
• Hand-made objects that impress you with their artistic value and "feel right" in your space.

- Natural objects, which bring more "life" with them than mechanical creations.
- Pets, which reflect who you perceive yourself as and demonstrate your love in the care you provide for them.
- Mirrors, which can change the view or the perceived size of a room, significantly changing the way each person reacts to the space.

Linn believes each thing you choose to bring into your space should be well considered. You should not allow things to multiply without thought, as gimcracks and trinkets often do. Objects in your home should be ones you love, and should add to your energy Anything you hate should be disposed of since it will pull you down every time you see it.

Minimalism: the Zen Aesthetic

Rather than surrounding themselves with toys and stuff, some Simplifiers take simplicity to its limits in their homes. They eliminate not only their clutter, but also much of their furniture. The resulting opening up of the space that surrounds them at home gives them a great deal of peace. Uncluttered surroundings contribute to an uncluttered state of mind. Having less stuff to clean and maintain gives them the space and time to do what they want with their lives.

Look around your home. What could you get rid of? Do you have pictures, chairs, or cabinets whose only purpose is to fill an empty wall? How would it feel to get rid of the furniture and have just the empty wall? Would it fill you with joy to have that much less to dust and take care of? Would it open up some space in your life, or would it make you uncomfortable? Try it and see.

You do not have to get rid of furniture to gain some benefit from this idea. Almost all of us have things that we display simply because they look pretty, or because we think they make a statement about our taste or our abilities. Think about the amount of time you spend dusting, stepping around, repairing and insuring your pretty things, as well as the time you spend worrying about them being stolen, and decide whether your life would be simpler without them.

Not-So-Big Can Be Better

Western culture's acquisitiveness creates a vicious circle: Once we have more stuff, our living space gets crowded, and we think we need a bigger house to put it in. Then, once we have the bigger place, we tend to clutter it up with still more stuff.

This keeps the McMansion developers happy, and it keeps the housewares manufacturers and retailers happy, but it doesn't make *us* happy. And makes at least one architect very unhappy.

Sarah Susanka is a residential architect who has found the big, cookie-cutter McMansions to be soulless. In *The Not So Big House*, Susanka suggests that part of the problem is with the scale of the interior spaces of many new homes:

> The current pattern of building big to allow for quantities of furniture with still more room to spare is more akin to wearing a sack than a tailored suit. It may offer capacity, but at the cost of comfort and charm. Spaciousness, although it can look appealing in a photograph, just isn't conducive to comfort. Many of the huge rooms we see in magazines today are really only comfortable to be in when they are filled with people. For one or two, or for a family, they can be overwhelming. And when they feel overwhelming, they don't get used.[3]

Susanka's solution is to have a living space that may not be huge, but is comfortable for the people who will actually live there. One of Susanka's ideas for building comfort into a home is to include a room for everyone in the family, even for each of the adults, where that person can pursue his or her own passions: from woodworking to yoga, from pottery to prayer. "Children have their own rooms typically, but, once coupled, adults share their private space, leaving no place for what I like to term 'inner listening' and self discovery," Susanka says.

Men have traditionally had a workshop or den to retire to (Lynne's father's refuge was the garage), but women often have not had a similar sanctuary. Their refuge could be rooms such as a formal dining room that the family uses perhaps once or twice a year and just sits there looking stately for the rest of the year; Susanka claimed space for her private room from the attic of her home..

World Decor

Westerners are not the only ones who surround themselves with beauty, but we are among the few who believe we must pay for that beauty. Rather than keeping decorative items that are beautiful for their own sake, native cultures around the world decorate their functional items to make them beautiful. They have to, because they cannot afford to trot down to the nearest big-box store every time the fashion gurus decree a new popular color for blenders.

You might consider taking this approach. Look around your home and turn your creativity loose. You might find that you do not need to make that trip to the big-box store to redecorate. And what you create will be *yours*. You, and not some decorating magazine editor, will get to decide what looks best in your home.

- Hang your "company dishes" or decorative platters on the walls as decorations. When company does come over, take them down and wash once, use until they leave, and then rehang on your walls.
- The ever changing picture. For example, create a shadow box picture frame to use to store your CDs. The CD at the front becomes the picture in the frame. For variety, rotate the CDs featured in the frame. This same idea could be used with books.
- Use storage containers to decorate. Use wicker baskets or decorative boxes to store items such as CDs/cassette tapes, office items, computer accessories such as diskettes, dresser items, etc.

Traditional Art Alternatives

If you feel you must hang pictures on the wall, try a different type of artwork. The most personal would be your own artwork, whether in the form of a sketch, painting, needlework, photograph or something else. Other ideas include:

- Display artwork created by relatives. Obviously it would need to be something that you like.
- Display artwork from local artisans. This might be material from the nearby college or art school that you can buy cheap or have for free just by helping clean out the accumulated art. Jonathan owns the set model for a theatre production he worked on as crew. It is a model of the stage, complete with flys, set pieces, and the paint scheme used for the actual show. Made with mixed media (fabric, wood, cardboard, wire, paint, and hardware cloth), it evokes strong memories of a fascinating show.
- The same fellow who did the stage model also helped Jonathan's wife Pam make stained glass windows for her kitchen cabinet doors. Now Jonathan and Pam can see the dishes in their cabinets and the colors in the stained glass match the colors in the kitchen floor.
- Decorate with pictures of one person, family, or thing per room.

Other Ideas

Here are some other ideas that you can use when decorating:
- Simpler furniture styles can be easier to care for and keep clean. Shaker and Craftsman styles, with simple lines and few crevices, make for a "clean" look and easy dusting.
- If Victoriana or Elizabethan art and furniture are of more interest to you, just be aware that all those rugs and the ornate carvings on the furniture are going to collect dust.
- You can decorate each room with a theme: nautical, seashore, lighthouse, desert Southwest, Western, or even by country. Jonathan's house has a German room that celebrates his wife's German heritage and doubles as the guest bedroom.

- You might decorate each room by a favorite color. Leave the walls painted a neutral color, and use colored objects and wall coverings instead of painting the walls.
- If you crave redecorating regularly, find ways to reuse your existing decorations. Rotating some of your materials through different rooms or storing a small set temporarily out of sight will help keep things fresh.
- Trade decorations with like-minded friends and family.
- Use slipcovers for existing furniture that can be turned over to expose a new color, or have a couple of sets of covers so you can change them once in a while.

Zen or Early Bric-a-Brac?

We realize that in this chapter, we have given you a range of ideas to consider, some of which are contradictory. Not every decorating style appeals to everybody. What VS promotes is the idea that the only person who knows what will make you comfortable and contented is *you* – not a magazine editor, not a retailer, not a McMansion developer. We hope that you have come away with a couple of ideas to try so that you can make your home more comfortable and more welcoming. The happier you are at home, the less you will feel the need to escape – to TV, to the mall, to an all-inclusive resort, and to all the other distractions that complicate our modern lives.

Practical To Dos

- Check yard sales, thrift shops, and junk shops for reclaimable furniture and decorating items.
- Beautify what you have. Learn, or improve your skills in, sewing, upholstery, or furniture refinishing. Make your functional things beautiful.
- Declutter. Consider the things you have on display and decide whether you would be more peaceful if you kept them around to dust, maintain, and look at, or got rid of them.

- Consider minimizing the furniture in your rooms to open up space. A less cluttered look can help bring you a less cluttered mind.
- Design (or retrofit) your house to provide you and your family with sacred space: a refuge for each of you.
- Decorate your house to please yourself.
- Check out your local Community Education program to learn skills you need.

Library Guide

- *The Furniture Doctor*, by George Grotz
- *The Weekend Refinisher* by Bruce Johnson
- *Sacred Space* by Denise Linn
- *The Not So Big House: A Blueprint for the Way We Really Live* by Sarah Susanka

Internet Resources

www.shopgoodwill.com
www.notsobighouse.com
www.simpleliving.net

Search Terms

furniture refinishing
sewing
quilting
upholstering

CHAPTER 24

A FEW FINAL WORDS

If you have read this far, we hope we have made a convincing case that you can live a simpler and saner life in the city. We need to leave you then, with some philosophy about transitioning your indenture from complexity and insanity, to the freedom of a simpler and saner life. As you can imagine, changing your lifestyle is not as easy as it might look.

Making the Transition to Voluntary Simplicity: Jonathan

Before Jonathan began practicing Voluntary Simplicity, he could have summed up his existence with a Twisted Sister song lyric: "Your life is trite and jaded, boring and confiscated." Jonathan and his wife had been consistently living within their means and paying down debt like fiends; so much so that they were nearing the end of their 15 year mortgage—10 years early.[1] Jonathan's wife came home with a borrowed copy of *Your Money or Your Life*, they read it together, and the die was cast.

Shortly after paying off the house he quit his crazy job,[2] went back to school full time for nine months to finish up the graduate degree he had already started, and started working the nine steps outlined in *Your Money or Your Life* in earnest. After a period of introspection and skipping the graduation ceremony because it was pointless and costly, he found himself re-employed making almost double his crazy job's salary, but this time with a difference. Not only does he find the new job interesting and fulfilling (though his life is still confiscated 10+ hours a day), but Jonathan has a plan for the future that includes not being a wage slave for the rest of his life. After living on $176 cash for nine months, he has discovered that there is much more to life than spending and acquiring stuff. Jonathan has a list of actions to accomplish that have intense personal and motivational meaning. He has an achievable vision of a life where he has the <u>choice</u>, not a <u>need</u>, to work.

Making the Transition to Voluntary Simplicity: Lynne

Lynne first spotted *Getting a Life* by Jacqueline Blix and David Heitmiller at a bookstore in late 1998. She had been through bankruptcy, divorce, and numerous layoffs; at that point, she and her daughters were living on Lynne's unemployment while she attended school to change careers. If there was one thing she needed, she reasoned, it was *a life*. Excited by what she read, she checked *Your Money or Your Life* out of the library. Even more excited, she bought a copy of her own.

Simplifying has allowed Lynne to more firmly identify the things she valued, and first and foremost among those values is her desire to raise her daughters to be happy and responsible adults. She found, moreover—as you may have found as you read this book—that she was already doing many things that Simplifiers do, without knowing that there was a name for somebody who did those things. Simplifying has been an education for Lynne, and she is the first to say that she is still learning. Practicing Voluntary Simplicity has not always been easy, but for Lynne, so far, it has always been worth it.

A word of warning

We have said this elsewhere in this book, but to reiterate: when following the VS path, you may find yourself swimming against the direction of the powerful Consumer Current, a.k.a. Western Civilization. One of the first things newcomers to VS notice is that their friends "just don't understand them anymore." Neither the Simplifier's behavior nor the things they want to talk about make much sense to those still enmeshed in the Consumer Culture.

This is to be expected, given the commercial media saturation we endure in the West, but it often comes as a shock to the novice Simplifier. The truth is that most of us have never really sat down and thought through exactly what it is we really believe in, what it is we really will stand up for, and what it is that makes our own existence meaningful to our deepest selves. This state of affairs is expected, given the shallowness of what we are taught in the public schools and what is expected of us in our public existence.

So much of Consumer Culture is centered on the media, particularly television, beating into the minds of all receivers what is good, bad, in, out, and so forth. Indeed, the more media outlets you are plugged into, the more advertising you are exposed to, the more likely it is that you are behaving the way that advertisers want you to behave: that is, you are buying the advertisers' products. We have a media machine in the West that is unmatched at warping public opinion to the way of thinking desired by the highest bidder.[3]

The end result is that many who would otherwise follow the path of Voluntary Simplicity give up because of the "static" they receive from their peers, friends, and acquaintances over seemingly trivial decisions:

- If it is time for a new car and you can afford the best on the market, why did you buy a good used car?
- If you have paid off your house, why are you still living here, and not moving up?
- If you have the money, why is your child attending public instead of private school?
- If you shop for organic food, why do you buy from the local food co-op in their rundown warehouse, or from a local farmer, instead of shopping the fancy organic food chain store?

- If you are so rich, why are your suits from JC Penney's instead of more prestigious stores?
- If you have a degree, why are you being a stay-at-home parent, or working for a trivial salary at something you happen to like more, when you could be making big money in your field?

The litany of questions that Consumer Culture aims at someone who is trying to live consciously is endless, and in a real sense derogatory and degrading of the asker. "How dare someone question what their TV told them," the asker seems to be saying to the Simplifier. The Simplifier has to be prepared to deal with these well intentioned, but brainwashed, people. And sadly, simplifying your life will sometimes drive away people you like, admire, and maybe even love, because they just will not take the time to understand your perspective and are unwilling to challenge their own assumptions the same way you are challenging (and changing) yours.

Rather than get hostile in return, the Simplifier often tries to seek out like souls. This has become easier with the advent of the Internet (see the resources section at the end of this chapter). But it is still a challenge, and an ongoing one for all Simplifiers, to live in a consumerist culture. Perhaps the best way to deal with the situation is to "cultivate a sublime contempt for *the opinions of others*," as one of our respondents put it. Some Simplifiers consider this strategy a bit harsh, and it is hard to do for the unsure, novice Simplifier, but it does work.

However, the news is not all bleak. The book *Cultural Creatives* shows that more than a quarter of the US population is part of the "counter consumer culture." There are indications that a similar level or more of "counter consumer culture" participation is happening elsewhere in the Westernized world. So the Simplifier is not alone, even if it sometimes looks and feels like it. With the world-wide recession and other events since the last half of 2000, more and more people are waking up without jobs, or facing reduced salaries and benefits at their old jobs, and wondering what this Consumer Culture is really all about, anyway.

You are not alone! Your situation, whatever it is, can most likely be improved, and living in the city can make the changes you are considering easier to make. Simplifying will take some thinking, time, and gumption on your part, but this is not rocket science. If you have the willingness to consider your personal situation carefully, you are on your way to living the examined life.

And take heart: the minimum you can bring to the table—*yourself*—is enough. The more you can shuck off the dead husks of Consumer Culture, the more your very best will shine through for all to see. We are all counting on you, because we know beyond doubt that you can.

We would love to hear how you make living simply in the city work for you; let us know how you fare. We would especially like to know if you think we have forgotten anything; your suggestions could end up in the second edition of this book! Please contact us through our website, www.ardeapress.com, or by e-mail: jonathanallan@ardeapress.com   and lynnecantwell@ardeapress.com.

We wish you Enough!

Things for You to Try

Looking for a way to jumpstart your journey down the path of Voluntary Simplicity? In every chapter of this book, this section has featured a handful of things for you to try. The Simplifiers who responded to our survey had so many other good ideas for this that we thought we would list them here. Some of the things in the list below are not actual things to do, but ideas to ponder. Several people had multiple good ideas, so you will see some names more than once.

You can probably think of other things that you can try that we did not include in this book. Write all those things on a piece of paper. Add to your list anything that looks interesting below, or you found interesting in any of the other sections of this book. Select the easiest or best looking one, and get busy.

- Voluntary Simplicity is not where you live, but a state of mind. (Maggie, Allentown, PA)
- Voluntary Simplicity can be challenging because it forces you to accept that you are the only person who can change your life. (Benjamin Freeman, Washington, DC)
- Know why *you* are getting into this. If it were easy, everyone would be doing it. Keeping your own vision in front of you sure makes it easier to stay on track when society and the world seem intent on pulling you off. (Joseph Beckenbach, San Jose, CA)
- By keeping your wants tiny, you won't go through life so whiny. (Tom Harrington, Ontario)
- Start low, go slow. It's not a competition. You don't have to be holier or simpler than anyone else. (MaryAnne Murray, Seattle, WA)
- Conserve your energy. Don't waste time on unimportant things. It takes extra effort to lead a less common lifestyle and it would be unfortunate to lose focus. (Catherine Barker, Brooklyn, NY)
- I would tell them that they have to WANT to practice VS before they can be successful at it. I would also ask them what they want out of life and if their present lifestyle is going to help them achieve that… Start with a couple of steps at a time, get used to those for a month or so, and then proceed to a couple more steps. Definitely read some books on the subject, such as *Your Money or Your Life* and *The Tightwad Gazette,* which will help you reduce expenses. (Marilyn, Baltimore Co., MD)
- Read some of the VS "classics" (use the library or a bargain web site like half.com) and find a group of like-minded people. (Mary Sullivan, Boston, MA)
- Read all you can, then decide why, and how. Choose one area in your life at a time to simplify. Get really good at it, then pick another. This isn't like kicking cigarettes. You don't go cold turkey, and there is no patch to keep you from shopping, or from spending money you don't have. (H. Brandenburg,

Vancouver, WA)
- Read some books and talk to those doing it. If you find that some folks are too way-out and think it's still 1970, keep looking. There are plenty of VS folks who wear suits and heels during the day. (Debra Pierce, Knoxville, TN)
- Take time to examine your behavior and see if you really enjoy how you're spending your time. Walking seems very inconvenient to most people, but if the alternative to walking is staring at the television, then I'll take a nice walk…. There's no one right way to live. It's a frightening quest, but finding out what works for you is probably the most fascinating and rewarding thing you can do with your life. (Rhett, Portland, OR)
- Throw out the TV set. That's the first step to *any* serious attempt to take back control over your life, whether you're in the city or in the country. (Jef Murray, Atlanta, GA)
- Start with what is pulling you toward VS, what it is that makes it attractive to you, then connect with other VS folks and listen to what they have done and how they feel about it. (Katherine Carter, Springfield, IL)
- Be sure you really want to do it. I see many people around me spending money to simplify! (Dena Sigman, Charlotte, NC)
- Every city has great frugal entertainment. You just have to look for it. (Amanda Graham, Baltimore, MD)
- Have lots of roommates and no car. Cars are more expensive than they're worth. Always try to find a way to avoid unsecured debt. There isn't always a job waiting to help you pay off all of those school loans. (Dede White, Seattle, WA)
- Have enough space to do yoga or other exercise in your apartment – protected space to relax and rest. Because if you always have to go out somewhere to unwind, you will end up spending money. (dodogrrl, Washington, DC)
- Go check the garbage on the street for wonderful things you can still use. Go to the street market after 4:00 p.m. and get all the leftovers for next to nothing. Lots of facilities here to get

things cheap or make your own. You do not need to live on a farm for that! (Anonymous, Amsterdam, The Netherlands)
- Ditch the car. (Lucy, Sheffield, UK)
- Do car sharing if you MUST have access to a vehicle. (Kyenne Williams, Portland, OR)
- Take advantage of the library and freebies that are available. (Howard Hill, Akron, OH)
- Bookstores, coffee shops/cafes and faith communities, particularly those located near an academic community, are excellent sources of connection to a VS lifestyle. Many libraries are hubs of information about free and low-cost municipal services (e.g., all of our libraries have free passes to the big museums – you just need to reserve it ahead of time to borrow the pass for a day). Check the library for citywide calendars of events. (Gretchen Kimber, Boston, MA)
- Cut up your credit cards. It can be done. (Bostongrrl, Malden, MA)
- If you learn the basics about money – how to save, spend, invest, etc. – you can enjoy the freedom of being an American, but the luxury of working less and taking long vacations like a European. In other words, you can enjoy life on your own terms, not the government's or someone else's. (Johnny Viper, North Las Vegas, NV)
- Getting a handle on your spending brings such freedom and joy! (Mary Sullivan, Boston, MA)
- Use your secondhand stores and garage sales. These are plentiful in our area and I have found many really good bargains in clothing and household items. (D.C., Portland, TX)
- If you have children and live in a city, do not compare yourself to singles or couples without kids living there. You are just in a completely different universe. (Melissa, San Francisco, CA)
- Take a look at your community. There are ample opportunities for volunteer work that will improve where you live. Everything you need is probably within a short bike ride if you just

take the time to look. You'll never go to the mall again. (Traci Freebairn, Tacoma, WA)

- Avoid the mall, the bars, the expensive ridiculous restaurants. Support the local farmers and always go out to nature, no matter how small. (Marianne Kimber, Boston, MA)
- Research what's available in your area. It surprises me people don't know about the car sharing concept. It's working great here! (VaLera Washburn, Portland, OR)
- Quit looking around you for validation, because there is so much going on in a city, so much that you are expected to make, expected to attend, expected to do. You will have to be more open and creative to find a living place that is both safe and cheap. (C.S., suburban Los Angeles, CA)
- Think outside the box about ways to make your dream/desire to live in the city a reality. If living in the city is your dream, think of how you can make that happen without owning your own place. I (half-joking) tell my wife that before I'd go back to work, I'd move in with one of our widowed neighbors and (by way of payment) help them continue to live on their own, rather than go back to the way we've done things in the past. It is only a phenomenon of this past generation or two that we all have to have our own houses. (Kevin Cornwell, Vancouver, WA)
- Remember that we have many choices and we do not have to follow the mainstream. We *can* live the abundant life we want and not get caught up in the rat race. (Everette Orr, McLean, VA)
- Seek like-minded people for encouragement and soak up as much culture and civic involvement as you can. (SMD, Michigan)
- Keep yourself focused on your goal and seek out other people who are also seeking the same thing. (Maggie, Allentown, PA)
- Look for a community – whether church, friends, or neighborhood. That is crucial! (Linda McDonough, Chapel Hill, NC)

- Check out university housing boards for good apartment listings. Read your local paper to see where you might be able to barter your services. (Bostongrrl, Malden, MA)
- Try to live within walking distance of frequented stores or near a bus line. (Margaret R., Austin, TX)
- Live near a bus stop or subway stop, so you won't need a car. Live as close to work as possible, so you'll have an easy mass transit (or walkable) commute. (Eucalyptus Tree, Berkeley, CA)
- Either live very close to work or find a walkable community. (Anonymous, Irvine, CA)
- Don't rule out a part of the city just because it has a reputation for being rough, or having poor schools. There are many neighborhoods in such areas that are stable and have much more affordable housing than the supposedly desirable areas. Consider living in inner-ring suburbs and in older parts of the city; they are much more affordable than the fancy downtown areas or the sprawled-out suburbs, and they have better public transportation than the outer suburbs. (Claire Schosser, St. Louis Co., MO)
- Get rid of your car(s). It will bring you the most bang for your buck! (Jane Zeender, Arlington, VA)
- Comparison shop for everything. (Katherine Kiger, Orlando, FL)
- Determine what you want out of life. Then do it. Don't become another "Consumer." (Johnny Viper, North Las Vegas, NV)
- Be true to yourself. Figure out what is important to you and don't be caught up in what is important to other people. (Linda Kay, Seattle, WA)
- Look first at the "real" lifestyle you lead—not the one you think you should be leading (i.e., do you really need a bigger house, a larger yard, a longer commute, more stuff). Look at your needs and not at your wants. Greater happiness and more "life" can be found by living with less. (Lindi Hulse, vagabond based in Los Angeles, CA)

- All of us have a "higher" self and a "lower" self. Taking care of and feeding the "higher" self leads to a more whole and healthy person. Feeding the "lower" self creates a voracious appetite for things that harm the self or others. VS is a way to feed the "higher" self. (Katherine Carter, Springfield, IL)
- If you haven't tried Voluntary Simplicity, you should for one month. You have nothing to lose and much to gain. The world is getting faster, smaller, more crowded, and crazier by the moment. Try VS for your own little peaceful corner in the world. (Catherine Barker, Brooklyn, NY)
- One cannot finance or lease early retirement. One either has the means to stop working or one doesn't. Most do not have the means and cannot afford to stop working because they have leveraged themselves far beyond their real means. (Jenny McKinney, London, England)
- Read *Your Money or Your Life* and follow the steps. For me, reading that book formed a turning point in my life. I'm 35, and should never have to work for money again. Ever. Sure, I'll certainly take paying jobs sometimes (there are lots of things I want to do which have the side effect of paying money), but I should never *have* to. I pinch myself, and wonder how this ever happened! (Fred Ecks, San Francisco, CA)
- I'd tell them how exhilarating life has been since I found VS in 1998. I will retire in September 2002, thanks mostly to *Your Money or Your Life* and the eye-opener it was for me. Because of VS, I've taken the time to sort out what "makes my heart sing" and I know it is not my 9-to-5 job. I will get up when I want, take vacations when I want, do volunteer work for causes important to me, take naps, live lightly on the earth, have time to read the unread books on my shelf – all because of VS. I'm so grateful for it. (Linda Kay, Seattle, WA•   )
- It's just as easy to practice all of the elements of VS in the city as it is in the country. Simple wishes make for such sweet living!!! (alex glenlee, St. Catharines, ON)

- We only get one crack at life. What are you going to enjoy more at 80? The constant upgrading of your kitchen and three piece suits? Or the experience of time with your children, traveling in different cultures, or whatever your passion is? (Lucy, Sheffield, UK)
- Don't spend your life listening to advertisers who are trying to get you to buy junk and go into debt. Think for yourself. Do you really need a car? Most city dwellers don't. Do you really need a McMansion in the suburbs, or would you be happier in a studio apartment in the city? Wouldn't you rather be walking around your neighborhood seeing the flowers and hearing the birds, rather than driving through it with your windows rolled up, listening to radio ads? (Eucalyptus Tree, Berkeley, CA)
- I think the biggest issue with city dwelling and Voluntary Simplicity is perception: your own perception that if you were truly the granola that you aspire to be, you'd move to the boondocks; your concern that all your neighbors think you're a freak; and your inner conflict regarding giving up all the trappings of "success" that you used to need. Work on the inner conflicts as you simplify the outer things. Otherwise [they] will derail you eventually. (Juli Parsons, Salt Lake City, UT)
- You are the one who makes the choice for yourself. No one else is going to do it for you. You can do whatever you want and there are ways to get there. I have always had the motto, "There is no harm in asking." Until you ask, you never know. (Souix Fox, Vancouver, BC)
- VS is about all aspects of your life: work, friends, love, home life. It's not about scrimping and saving. It's just knowing what is important to you and your family. (Betty, Washington state)
- Given September 11[, 2001] and all we've heard about how hated we are, I hope Americans will take a look at their personal lives and think how that impacts on what other people don't have. How many TV sets do we need? Why do we drive vehicles that get 15 m.p.g. when we are depending on foreign oil and we claim to hate Gulf and Alaska drilling? How does credit card

usage ruin our lives and contribute to "stuffitis" that spoils our kids and has us substituting shopping for hobbies, fun with friends and family, and volunteer work? Our society is truly Bowling Alone, as Robert Putnam has said. If we would stop spending so much, we could stop working so much. We could get our lives back and look around at our neighborhood and its school, our larger community and its government. What we do as a family does matter in the world. When we have used every natural resource on earth, they will be gone. We're a greedy nation, tattooed with a sense of entitlement. I hope our peek into life across the world will touch us and help us learn to live better with less. (Debra Pierce, Knoxville, TN)

- Life is short. Do you really want to use it up "getting and spending"? (Wordsworth: "Getting and spending, we lay waste our powers/Little we see in Nature that is ours...") (Starlight, Beaverton, OR)

- Your life is too precious *not* to take control of it. We only have so much time and energy to do whatever it is we're called to do on this earth. And if your life is nothing like what you hoped it would be, or if you're so stressed out that you don't even *know* what your life should be about, VS offers you tools to begin to heal, to begin to transform. The best time to start this process for most of us was perhaps ten years ago, but the next best time is right now. (Jef Murray, Atlanta, GA)

- Begin. (C.S., suburban Los Angeles, CA)

Internet Resources

www.culturalcreatives.com (The web site associated with the book *Cultural Creatives* by Ray and Anderson)

www.simpleliving.net

www.futurenet.org (Home of "Yes" magazine)

NOTES

Chapter 1:   What Is A City?

¹ *It Takes a Village Idiot*, p. 57.
² Justice Potter Stewart: *Jacobellis v. Ohio*, 378 U.S. 184, 197 (1964).
³ *Suburban Nation*, p. 39.
⁴ Ibid., p. 43.
⁵ Ibid., p. 245.
⁶ *Voluntary Simplicity*, p. 25.
⁷ *Five Acres and Independence*

Chapter 2: Choices and Values

¹ Marie Sherlock, *Living Simply with Children*, pp. 26-33.
² The way you spend money also points out some of your true values. After all, money is only another form of your life energy.
³ Juliet B. Schor, *The Overworked American: The Unexpected Decline of Leisure*, p. 129.
⁴ Real cheapskates will have to get another piece of already used paper. You know who you are—smile and enjoy! Now get your stub out of that pencil sharperner and start writing...
⁵ As mentioned in Malcolm Gladwell's book, *The Tipping Point*, this is exactly how the New York subway system was rescued from near total destruction. By cracking down on subway fare cheaters and keeping the subway cars painted nicely, the criminal element did not have the implicit permission to run amok. Once everyone started to believe a subway ride could be pleasant, they became so, and the violent criminal element has largely abandoned the subway system for easier pickings where people don't care.

Chapter 3: Advertising

[1] Jerry Mander, *Four Arguments for the Elimination of Television*, p. 124.

[2] Juliet B. Schor, *The Overspent American*, p. 78.

[3] "Can Mom and Pop Hold the Line?" Justin Lahart: http://money.cnn.com/2002/08/08/news/consumer/index.htm

[4] "Wary Eye on Wall Street and Washington", Gretchen Morgenson, The New York Times, July 21, 2002.

[5] "Ad Nauseam; Ad Creep: Ads are literally everywhere today, and an increase in venues only promises more for the future," Charles Pappas, Advertising Age, July 10, 2000.

[6] Ibid., p. 27.

[7] Mark Crispin Miller, *Boxed In: The Culture of TV*. Evanston, IL: Northwestern University Press, 1988. ISBN 0-8101-0792-9. Mander makes the same point in *Four Arguments for the Elimination of Television*, p. 195, but it is on this single point that Mander is repeatedly dismissed as a crank.

[8] However, there are scattered reports in the press of graphic artists in the catalog and magazine industries putting hidden messages in the ads. See http://abcnews.go.com/sections/science/DailyNews/subliminal000912.html and www.subliminalworld.com for more details.

[9] Kilbourne, Deadly Persuasion: Why Women and Girls Must Fight the Addictive Power of Advertising. Free Press, 1999, pp. 258-259.

[10] Kilbourne, lecture at Mayo Clinic, June 2000.

[11] Kilbourne, ibid., p. 97.

[12] Ibid., p. 270.

[13] Ibid., pp. 196-198.

[14] Ibid., p. 27.

[15] Ibid., p. 229.

[16] Ibid., pp. 300-301.

[17] Ibid., p. 224.

[18] Ibid., p. 225.

[19] Ibid., p. 308.

[20] Miller, ibid., pp. 14-15. James was originally quoted in "TV Guide," January 10, 1987, p. 18.

[21] Ibid., p. 15.

[22] Mander, ibid., p. 125.

[23] Ibid., p. 137.

[24] Ibid., pp. 299-311.

[25] Betsy Taylor and the Center for a New American Dream, "More Fun, Less Stuff Starter Kit." Takoma Park, MD: Center for a New American Dream, 2001. ISBN 0-9707727-0-X

Chapter 4: Downsize Your TV

[1] The TV figures come from http://www.tvb.org/tvfacts/tvbasics/basics1.html, the plumbing figures from http://www.census.gov/hhes/www/housing/census/historic/plumbing.html. The 1990 census showed 98.9% of US households with complete bathrooms as opposed to 98.2% of US households with TVs.

[2] http://www.cbsnews.com/stories/2002/01/31/health/main326995.shtml. See also http://www.sleepfoundation.org.

[3] Television and the Quality of Life, pp. 70-71. The research study did not cover the hours of 10pm to 8am (41% of time) on the theory that people do not watch while they are sleeping. 27.5% of time was spent working. In 1988, 10% of the remaining time, 1.4 hours per day, was spent with TV as a primary or secondary task. Average TV viewing time has been reliably reported at over 3 hours per day in 2000, indicating even more time is spent with TV now than the 1988 study.

[4] Mark Crispin Miller, Boxed In: The Culture of TV, p. 327.

[5] Much of this section and the following one is adapted from Jerry Mander, Four Arguments for the Elimination of Television.

[6] Television and American Culture, p. 171.

[7] Television and the Quality of Life, pp. 101 – 104.

[8] Television and the Quality of Life, p. 170. Have you ever noticed that people who watch the most TV are also the ones that are chronically tired?

[9] Television and the Quality of Life, pp. 139-140, discusses the orienting reflex and how TV's technical wizardry plays up to it, jerking our attention around.

[10] Television and the Quality of Life, pp. 124-140.

[11] Robert D. Putnam in Bowling Alone, ISBN 0-684-83283-6 (2000).

[12] Cronkite was quoted in "Troubled Times for Network Evening News," Howard Kurtz, The Washington Post, March 10, 2002.

[13] "At ABC, A Shaken News Dynasty," Howard Kurtz, The Washington Post, March 5, 2002.

[14] Kurtz quotes from a Pew Research Center survey in "Troubled Times for Network Evening News," ibid.

[15] "Who People Trust — by Profession," Daniel Wood, Christian Science Monitor, November 28, 2000. A Harris Poll in late 2001 also ranked journalists near the bottom of the heap, with trade union leaders, members of Congress, and business leaders. http://www.harrisinteractive.com/harris_poll/index.asp?PID=273

[16] http://people-press.org/reports/print.php3?ReportID=159

[17] This is nothing new. For the story of how most of the Hanna-Barbera cartoons were conceived, pitched, and sold, read pp. 131-177 of Joseph

Barbera's autobiographical My Life In Toons, ISBN 1-57036-042-1, Turner
Publishing Company. This gives a fascinating, if stomach turning, history
of how many of our favorite cartoons were conceived merely to sell products, mostly breakfast cereal. For example, Johnny Quest's dog Bandit was
added to the script in order to market a fluffy toy dog.

[18] "Disney Finishes Fox Family Deal," Broadcasting & Cable, October 25,
2001.

[19] "Who'll Buy Fox's Kids?", Broadcasting & Cable, January 21, 2002.

[20] Unplugging the Plug-In Drug, pp. 9-14. Winn offers many powerful reasons why children should not be exposed to TV until after the age of four, if
not later. Pp. 139 – 147 are yet more good reasons why adults, especially
parents, should seriously consider getting rid of their TVs permanently.

[21] Television and the Quality of Life, p. 201.

[22] Ibid., p. 134.

[23] Ibid., pp. 202-208.

[24] Jonathan even went so far as to magnet a "Free Your Mind, Kill Your TV"
bumper sticker to his filing cabinet at work; people still do not believe he
can live without watching TV.

Chapter 5: A Bathtub Model of Cash Flow

[1] Unless you choose to prepay the loan. The more principal you prepay, the
less interest you will pay, so this is why you can choose to pay less interest
on a self-amortizing loan. This statement does not apply to certain types of
loans: "Sum of Digits" and "Rule of 78s Method" loans are two examples.
These loans are typically found on consumer items like boats and recreational vehicles. Your state may not even allow such loans; they front-load
so much interest that many states have outlawed them as unfair to the consumer.

[2] alex is a Buddhist and does not capitalize either his name or the personal
pronoun for himself.

Chapter 6: More Money

[1] This section, and next few following, are abstracted from Do What You
Love, the Money Will Follow, by Dr. Marsha Sinetar.

[2] If you want a detailed, guided tour through this exercise, check out The
Passion Plan by Chang or Creating Your Future by Ellis.

[3] Yes, weaknesses are important to note. Just like you don't use a screw

driver to put in nails, your calling should play to your strengths and require little reliance on your weaknesses. Or if your dream demands you build up a weak area, then you have to find ways to strengthen that part of yourself, or to compensate — if, for example, your math skills are poor, you could learn to use a spreadsheet program, or hire an accountant. Either way, the intent of listing weaknesses is to help avoid falling into those potholes unaware. A full discussion of strengths and weaknesses can be found in *Now, Discover Your Strengths* by Marcus Buckingham.

[4] Do What You Love, the Money Will Follow, pp. 141-142.

[5] We really do mean every penny! We know that this is a difficult habit to start, so be as diligent as you possibly can and don't sweat it if you lose track of a day or two. You are likely to get the same answers anyway.

[6] Of course, we recommend you do this for longer than that—Jonathan has 5+ years of data already and no intention of stopping tracking. But for purposes of this exercise, commit yourself for that limited period of time, say a month, and then evaluate the usefulness of tracking after doing the exercise.

[7] Gleefully taken from Your Money or Your Life, pg. 112.

Chapter 10: Entertainment

[1] Associated Press, as reported in the Rochester Post Bulletin, July 4, 2002.

Chapter 11: Simple Politics

[1] L. J. Hanifan, as quoted in Bowling Alone, p. 19.
[2] Ibid., p. 21. Although there are downsides to social capital as well: see Bowling Alone, chapter 22.
[3] Among them the Rouge Valley, near Ashland, Oregon. http://www.co-intelligence.org/P-wisdomcouncil.html
[4] Dr. Marshall Rosenberg's book, Nonviolent Communication, describes a communication process that makes it easier for everyone to comprehend others' feelings and needs.
[5] Practical Politics, p. 152.
[6] See http://plato.stanford.edu/entries/prisoner-dilemma/ for many more details and variations on tit-for-tat.

Chapter 12: Retirement

[1] One of Howells' titles is Choose the Southwest for Retirement: Retirement Discoveries for Every Budget (3rd ed.), Guilford, CT: The Globe-Pequot Press, 2001. Howells has also written about retiring in Mexico, Spain, Costa Rica, and several regions of the United States.

[2] Quoted by Ric Edelman in "Will You Ever Retire?", http://www.ricedelman.com/planning/retirement/retire.asp

[3] From Gordon's December 6, 2001, column in the Toronto Star, http://www.baycrest.org/column/gordon.html#volunteerism

[4] See Chapter 9 in Your Money or Your Life, pp. 298–305 for the full argument.

Chapter 13: Transportation

[1] Check your library for the book by this title; a good read and just stuffed with good transportation facts.

[2] Ad Age, as quoted by Ken Avidor at the Living Green Exposition, April 27, 2002.

[3] Divorce Your Car!, pp. 228 and 229; the Circle Game. Most people walk at a rate of three to four miles per hour.

[4] One company frequently mentioned is http://www.bikesatwork.com. There are many others.

[5] http://www.mwcog.org/commuter/Bdy-GRH.html

[6] Although not technically a state, Washington, DC, allows employers to do this. http://www.wmata.com/riding/metrochek/metrochek.cfm

[7] In 2001, Minnesota companies could do this.

[8] Research Note: DOT HS 809 439, April 2002. 2001 Motor Vehicle Traffic Crashes Injury and Fatality Estimates Early Assessment, by Judith Hilton and Umesh Shankar.

[9] Table value multiplied by ten from http://www.fta.dot.gov/library/intro/fy2ppg1.htm.

[10] http://www.transit-safety.volpe.dot.gov/Publications/Safety/SAMIS/SAMIS99/sheet002.htm

[11] Figures derived from Delucci, M.A. et. al., 1996, The Annualized Social Cost of Motor Vehicle Use in the United States, Based on 1990-1991 Data, and U.S. Government publication FHWA-PD-93-015, Case Study No. 15: The Environmental Benefits of Bicycling and Walking. The 1991 costs were then adjusted to year 2000 constant dollars.

[12] Mark Singer, speaking at the Living Green Exposition in Minneapolis on April 27th, 2002. Also corroborated in 2002 by http://www.edmunds.com/advice/specialreports/articles/59897/article.html. A figure of $3,000 for 1998 is quoted in Divorce Your Car!, p. 101.
[13] Divorce Your Car!, p. 110. The upper limit was estimated around $15,000.
[14] http://www.AlexRide.org/carsharing.html
[15] See also Divorce Your Car!, pp. 225 – 229.

Chapter 14: Building Community

[1] Doug Carroll comments: "But even nowadays in Iowa, you drive to town to get groceries, they'll watch you and they know where you live when they see your car go by. They'll go out and steal your tools on the farm. Even the farms all have to lock up nowadays. So no matter where you live you have to lock things up. You don't leave your houses open; you don't leave things lying around."
[2] We use Putnam, Bowling Alone, as the source of much of the information in this chapter.
[3] Putnam, pp. 283-84.
[4] In recent years, however, Tupperware had begun to see its bottom line slip. In response, it is once again selling via retail outlets, including stand-alone kiosks in some shopping malls and on the Home Shopping Network. http://order.tupperware.com/
[5] http://www.dsa.org/research/numbers.htm#SALES
[6] Jaida N'Ha Sandra and Utne Reader, The Joy of Conversation: The Complete Guide to Salons, 1997 (ASIN 0965381609). Sandra also co-authored a more recent book on this topic with Jon Spayde called Salons: The Joy of Conversation (ISBN 0865714444).
[7] See http://www.conversationcafe.org for more details and a listing of where and when some cafés meet.

Chapter 15: Complicated Relationships

[1] Tightwad Gazette.
[2] 1 Timothy 6:10.
[3] There are good reasons for prenuptial agreements, among them: having large business assets prior to the marriage, or having a child with special needs. The vast majority of us do not need one.
[4] The Overspent American, p. 100.

[5] Your Money or Your Life, p. 8 for starters; there are other surveys that show the same thing.

[6] In the cartoon strip Doonesbury, Elmont and Alice inherit from Lacey Davenport and change from living on the streets to a nice apartment. They eventually end up back on the street, to their relief.

[7] Among them is the tape course "Transforming Your Relationship with Money" that preceded Your Money or Your Life by Dominguez and Robin.

[8] Your authors do not really like to recommend this tactic, but it has been known to work. Use at your own risk.

Chapter 16: Simple City Pets

[1] "Snakehead's Luck Puts Pond in Soup," The Washington Post, July 12, 2002.

[2] The declawing procedure removes everything beyond the first joint of the cat's "fingers." Because of this, many people consider this procedure inhumane.

Chapter 17: Consumer Culture

[1] http://www.adage.com. Coen's spending totals for 2001 advertising. Total advertising spending in all media in 2001 was $231.3 billion.

[2] The Complete Tightwad Gazette. Dacyzyn's newsletters have been collected in book form; her first reference to a price book is on p. 33.

[3] Even the voice of Bugs Bunny spit his raw carrot-chewings into a wastebasket. That's Not All, Folks!, Mel Blanc and Philip Bashe, ISBN 0-446-39089-5, p. 87.

[4] The Complete Tightwad Gazette, pp. 584-6.

[5] http://www.interfacesustainability.com/

[6] www.container-recycling.org/publications/ trashedcans/TCExecSum.pdf

Chapter 18: Gardening

[1] The Contained Garden by Kenneth Beckett, David Carr, and David Stevens from Penguin Books has many creative container ideas as well as information on designing container gardens and plants suited for containers. This book also shows ways to layer plants using stairs, railings, and balconies.

² Gardening in Small Spaces by Jack Kramer gives plans and instructions on how to construct planters, trellises, vertical and modular gardens to make the best use of patios, porches, balconies, rooftops and atriums.

³ Mel Bartholomew's Square Foot Gardening lists when growing seasons for a variety of vegetables and herbs.

⁴ Container Gardening from the American Horticultural Society's Illustrated Encyclopedia of Gardening has some great ideas for trellises that you can make. If these projects are a bit beyond your abilities, you can still get some ideas on how to use items like trellises, modular containers, etc.

⁵ "Compost worms" such as Red Wiggler, Red Hybrid, or California Red can be purchased from specialized companies. Look for advertisements for these companies in gardening magazines.

⁶ Mary Appelhof's book, Worms Eat My Garbage, gives detailed information on worm-composting.

⁷ The Budget Gardener by Maureen Gilmer.

⁸ Home solutions can be found in Your Organic Garden with Jeff Cox by the Editors of Rodale Garden Books or The Big Book of Gardening Skills by the Editors of Garden WayPublishing. The Environmental Protection Agency, www.epa.gov, has a trove of information about common chemicals.

Chapter 19: Simplifying With Kids

¹ Marie Sherlock, Living Simply with Children, New York: Three Rivers Press, 2003 (ISBN 0-609-80901-6), p. 4.

² "Rushing to Cash In on the New Baby Boom," Wendy Bounds, The Wall Street Journal, August 9, 2000.

³ "Tips for Parenting in a Commercial Culture," Center for a New American Dream.

⁴ http://www.newdream.org/campaign/kids/press-release2002.html

⁵ http://www.sweden.se/templates/Article____3143.asp.

⁶ "Pushing Plastic to Teens," Michelle Singletary, The Washington Post, August 20, 2000.

⁷ Ibid., quoting a survey done by the American Savings Education Council.

⁸ Manning was quoted in "Just One Word: Plastic," Hank Stuever, The Washington Post Magazine, June 16, 2002.

⁹ "Debt and a Degree", Knight Ridder Newspapers, Rochester Post-Bulletin, June 6, 2003.

¹⁰ "It's Not Just a Toy, It's an Indoctrination," Daphne White, The Washington Post, August 13, 2000.

¹¹ "Born to Shop," James McNeal and Chyon-Hwa Yeh, American Demo-

graphics, June 1993, as quoted in "Tips for Parenting in a Commercial Culture," ibid.

[12] Marie Winn, The Plug-In Drug: Television, Children, and the Family, p. 102.

[13] Lasn's book is quoted by Marie Sherlock in Living Simply with Children, p. 127.

[14] Ibid.

[15] Four Arguments for the Elimination of Television, pg. 265. One immediately has to wonder what TV does to an adult, and if TV's effect on adults includes the degenerating social skills that we see in public nowadays.

[16] "Sponsored Schools and Commercialized Classrooms: Schoolhouse Commercializing Trends in the 1990s," Alex Molnar. Arizona State University Education Policy Studies Laboratory, 1998. http://www.uwm.edu/Dept/CACE/

[17] Ibid.

[18] "L.A. schools ban sodas," Reuters, August 27, 2002.

[19] "Spanish Immersion: In Guatemala, the Author's Young Daughter Learns that All Americas Are Not Alike," Lonnae O'Neal Parker, The Washington Post, December 23, 2001.

[20] Living Simply with Children, p. 47.

[21] Ibid., p. 187.

Chapter 20: Energy

[1] Newer double and triple pane windows have the pleasant side effect, when closed, of cutting down on the exterior noise that comes straight through old single pane windows.

[2] Newer refrigerators may not have coils. See the manufacturers web site for exact cleaning instructions for your model.

[3] Microwaves use about one-third the energy of a regular oven.

[4] The 25W bulbs are lit an average of an hour a day. $5*(40-25)W*1h/1000*365=27.4KWh$/year. At 10 cents per KWh, that's $2.74 saved, on top of the cost difference between the bulb sizes. And there is no net loss of bathroom utility with the smaller wattage bulbs, so there is no change to our lifestyle. Would you pick up $2.74 lying on the ground when no one was in sight?

[5] Infill construction has detractors, and often for good reasons. Consider the value of any infill development carefully.

[6] Atlantis SunSlates. http://www.stli.com/atlantis/residential.html

[7] PV Shingles: http://ovonic.com/unitedsolar/roof.html

[8] Field applied roofing laminate: http://ovonic.com/unitedsolar/roof.html. These are amorphous silicon products.

[9] Still a custom made product however. See also: http://wwweng.uwyo.edu/ electrical/doeepscor/delephoarrays.html and http://www.pacificsites.com/ ~sps/info.html

[10] This is what insurance is for. An umbrella policy can be purchased for a reasonable fee that should cover these sorts of very remote hazards. Most cities and utilities progressive enough to deal effectively with solar systems have very modest insurance requirements, if any. Check with the appropriate authorities and see what your jurisdiction requires.

[11] Home Power #37, pp. 10-13.

[12] Home Power #96, pp. 26-31.

[13] The technical term is "grid intertied".

[14] Sometimes by contract, sometimes by a general agreement enforced by the state called net metering. In the US, net metering availablility varies by system size, type, and area of the country. In other countries, your first action should be a call to your utility company.

[15] There is great argument about the "lightness" of PV panels because many models use crystalline silicon that is processed like computer chips: energy intensive and sometimes a pollution problem. However, manufacturing processes have gotten better over time and the resulting panels often produce more energy in the first two years of use than it took to make them in the first place (their embodied energy). So every year after 2, up to the 25 or 30 years a crystalline silicon panel can be expected to last, is a net energy gain for little or no further environmental cost. By contrast, amorphous solar panels have a much lower initial embodied energy, and they return less energy over time (they are much less efficient on a per square inch basis). Like crystalline panels, amorphous panels are hazardous waste when they no longer work. No one has managed to solve this one yet, and they may never do so because the materials used are inherently hazardous. Note however that the hazardous waste represented by a dead solar panel is all in one place and easily contained; unlike the filth spewed from a coal-fired power plant for the same 30 years of electrical power output.

Chapter 22: Finding Time

[1] The Overworked American, Schor, p. 129.

[2] Living the Simple Life. Elaine St. James, p. 56.

[3] Managing Management Time. William Oncken, Jr., ISBN 0-13-511086-4, Prentice Hall. Pp. 128 – 138 have a complete theory of monkey management.

[4] The Seven Habits of Highly Effective People. Stephen R. Covey, 1989, ISBN 0-671-66398-4, Simon & Schuster. Pp. 156-158.

Chapter 23: Your Home As Art

[1] "A New Lease", by April Thompson. Natural Home, July/August 2002, p. 38.
[2] A rather "New Age" book, but she does provide some practical ideas, even if you don't share her views on the spiritual realm.
[3] From Susan Susanka, The Not So Big House: A Blueprint for the Way We Really Live. Quoted at http://www.notsobighouse.com/simplicity.html

Chapter 24: A Few Final Words

[1] We intentionally bought less house than we could afford because the economy was slack at the time and we wanted a place we could afford if we were both flipping burgers part time. In hindsight, this under-buy was an excellent financial move and we now recommend underbuying to everyone.
[2] Exactly 42 days later in fact, just after the notice from the bank on the loan payoff was properly recorded. The day after they got the notice of the pay-off, Jonathan turned in his resignation.
[3] Four Arguments for the Elimination of Television, p. 136.

BIBLIOGRAPHY

Here are some books you may be able to find at your local library. Either we referenced these multiple times, they are definitive works in the field, or they are good introductions to the topic listed. Regardless of why they ended up in this list, we think you will find them worthwhile reading. We have included a couple sentences about each to help you choose what to read more easily. Enjoy!

Alvord, Katie. *Divorce Your Car!* Gabriola Island, BC, Canada: New Society Publishers, 2000.
Alvord makes the case, with meticulously researched statistics, that ridding your existence of cars is one of the better things you can do for yourself. She lives and bicycles year-round in Michigan.

Andrews, Cecile. *The Circle of Simplicity: Return to the Good Life.* New York: HarperCollins, 1998.
This book gives you a framework for creating your own simplicity circle — a way to foster community and connect with others disenchanted with the consumer culture.

Blix, Jacqueline, and David Heitmiller. *Getting a Life.* New York: Penguin, 1999.
Blix and Heitmiller have achieved financial independence by following the steps outlined by Dominguez and Robin in *Your Money or Your Life.* They talk about their own journey, and that of others who have done the same thing — and who have not moved to the sticks to get there. This is a good book for inspiration.

Bolles, Richard Nelson. *What Color is Your Parachute? A Practical Manual for Job-Hunters and Career-Changers, 32nd Ed.* Berkeley, CA: Ten Speed Press, 2002.

The perennial guide to finding a new job, a better job, or a new career. Filled with practical advice on how to market yourself to an employer. Companion workbook also available.

Briand, Michael K. *Practical Politics: Five Principles for a Community That Works.* Champaign, IL: University of Illinois Press, 1999.

Discusses why politics in the United States is broken and a practical way to fix it, at least at the community level. Briand lays out five principles for making politics work, and identifies the seven C's required to get and keep citizens involved in the political process.

Cameron, Julia. *The Artist's Way: A Spiritual Path to Higher Creativity.* New York: J.P. Tarcher, 1992.

Consider this a 12-week boot camp for your creativity. Cameron is a poet-playwright-scriptwriter-journalist who developed the steps she outlines in this book during a personal period of writer's block.

Chang, Richard Y. *The Passion Plan.* San Francisco: Jossey-Bass, 2001.

A step-by-step guide for discovering and achieving your passions.

Chilton, David. *The Wealthy Barber.* New York: Prima Publishing, 1998.

This book tells the tale of a barber who, given some good business advice, handles his personal money adroitly, raises his net financial worth to a large amount, and turns the local barber shop into a money-making machine. All this, even though he is a "lowly" barber and started off in a bad situation due to a family crisis.

Covey, Stephen R. *The Seven Habits of Highly Effective People.* New York: Simon & Schuster, 1989.

A step-by-step guide to the seven habits that successful people practice in one form or another.

Dacyzyn, Amy. *The Complete Tightwad Gazette*. New York: Villard, 1983.
The collected Tightwad Gazette newsletters. Packed with frugal ways to do darned near anything.

De Graaf, John, David Waan, and Thomas H. Naylor. *Affluenza: The All-Consuming Epidemic*. San Francisco: Berrett-Koehler Publishers, Inc., 2001.
De Graaf co-produced two PBS series by the same name. The authors define affluenza as "a painful, contagious, socially-transmitted condition of overload, debt, anxiety and waste resulting from the dogged pursuit of more."

Devine, William Frances, Jr. *Women, Men & Money*. New York: Crown Publishers, Inc., 1998.
Subtitled: The Four Keys for Using Money to Nourish Your Relationship, Bankbook, and Soul, this author describes his personal quest for money, what went right, what went wrong, and how these events affected his relationships with his family, himself, and his customers.

Dominguez, Joe, and Vicki Robin. *Your Money or Your Life*. New York: Penguin Books, 1992.
A pragmatic text, this book shows one practical way (and points out a veritable plethora of others) to simplify your life by focusing on the money you spend and aligning your spending around your values.

Duany, Andres, Elizabeth Plater-Zyberk, and Jeff Speck. *Suburban Nation: The Rise of Sprawl and the Decline of the American Dream*. New York: North Point Press, 2000.
A look at how car culture has hurt the viability of the city neighborhood and the mixing of cultures found there. The authors assert that the American Dream has been seriously compromised by the building of suburbs and the resultant lack of social mixing found in development pods sprawled around the city.

Elgin, Duane. *Voluntary Simplicity*. New York: William Morrow and Company, Inc., 1993.

First printed in 1981, this text contributed the term "Voluntary Simplicity" to the public discourse. Following on the footsteps of *The Population Bomb* and similar works by others, the research behind *Voluntary Simplicity* showed that an aesthetic lifestyle need not mean continued over-consumption and planetary degradation.

Ellis, David B. *Creating Your Future*. New York: Houghton Mifflin Company, 1998.

Ellis lays out five steps for identifying what you want in life and then achieving those things. Although his process is a bit intense for working as an individual, working the steps in a small group, or even just with your SO, will aid in your success with the ideas.

Kains, Maurice G. *Five Acres and Independence*. Mineola, NY: Dover Publications, 1973..

A 1940s back to the land book, with a great title. How to live the self-sufficient life on a small farm. Not exactly what you want to be reading if you want to live in the city.

Kilbourne, Jean. *Deadly Persuasion: Why Women and Girls Must Fight the Addictive Power of Advertising*. New York: Free Press, 1999.

Kilbourne is a former alcohol and tobacco addict who has fashioned a career for herself by crusading against the advertising industry. She documents the ways in which ads for alcohol and tobacco make the products seductive, particularly to young people and to those already addicted to the products. Kilbourne is clearly a feminist, and readers who are not so inclined may find her arguments a bit overstated.

Kubey, Robert, and Mihaly Csikszentmihalyi. *Television and the Quality of Life: How Viewing Shapes Everyday Experience*. Mahwah, NJ: Lawrence Erlbaum Associates, Inc., 1990.

A scholarly book, filled with good references and research about the evils of TV. After reading chapter 10, you will want to destroy your set and ensure your children are never exposed to unsupervised TV anywhere else.

Lamott, Anne. *Bird by Bird: Some Instructions on Writing and Life.* New York: Anchor Books, 1994.

Anne Lamott is a single mother, a writer, and a teacher of writing. If you enjoy dark humor or want to learn about the personal craft of writing, this is a good starter text and fun to read besides.

Lowe, Carl, ed. *Television and American Culture.* Bronx, NY: The H.W. Wilson Company, 1981.

A collection of articles on the presence of TV in US culture, TV's known and speculated effects on people and the culture they make, and a brief discussion on how TV programming is put together. Also includes some speculation on TV's future role in the public discourse, the effects of cable TV, and how the US lifestyle might change in the TV age. Details how TV mightily affects the political process.

Mander, Jerry. *Four Arguments for the Elimination of Television.* New York: William Morrow and Company, Inc., 1978.

Why watching TV warps your mind, rots your soul and your teeth, helps the advertisers win the war for your dollar, and makes you a machine that jumps at the whim of the highest bidder. Free your mind and your time; kill your TV!

Mendel, Peter, Charles C. Mann and Peter Kennedy. *Material World: A Global Family Portrait.* San Francisco: Sierra Club Books, 1994.

A pictorial essay, backed by relevant statistics, about the "stuff" people own in various countries across the world. It is instructive to ponder our extravagance after seeing Mali or Bhutan or …

Mullen, Jim. *It Takes a Village Idiot: Complicating the Simple Life.* New York: Simon & Schuster, 2001.

A sarcastic look at living, and messing up, the simple life in the Catskills by a formerly "second homeless" Manhattanite. A must read for all those flatlanders tempted to own a "country place". Ahhh, the smell of steamed dandelion greens!

Mundis, Jerrold J. *How to Get Out of Debt, Stay Out of Debt, and Live Prosperously.* New York: Bantam Books, 1988.

An exploration of the thinking behind Debtors Anonymous and Mundis' experience using the plan to pay down his own debts.

Nearing, Helen, and Scott Nearing. *The Good Life: Helen and Scott Nearing's Sixty Years of Self-Sufficient Living.* New York: Schocken Books, 1989.

Comprised of two books, *Living the Good Life* and *Continuing the Good Life*, this is the story of the Nearings as they went back to the land to live the examined life free from the corporate and academic chains they had rejected. *Living the Good Life* is often discussed as the progenitor of the 1960s "back to the land" movement.

Pierce, Linda Breen. *Choosing Simplicity.* Carmel, CA: Gallagher Press, 2000.

A general look at Voluntary Simplicity, and a deeper discussion of the types of people who are drawn to the movement.

Poynter, Dan, and Mindy Bingham. *Is There a Book Inside You? Writing Alone or with a Collaborator* (5th ed.). Santa Barbara, CA: Para Publishing, 1999.

This text is about deciding if you want to be a writer and, if you do, the mechanics of actually writing your book. Covers the writing process from the beginning idea through the end of the book's life, with emphasis on self-publishing.

Quinn, Jane Bryant. *Making the Most of Your Money.* New York: Simon & Schuster, 1997.

A good book for a general overview of investments. She thinks stocks are the best things since sliced bread, but knowing her bias, you can evaluate the rest of her opinions accordingly. Recommended for learning the vocabulary of investing, not its investment advice.

Ray, Paul H., Ph.D., and Sherry Ruth Anderson, Ph.D. *The Cultural Creatives: How 50 Million People Are Changing the World.* New York: Three Rivers Press, 2000.

Research showing, among other things, that a large mass of people is becoming disenchanted with modern Western culture and casting about for a better way to live, play, and work.

Schor, Juliet B. *The Overspent American: Why We Want What We Don't Need.* New York: HarperCollins, 1999.

Heavy with statistical analysis, this book is nevertheless eye-opening reading. Schor documents that no matter how much Americans make, we never feel rich enough. She lays the blame for this on our consumer culture, and includes profiles of downshifters who have opted out of the work-and-spend madness.

————. *The Overworked American: The Unexpected Decline of Leisure* (reprint ed.). New York: Basic Books, 1993.

Which would you rather have, overtime pay or comp time? Schor's findings in this statistically-laden book indicate that we'd much rather have the time off — and more vacation time, and a shorter work week in general. She discusses whatever happened to the early 20th century trend toward shorter work weeks, why American industry discourages part-time work, and the amount of vacation time Europeans get (hint: it's a lot more than Americans get).

Schor, Juliet B., et al. *Do Americans Shop Too Much?* Boston: Beacon Press, 2000.

A collection of essays started by Juliet Schor advocating the simpler lifestyle. Other economists then respond to her various points and Schor then wraps up with a few responses. The most disturbing of the responses is James Twitchells' "The Stone Age", in which he advocates creating a religion around consumption. Obviously he's the one living in the Stone Age, because we already have...

Sher, Barbara. *Wishcraft: How to Get What You Really Want.* New York: Ballantine Books, 1986.

If you have what seems an impossible dream, this book can help you get there. Sher suggests exercises so that you can pin down what you really want. Then she gives you strategies for going after it.

Sherlock, Marie. *Living Simply with Children.* New York: Three Rivers Press, 2003.

Sherlock provides tips from real parents who are raising their children simply today. A great resource for parents who would like to simplify but who are having trouble getting their kids to cooperate.

Sinetar, Dr. Marsha. *Do What You Love, The Money Will Follow.* New York: Dell Publishing, 1987.

Written by a psychologist, this book explores "right livelihood". Explores how to work doing what you love, instead of being a weekend warrior. Also touches on what makes people successful in the long run.

St. James, Elaine. *Living the Simple Life.* New York: Hyperion, 1996.

A tiny little book filled with 100 thoughts about how she simplified her life.

————. *Simplify Your Life with Kids.* Kansas City, MO: Andrews McMeel Publishing, 1997.

A fat little book with 100 ways to simplify your existence with children (your own or someone else's).

Stanley, Thomas, and William Danko. *The Millionaire Next Door.* New York: Pocket Books, 2000.

A fascinating look into the demographics of US millionaires: they aren't what you think. The chapter titled "Frugal, Frugal, Frugal" just about says it all.

Thau, Annette. *The Bond Book.* New York: McGraw-Hill, 2001.

This book is perhaps the most accessible material currently in print on the various aspects of investing in bonds. While the book can be technical in spots, and drier than a desert to read occasionally, it is chock full of good information for the beginning investor interested in the bond market. Well worth the time to puzzle through some of the vocabulary. It helps to have a calculator or spreadsheet that has financial functions.

Thoreau, Henry David. *Walden and Other Writings.* New York: Dorset Press, 1994.

Perhaps the original "back to the land" book in the New World, *Walden* advances the idea that life should be lived and enjoyed without some required amount of material "stuff" lying about and consuming your energies.

U.S. Department of Health and Human Services, Public Health Service, with the National Institute of Mental Health. *Television and Behavior: Ten Years of Scientific Progress and Implications for the Eighties, Volume 1: Summary Report.* Washington, DC: Government Printing Office, 1982. A survey of entertainment TV, the study provides disturbing information about TV's ability to promote cognitive and emotional function; the effects of violence and aggression portrayed; imagination, creativity, and prosocial behavior in children exposed to TV; social reality; interpersonal relations; and TV's effects on social and political institutions.

Winn, Marie. *The Plug-In Drug: Television, Children, and the Family* (rev. ed.). New York: Viking Press, 1985.
This is the seminal work on the effects of TV on children. Winn explains why your kids are a pain in the butt after they have spent a morning watching the boob tube and eating Chocolate-Frosted Sugar Bombs — and what that does to family life.

————. *Unplugging the Plug-In Drug: Help Your Children Kick the TV Habit.* New York: Penguin Books, 1987.
Packed with tips for weaning yourself and your kids off the idiot box, the book also suggests ways to unplug your school, your city, or any other large group.

Ziglar, Zig. *See You at the Top.* Gretna, LA: Pelican Publishing, 1977.
One of the many motivational books with a mission to change the way you think about work and avoid "hardening of the attitudes".

Printed in the United States
R283200001B/R2832PG14947X00025B/145

9 780972 711234